Rock Climbing
Boulder Canyon

Richard Rossiter

CHOCKSTONE

A FALCON GUIDE

HELENA, MONTANA

A FALCON GUIDE®

Falcon Publishing is continually expanding its list of recreation guidebooks. All books include detailed descriptions, accurate maps, and all the information necessary for enjoyable trips. You can order extra copies of this book and get information and prices for other Falcon® guidebooks by writing Falcon, P.O. Box 1718, Helena, MT 59624 or calling toll free 1-800-582-2665. Also, please ask for a free copy of our current catalog. Visit our web site at http://www.falconguide.com

©1999 Falcon® Publishing Inc., Helena, Montana

Printed in the United States of America

1   2   3   4   5   6   7   8   9   0   PU   04   03   02   01   00   99

Send all corrections, inquiries and new route information to:

Richard Rossiter c/o Falcon Publishing Co., Inc. P.O. Box 1718, Helena, MT 59624.

All text photos are by Richard Rossiter.

Cover photo: Jane Sears on *Country Club Crack* (5.11 b/c). Photo by Dan Hare.

Library of Congress Cataloging-in-Publication Data
Rossiter, Richard, 1945–
    Rock climbing Boulder Canyon / by Richard Rossiter.
        p.   cm. -- (A FalconGuide)
    Includes indexes.
    ISBN 1-56044-750-8 (pbk. : alk. paper)
    1. Rock climbing--Colorado--Boulder Canyon--Guidebooks.
2. Boulder Canyon (Colo.)--Guidebooks.   I. Title,   II. Series:
Falcon Guide.
GV199.42.C62B6874   1998
796.52'23'0978863--dc21
                                98-42941
                                  CIP

Text pages printed on recycled paper.

Table of Contents

About This Book

ARRANGEMENT OF TEXT

All crags and routes in this book are catalogued from left to right as they are normally viewed on approach. I have used this format simply because books published in western languages are paginated from left to right. This lends a visual logic to the information as one leafs through the drawings and text. I considered listing the whole of Boulder Canyon in this manner, which would have dictated describing first the south side from Boulder to Nederland, followed by the north side from Nederland to Boulder. But since nearly everyone enters Boulder Canyon from the east, I decided to make an exception and list the crags as they are encountered left and right driving west up the canyon. Crags accessed from a single approach, however, are still listed from left to right.

RATINGS

The system used for rating difficulty in this book is a streamlined version of the so-called Yosemite Decimal System. The class five designation is assumed, so that 5.0 through 5.14 is written as 0 through 14 without the 5. prefix. The Welzenbach classes 2 through 4 have been retained and appear in route descriptions as (cl3), (cl4), and are written out in route names as Class 3 or Class 4. The Roman numeral grades I through VI for overall difficulty are not used.

The potential for a long leader fall is indicated by an s (serious) or vs (very serious) after the rating of difficulty. A climb rated s will have at least one notable run-out and the potential for a scary fall. A climb rated vs typically will have poor protection for hard moves and the potential for a fatal or near-fatal fall. The absence of these letters indicates a relatively safe climb providing it is within the leader's ability.

Remember that the ratings of climbs are not absolute, but represent an informal consensus of opinion. Some of the routes in this book may never have been repeated which makes their ratings extremely subjective. But even the ratings of long-established routes are still debated — all of which should serve as a warning to not rely entirely on numbers. Look at the route on location and use your best judgment before proceeding.

EQUIPMENT

Appropriate climbing hardware can vary drastically from one route to another, and what a climber chooses to carry is a matter of style and experience. Sport climbs require only quick-draws unless otherwise noted. All other routes require a selection of gear based on crack width. Thus, a "standard rack" (SR) for the Boulder area might consist of the following gear:

A set of RPs

Wired stoppers up to one inch

2 or 3 slung stoppers, Hexes, or Tri-cams

Various camming devices up to two inches

6 or 7 quick draws (QDs)

TOPO LEGEND

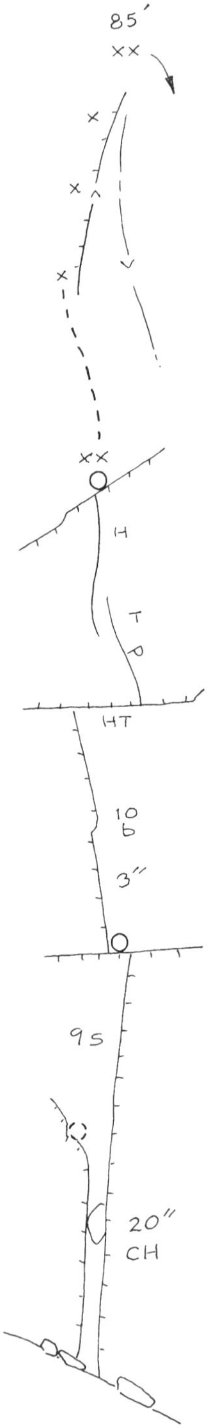

85'
xx
lower off or
rappel 85 feet

arête (left)

inside corner (right)

face climbing with bolts

belay on ramp with
bolt anchor

hand crack

thin crack with fixed pin

roof

right-facing dihedral
rated 10b with
three-inch crack

10
b

3"

belay on ledge

left-facing dihedral
rated 9 with poor pro

9 s

optional belay

20"
CH
20-inch chimney
with chockstone

ground/talus

 tree	
ʍ	tree (cut away for view)
O	belay
O.... O	move belay
◭	cairn
×	bolt
ρ	piton
× ×	bolt anchor
✓	direction of route
 ---→	walk off
HT	hand traverse
UC	under cling
LB	lieback
CH	chimney
OW	off-width
FIST	fist
H	hand crack
F	finger crack
T	thin crack

3 to 5 runners long enough to wear over the shoulder

1 double-length runner

6 to 8 unoccupied carabiners (usually with the runners)

ENVIRONMENTAL CONSIDERATIONS

To preserve the natural beauty and ecological integrity of our climbing environment, a few suggestions are offered. Use restrooms or outdoor toilets where possible. Otherwise, deposit solid human waste far from the cliffs and away from paths of approach and descent. Do not cover solid waste with a rock but leave it exposed to the elements where it will deteriorate more quickly; or better, carry a small garden spade and bury it. Carry used toilet paper out in a plastic bag or use a stick or Douglas fir cone. Do not leave man-made riff-raff lying about. If you pack it in, pack it out. Take care to preserve trees and other plants on approaches and climbs. Scree gullies and talus fields usually have sections that are more stable; thrashing up and down loose scree causes erosion and destroys plant life. Always use trails and footpaths where they have been developed and demonstrate human evolution by removing obstructions, stacking loose rocks along trail sides, and picking up trash. Dogs are best left at home as there is no way they can be attended to while one is climbing. Unattended dogs are often a nuisance or even a hazard to others.

Fixed protection has become a major point of contention with park managers and powerful wilderness lobbies such as the Audubon Society. The very concept of "climbing management" and resultant closures and restrictions has developed around climbers' use of bolts and other forms of fixed anchors, especially in high profile areas. If we are to have access to public lands and preserve the freedom that we have enjoyed in the past, it is critical that we promote a sensible and responsible public image. Climber organizations such as the Access Fund do much to help this cause, but our actions in the field are even more important.

The use of fixed protection is currently not restricted in Boulder Canyon as it is in all other climbing areas around Boulder. As a result, this beautiful canyon has become one of the best sport climbing areas in Colorado. It is up to us as climbers to ensure access and the freedom to enjoy our great sport in this excellent venue. Be kind, be courteous, and keep it clean.

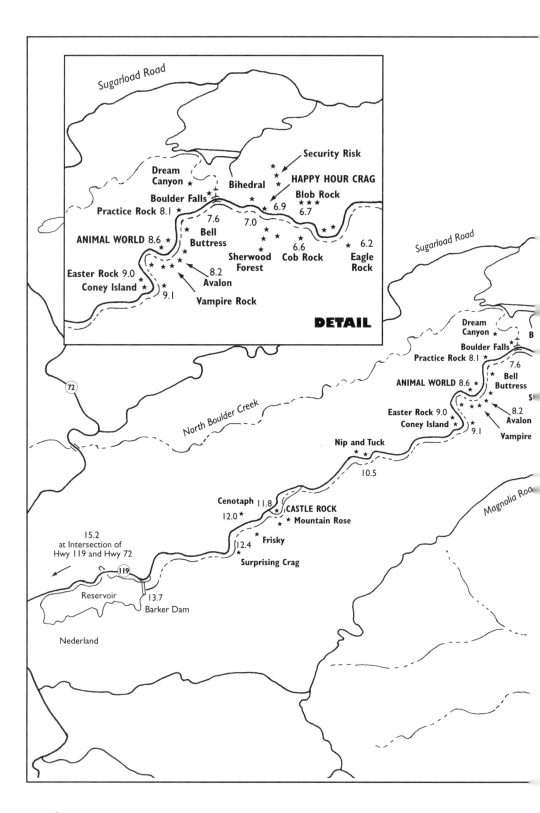

Sugarloaf Road

DETAIL

Security Risk

Dream Canyon

Bihedral

HAPPY HOUR CRAG

Boulder Falls

Blob Rock

Practice Rock 8.1

6.9

6.7

7.6

7.0

ANIMAL WORLD 8.6

Bell Buttress

Sherwood Forest

Cob Rock

6.6

6.2

Eagle Rock

Easter Rock 9.0

8.2

Coney Island

Avalon

9.1

Vampire Rock

Sugarloaf Road

Dream Canyon

B

Boulder Falls

Practice Rock 8.1

7.6

ANIMAL WORLD 8.6

Bell Buttress

S

Easter Rock 9.0

8.2

Coney Island

Avalon

9.1

Vampire

72

North Boulder Creek

Nip and Tuck

10.5

Cenotaph 11.8

CASTLE ROCK

12.0

Mountain Rose

Magnolia Road

15.2
at Intersection of
Hwy 119 and Hwy 72

12.4

Frisky

Surprising Crag

119

Reservoir

13.7

Barker Dam

Nederland

4

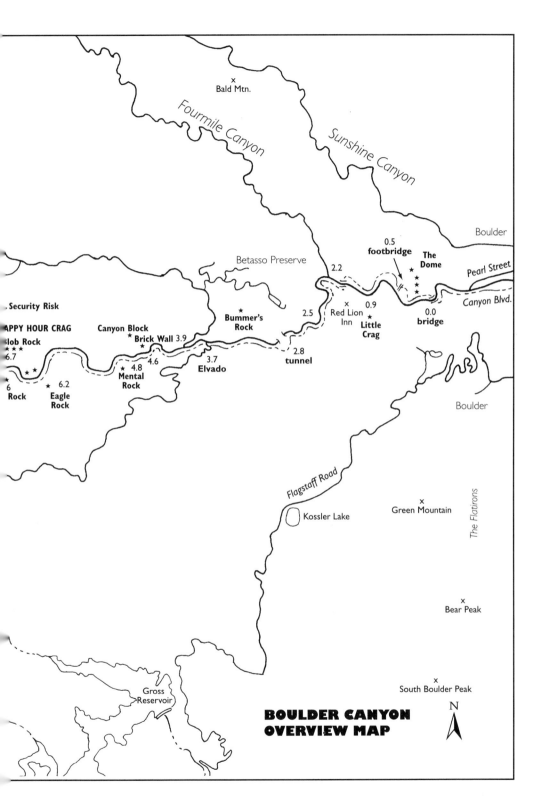

Bald Mtn. ×

Fourmile Canyon

Sunshine Canyon

Boulder

0.5
footbridge

**The
Dome**
★ ★ ★

Betasso Preserve

2.2

Pearl Street

Security Risk

APPY HOUR CRAG

lob Rock
★ ★ ★
6.7

2.5

Red Lion
Inn ×

0.9

**Little
Crag**
★

0.0
bridge

Canyon Blvd.

**Bummer's
Rock**
★

Canyon Block
★ **Brick Wall** 3.9
★

6 ★
Rock

★ ★

★ 6.2
**Eagle
Rock**

★ 4.8
**Mental
Rock**

4.6

3.7
Elvado

2.8
tunnel

Boulder

Flagstaff Road

Kossler Lake

Green Mountain ×

The Flatirons

Bear Peak ×

South Boulder Peak ×

Gross
Reservoir

**BOULDER CANYON
OVERVIEW MAP**

N
↑

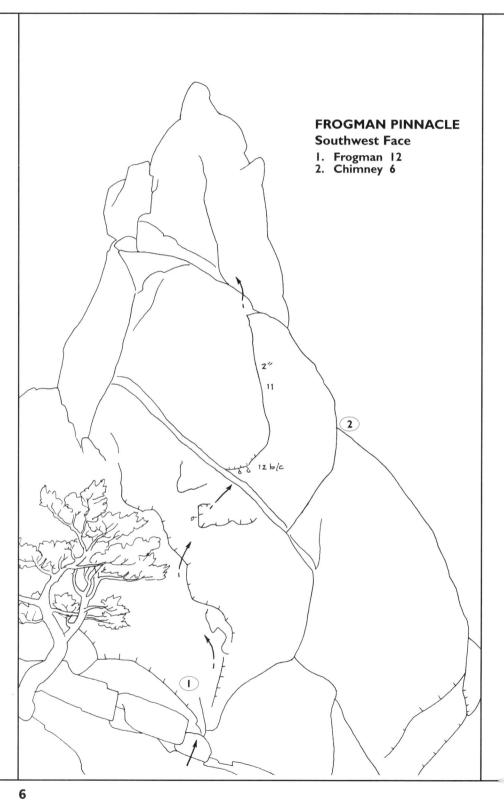

FROGMAN PINNACLE
Southwest Face
1. Frogman 12
2. Chimney 6

2"
11

12 b/c

The Dome Area

Less than a mile up the canyon and on the right is a very popular group of crags. There is a pull-out on either side of the highway at 0.5 mile and a steel footbridge where the Boulder Creek Path crosses Boulder Creek. A hundred yards or so further west is another bridge where a steel water pipe crosses the creek. The smaller crags of the group lie west along the creek path, but Frogman Pinnacle, The Dome, and the Elephant Buttresses are reached from a lesser path that heads east along the bank of the creek, and by hiking along the steel water pipe. This area may be reached easily and safely by bicycling on the Boulder Creek Path as well as by automobile.

THREE BUFFOONS

North from the waterpipe crossing is an obscure rock with a conspicuous wide crack in its south face. Other than the wide crack, one may top-rope the seam at left (11c) or jam an easy finger crack on the right.

ANUS GREAT 8+
FA: Pat Ament, Van Freeman, and Jim Dahlstrom, 1970.
Climb the perfect four-inch crack at the right side of the south face.

AMENT'S ROCK

About halfway between Three Buffoons and Frogman Pinnacle is a short south-facing wall with a roof slashing across its base.

1.   AIDS 9 ★
FA: Pat Ament and Linda Schneider, 1984.
Begin just left of the roof and climb an elegant (if short) hand and finger crack.

2.   WIGGLY SEAM 9+ s
Undercling left along flakes, then climb a wiggly seam up the right side of the face.

FROGMAN PINNACLE

As one crosses the footbridge over Boulder Creek, Frogman Pinnacle looms up just to the right above the aqueduct.

1.   FROGMAN 12
FA: Skip Guerin and Chip Ruckgaber, 1982
Climb up the middle of the south face via flakes and thin cracks. Some fixed pins may be in place.

2.   CHIMNEY 6
Climb a chimney on the east side.

THE DOME

With a warm southern exposure, metropolitan proximity, and good assortment of moderate routes, The Dome was destined for stardom. It stands high on the hillside between Frogman Pinnacle and the First Elephant Buttress and is easily viewed from the road. To reach The Dome, cross the footbridge, and hike east on a footpath that runs along Boulder Creek. After about 200 feet, turn left and hike up a short trail to a water ditch (aqueduct). Walk back west along the ditch, cross on a boulder, then follow a steep trail up the hillside to the base of The Dome. Descend from the top by scrambling down to the east or west.

THE DOME
FROM THE SOUTH
6. Gorilla's Delight 9+ ★
14. East Slab 5 or 6 ★

1.   EVENING STROLL 10D VS
FA: DUNCAN FERGUSON AND JIMMY HOFFMAN, 1970.

Begin at the west side of the crag and climb the slab left of a gully that is used as a down-climb (10a, a hook may be placed in a hole halfway up). Belay on the shoulder of the slab. Move down and right, then undercling right along and flake (crux), and jam a steep crack just above the descent gully (9+).

2.   PRELUDE TO KING KONG 9 ★
FA: ROB CANDELARIA, C. 1974.

About halfway up a lower ramp and left of a black streak climb a shallow left-facing dihedral to a thin crack that leads directly up to the belay niche on *Gorilla's Delight*.

3.   BLACK PLAGUE 10D S
FA: DAVE WEBER AND DAN HARE, 1984.

This takes the right-facing dihedral just left of the black streak.

4.   PINNACLE 10A, 11A OR CLASS 4
FA: ROB CANDELARIA, C. 1975.

Just right from the black streak is a pointed flake. The left crack is easier. The corner on the right is Class 4 and makes a good start for *Left Edge*.

5.   LEFT EDGE 5 OR 7 ★

Begin a short way up left from the low point of the wall. Climb onto a ramp and follow it up and left to belay beneath left side of a huge A-shaped roof. Traverse left past a roof and climb a corner to the top (7), or move further left and climb an easier crack to the down-climb gully.

6.   GORILLA'S DELIGHT 9+ ★
FA: PAT AMENT AND GEORGE HURLEY, 1965.

This route may be started with *Left Edge*, *Prelude To King Kong* or any other that leads to the belay beneath the left side of the big A-shaped roof. From the belay, climb a steep left-facing corner, then move right and climb a finger crack. A variation takes the finger crack just above the initial corner (10b).

7.   SUPER SQUEEZE 10D ★
FA: DAVE REARICK AND LEE HERRELL, 1963. FFA: PAT AMENT, 1969.

Begin with *Prelude To King Kong* or the like and belay from two pins beneath the awesome A-shaped roof to the right of *Gorilla's Delight*. Climb up into the apex and out through a slot.

8.   THE UMPH SLOT 8+ (10) ★
FA: PAT AMENT AND WAYNE GOSS, 1964. FFA: CHUCK PRATT, 1965.

Take any line up to the lower right side of the big A-shaped roof. Climb up and right in a Yosemite-like slot, then up a finger crack on the left (9). Most folks find the slot to require more umph than would be indicated by its original rating (8+).

9.   FAMILIAR FACE 10 S
FA: STEVE DIECKHOFF AND GEORGE BRACKSIECK, 1989.

Turn the roof above *The Umph Slot*, then climb straight up to an eight-inch-long crack (small stoppers) and continue to the top.

10.   THE OWL 7 ★

The following version of the route is called *Kor Direct* and was first climbed by Layton Kor and Ben Chidlaw in 1959. The original route climbed up to *The Umph Slot*, then traversed right beneath the big block to the hand crack. Begin near the low point of the rock. Work up and left over easy rock and

THE DOME

1. **Evening Stroll** 10d vs
2. **Prelude To King Kong** 9 ★
3. **Black Plague** 10d s
4. **Pinnacle** 10a, 11a or Class 4
5. **Left Edge** 5 or 7 ★
6. **Gorilla's Delight** 9+ ★
7. **Super Squeeze** 10d ★
8. **The Umph Slot** 8+ (10) ★
9. **Familiar Face** 10 s
10. **The Owl** 7 ★

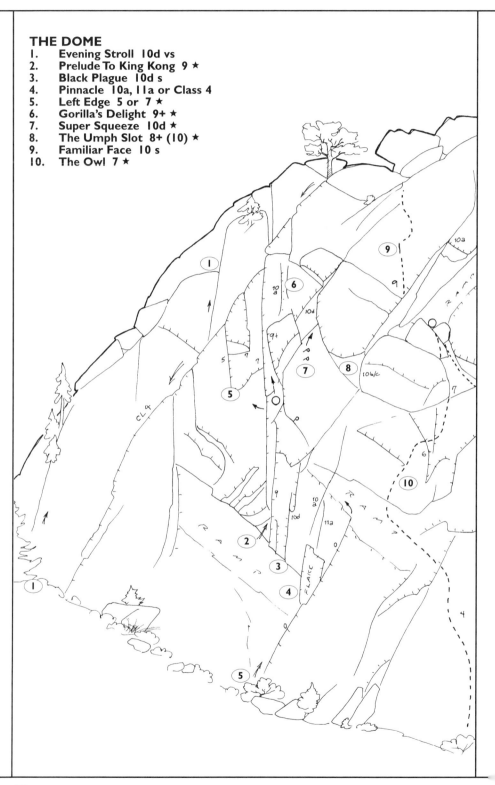

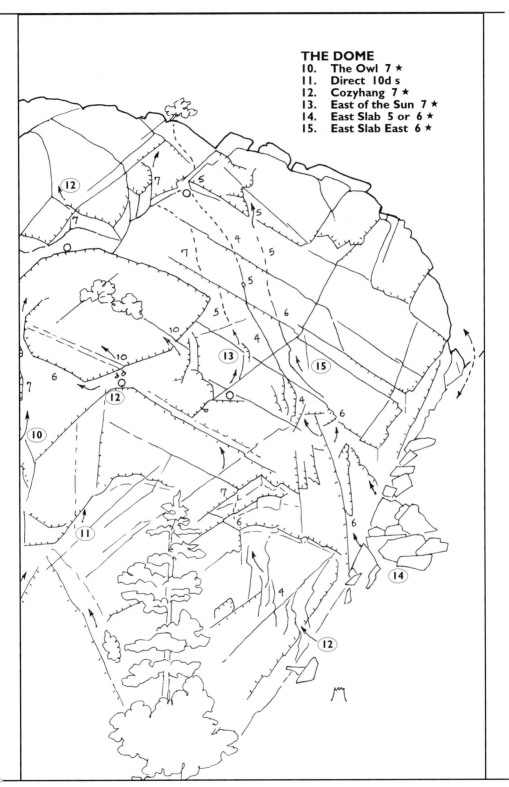

THE DOME
10. The Owl 7 ★
11. Direct 10d s
12. Cozyhang 7 ★
13. East of the Sun 7 ★
14. East Slab 5 or 6 ★
15. East Slab East 6 ★

11

belay on a ramp below the overhanging block of *Umph Slot*. Climb up toward the block, then move right at a horn and jam a steep hand crack along the right side of the block. Belay at the low end of a ramp. Finish with a crack on the left (9), a flake directly overhead (10a), or one of three exits farther to the right (7, 7, or 5).

11.   DIRECT 10D s
FA: ROB CANDELARIA, 1980s.

The low point of The Dome is formed by a blunt triangular buttress. Climb either side of the buttress to its top, then go up and right and follow a black groove to the first belay on *Cozyhang*.

12.   COZYHANG 7 ★
FA: MIKE O'BRIEN AND JIM CRANDLE, 1953.

Begin about 75 feet up and right from the low point of the face.
P1. Follow cracks up and left to a triple roof. Turn the upper roof at a crack (7), then follow a narrow ramp up and left to a stance under the big roof in the middle of the face. P2. Traverse left, do an awkward mantle, then climb through a slot and belay at the west end of a ramp as for *The Owl* (7). Move the belay up the ramp to an A-shaped roof. P3. Turn the tricky roof and continue to the top of The Dome (7).

The following three routes turn the big roof above the first belay on *Cozyhang*.

12A. COZY OVERHANG 10C
FA: CHRIS REVELEY AND DUNCAN FERGUSON, 1974.

Turn the big roof on the left.

12B. GROOVE 10D
FA: MARK WILFORD AND SCOTT BLUNK, 1977.

Just above the first belay on *Cozyhang*, turn the big roof at a channel formed by a dike.

12C. PUSSYCAT 10
FA: ALEC SHARP, DAN HARE, CHRISTIAN GRIFFITH, JOEL SCHIAVONE, 1981.

Follow a thin crack through the right side of the big roof above *Cozyhang*.

13.   EAST OF THE SUN 7 ★
BUT WEST OF THE MOON .... A LITTLE-KNOWN-BUT-GREAT VARIATION.

P1. Begin with *Cozyhang*. Turn the roofs and start up the narrow ramp, then break right at a right-leaning, right-facing corner with a fixed pin and belay on a good ledge to the right (7). P2. Climb up and right (not up the chimney) from the belay, back left along a dike/ramp, then straight up the face on tiny holds, and gain a sloping ramp that runs across the wall below some roofs (7). P3. Turn the roof at an overhanging hand crack about 12 feet left of *East Slab*, then continue more easily to the top (7).

14.   EAST SLAB 5 OR 6 ★

This is a great climb – one long pitch on perfect granite. Begin about 60 feet up and right from the dirt platform at the start to *Cozyhang*. Climb straight up a steep corner (6), or begin more easily by climbing in from the right. Pull over a bulge, then jam a discontinuous hand crack to a slab. Climb to an apex in the roof at the top of the slab and turn the roof by cranking off a down-pointing flake. A few easy moves lead to a pine tree at the top of The Dome.

15.   EAST SLAB EAST 6 ★

This is an excellent alternative when the *East Slab* is clogged with guides, clients, land tunas, and irreverent, politically incorrect, helmetless free soloists. Climb in from the right as for the regular route, but break right early and climb a tricky slot through a bulge (6). Climb discontinuous cracks about six feet right of the regular route and pass the upper roof about 20 feet down and right from the apex.

Jeff Lowe on *Left Wing*, Third Elephant Buttress.

Second
Buttress

Third Buttress

Fourth Buttress

16

22

ELEPHANT BUTTRESSES

One-half mile up the highway, on the north and right of The Dome, stand four bulky towers known as the Elephant Buttresses. These features are numbered one through four from north to south and are among the most popular crags in Boulder Canyon. Approach as for The Dome, but hike south along the ditch to a section of steel waterpipe. Continue south along the pipe until directly below the buttresses. To descend from the top of any route, scramble off the east side and traverse north to the slope between The Dome and the First Elephant Buttress, then hike down to the water ditch. One may also down-climb the steep gully between the Second and Third Buttresses. For those who don't mind the deep and dark, descend to the southeast, then wade back through a water tunnel under the Fourth Buttress. Routes are numbered continuously across all four buttresses.

First Buttress

1.   FLASH DIHEDRAL 8+
FA: PAT AMENT, C. 1970.
Climb an obvious dihedral system along the northwest aspect of the buttress.

Second Buttress

2.   ELEPHANTIASIS 10
FA: DAN HARE AND DAN MICHAEL, 1980.
Begin well up in the gully along the left side of the buttress. Undercling over a bulge (9) and continue to a belay. Climb a thin crack over a bulge along the left edge of the face to the left of *Tough Situation*.

3.   TOUGH SITUATION 9 ★
FA: DUNCAN FERGUSON, 1972.
Scramble up an easy gully to a platform below the summit block, then climb the roof and left-facing dihedral left of the prow.

4.   AVALON RISING 12B/C
FA: "SPIDER" AND IAN AUSTIN, 1988.
Also known as *La Chanson Pour Les Morts*. Climb the arête left of *Classic Finger Crack*. Four Bolts. Bring a #6 Rock.

5.   CLASSIC FINGER CRACK 9 ★
Approach as for the preceding routes. Start up the corner on the right, then step left at a flake and climb a thin crack up the beautiful face.

6.   PINE TREE ROUTE 4
Begin a short way up the gully, then climb a dihedral and crack system left of a deep chimney.

Third Buttress

7.   WINGTIP 10C ★
FA: CHIP CHASE AND PAUL LEVIN, C. 1982.
Begin about 100 feet up the gully along the north side of the buttress. Traverse right into a steep, left-facing dihedral left of *Left Wing*.

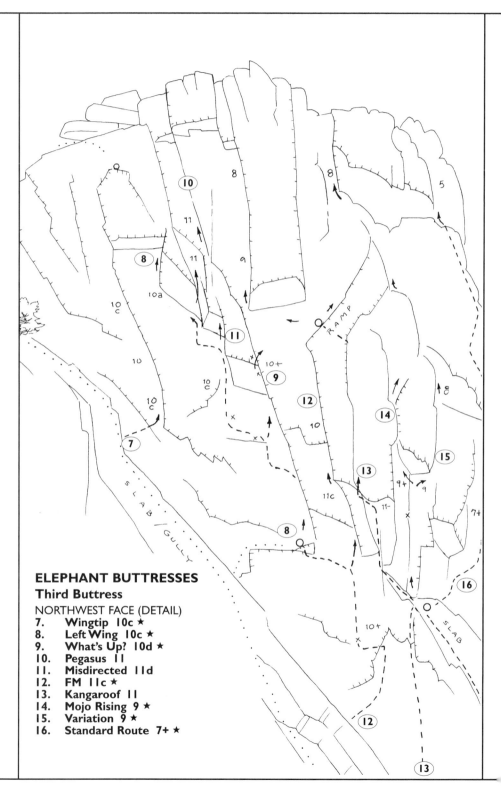

ELEPHANT BUTTRESSES
Third Buttress
NORTHWEST FACE (DETAIL)
7. **Wingtip** 10c ★
8. **Left Wing** 10c ★
9. **What's Up?** 10d ★
10. **Pegasus** 11
11. **Misdirected** 11d
12. **FM** 11c ★
13. **Kangaroof** 11
14. **Mojo Rising** 9 ★
15. **Variation** 9 ★
16. **Standard Route** 7+ ★

ELEPHANT BUTTRESSES

Third Buttress

17. Monster Woman 8+ ★
18. Ah Maw 10a s ★
19. West Face 7 ★

Fourth Buttress

FROM THE NORTHWEST
20. Flake 10c ★
21. Zolar Czakl 9+ ★
21A. Zolar Direct 10a s ★
22. Northwest Face 8 ★
23. The Heartland 9+ ★

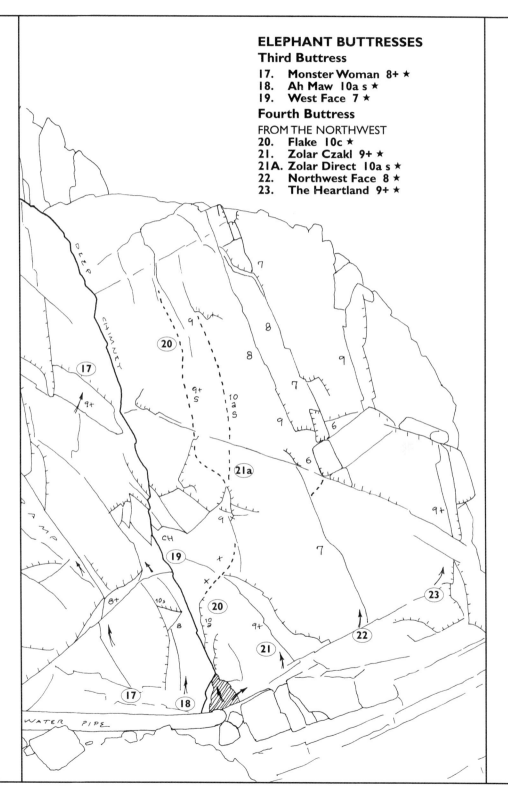

8. LEFT WING 10c ★
FA: JIM MCMILLAN, AID SOLO, 1969. FFA: ROGER BRIGGS AND ART HIGBEE, 1972.

Scramble about 70 feet up the gully between the Second and Third Buttresses and belay on a ledge to the right. This ledge may also be reached by climbing the first part of *FM*. Follow the left-leaning, left-facing dihedral and roof system to the top of the tower.

9. WHAT'S UP? 10d ★
FA: JIM AND JOHN MCMILLAN, 1969. FFA: ROGER AND BILL BRIGGS AND CHRIS REVELEY, 1973.

Climb the first 50 feet of *Left Wing*, then, undercling and lieback around a large square roof. Continue straight up a left-facing, left-leaning dihedral to the top of the tower.

10. PEGASUS 11
FA: ALEC SHARP, 1979.

Climb *Left Wing* past the roof of *What's Up?*, then follow a thin crack through the overhang and on to the top of the tower.

11. MISDIRECTED 11d
FA: CHRIS PEISKER, 1979.

Begin with *Left Wing*, then break right in a small groove between *What's Up?* and *Pegasus*. Climb past a fixed pin and join the crack of *Pegasus*.

12. FM 11c ★
FA: TOM FENDER AND JIM BURBANK, 1967. FFA: ROGER BRIGGS AND LUKE STUDER, 1974.

This stupendous route ascends the overhanging, left-facing dihedral right of *Left Wing*. Begin a short way up the gully from the pipe and climb into an A-shaped roof. Move left, then straight up into the fray. Bring an assortment of RPs and small stoppers.

13. KANGAROOF 11
FA: ALEC SHARP AND GREG CHILDS, 1979.

Start just down and right from *FM*. Climb the wall (8+) to a west-facing ramp and belay at its top. Follow a crack out through a big roof just right of *FM* (crux) and continue to a common belay for *FM* and *What's Up?*. Climb up past a small triangular roof and follow a right-facing dihedral to the top.

14. MOJO RISING 9 ★
FA: (?) RICHARD ROSSITER AND BONNIE VON GREBE, 1991.

Begin with *Kangaroof* or *Standard Route* and belay at the top of the ramp. Climb a shallow, right-facing dihedral with a fixed pin, undercling left at a roof (9), then follow a crack to a final roof that is passed on the left.

15. VARIATION 9 ★

Begin with *Kangaroof* or *Standard Route* and belay at the top of the ramp. Climb a shallow, right-facing dihedral with a fixed pin, go right around a roof, then follow dihedrals and cracks to a final roof that is passed on the left.

16. STANDARD ROUTE 7+ ★

Begin climbing from the water pipe at the northeast corner of the buttress. Climb a dihedral and belay near the top of a large ramp. Move right and climb a tricky overhanging corner, go up a crack to an easy section, up the right side of a smooth wall, back to the left, then up a short crack to the top. Just around to the right from the final section, two steep cracks may be led or top-roped (10a and 11a).

17. MONSTER WOMAN 8+ ★
FA: STAN BADGETT AND FRANK PRESCOT, 1969.

This is a more difficult start to *Mojo Rising*, *Standard Route*, et cetera. Begin at a slab with a large eye-bolt about 15 feet right of *Standard Route*. Turn the roof at a shallow, left-facing corner and continue to the communal belay near the top of the ramp. The original route climbed through the crux of *Standard Route*, then traversed left and finished as for *Variation*. It is also possible to climb straight through the crack in the initial roof (9). FA: Pat Ament in the early 1970s.

18. AH MAW 10a s ★
FA: ROB CANDELARIA AND TOM LACOMER, 1973.
Begin just right of a smooth dihedral with a square roof and climb the steep slab to a prominent roof. Turn the middle of the roof and continue up to join *Standard Route*. A variation called *Speed Trap* (10a) climbs past the right end of the main roof. FA: Dan Hare and Alan Bradley, 1984. Another variation takes the clean dihedral and roof just right of *Monster Woman* (10), then continues up to the main roof. FA: Rob Candelaria and Tom Lacomer, 1973.

19. WEST FACE 7 ★
This route climbs the southwest corner of the buttress. Begin about 25 feet from the south end of the steel water pipe. Start at a shallow, right-leaning dihedral, then follow cracks straight up the rounded arête. Pass a roof on the right and continue up steep rock to a shoulder below the top. Traverse left and finish as for *Standard Route*.

The large chimney between the Third and Fourth Buttresses is called *Pigeons' Paradise* (4), but no one in their right mind would want to climb through the reeking mess.

Fourth Buttress

This is the farthest south of the buttresses. The first four routes begin from the south end of the water pipe at the opening of a tunnel that runs beneath the Fourth Buttress. The remainder begin from a grassy ramp that angles up and left across the bottom of the buttress, and farther to the east.

20. FLAKE 10c ★
FA: STAN SHEPHERD AND ALLEN BERGEN, 1959. FFA: ART HIGBEE AND LUKE STUDER, 1972.
Begin from the end of the water pipe at the north corner of the tower. Climb an overhanging flake/crack (crux), pull around to the right side of the arête, then climb up and right past an old bolt to a roof with a fixed pin. Crank over the roof and step left to some good holds, then work straight up the left side of the steep face (9+).

21. ZOLAR CZAKL 9+ ★
FA: STAN SHEPARD AND ALLEN BERGEN, 1961. FFA: ROB CANDELARIA, SOLO, C. 1974.
Step right off the water pipe and gain a shallow dihedral that angles up to the left. Climb the awkward corner (9+) and join *Flake* at the roof.

21A. ZOLAR DIRECT 10a s ★
This is the best of all options. Once above the roof, step right into a tiny left-facing corner, then climb straight up the face between *Zolar Czakl* and *Northwest Face*. After the first ten feet above the roof it is possible to traverse right into the left hand crack of *Northwest Face* (9).

22. NORTHWEST FACE 8 ★
Begin from the south end of the water pipe, step across and pull onto a ramp, then traverse up and right along the ramp for about 30 feet and gain the bottom of a crack system that angles up and left. Follow the crack for about 50 feet, then move right and gain the top of a detached block. Step left and jam the right of two cracks to the top. It is possible to stay left and climb the left crack but is more difficult (9).

23. THE HEARTLAND 9+ ★

FA: DAN HARE AND ALAN BRADLEY, 1981.

From the pipe, traverse out right past the crack of *Northwest Face*. Climb a thin crack to a big ledge and belay (9+). Move left around an arête and jam a curving thin crack to the top.

The following routes begin from or near a long grassy ramp that runs up and left across the bottom of the south face.

24. SOUTHWEST CHIMNEY 4

Begin from the top of the ramp, and climb the chimney just left of a prominent rib. A variation called *Fool on The Hill* underclings right around a roof where the chimney becomes a deep slot. FA: Jim Erickson, solo, 1974.

25. SOUTH FACE ROOF 7 A3

Begin about 30 feet right of *Southwest Chimney* beneath a large roof. Climb a diagonal crack out through the roof and follow an easier crack system to the top.

26. ENDGAME 10A

FA: JIM ERICKSON, SOLO, 1973.

Following is a quote from Jim Erickson's guide book, *Rocky Heights*: "Begin as with *Mickey Mantle*. Go left up the decomposed rock to a large ledge, then traverse 40 feet back right to a short, one-inch crack (10-) in a large flake. Head left, and climb a thin, 5.8 crack or an easy dihedral still farther left to 'the end.'"

27. CANDELARIA'S CRACK 8

Begin with *Endgame* and climb a to narrow ledge. Jam a steep crack up the center of a big block.

28. MICKEY MANTLE 9

FA: JOE FRANK AND STEVE HALL, 1976.

Begin near the bottom of the long, grassy ramp that runs across the bottom of the south face. P1. Climb a shallow, right-facing dihedral, go up and left, then climb a left-facing dihedral, step left and belay on a sloping ledge with a cave. P2. Mantel onto a ramp above the west side of the ledge, then climb a crack to a higher ramp and go to its top. Move onto the face and step right into a crack that leads to the top of a small pillar.

29. AZIMUTH 10B

FA: DAN HARE AND STEVE MATOUS, 1985.

This route ascends an obvious finger crack in a small buttress above the start to *Mickey Mantle*.

30. MR. ATROPHY 12A

FA: ERIC DOUB AND DAN HARE, 1985.

Start up *Mickey Mantle*, turn a small roof on the right, then climb the right of two flared cracks to the right of *Azimuth*.

31. WAIT UNTIL DARK 10

FA: DAN HARE AND KURT KLEINER, 1980.

Begin about 50 feet right from the bottom of the long, grassy ramp. Climb a short, left-leaning hand crack to a grassy ledge with bushes.

32. AFTER DARK 10D
FA: DAN HARE AND GREG DAVIS, 1984.

From the ledge atop *Wait Until Dark*, scramble up to a steep wall and climb the right of two thin crack and belay on a sloping bench. Turn a roof at the top of the ramp and continue up obvious cracks on the wall above.

33. CLODDY CORNER 6
Climb a short, left-facing dihedral at the upper east side of the south face.

Topknot
The Fourth Elephant Buttress tops out in a steep block with several good cracks in the west side, all about 7 or 8 in difficulty. The following route may be among of them ... or maybe not.

34. GRAND JAM 7
Jam a crack in a 50-foot block near the top center of the south face.

LITTLE CRAG
1. **Belladonna 10**
2. **Short But Cute 10 vs**
3. **Nothing To Fear 10c s**
4. **Cool Operator 11d vs**

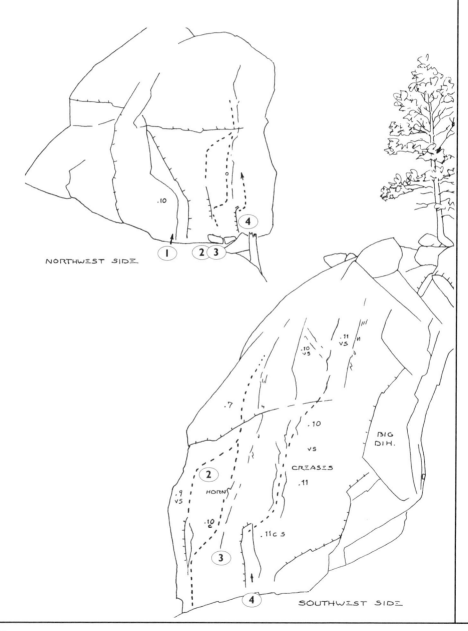

NORTHWEST SIDE

SOUTHWEST SIDE

Road Routes I

The following routes and minor crags are found along the highway between The Dome area and Cob Rock, and are described sequentially (left or right) as one drives west up the canyon.

ROCK ISLAND I

Just east of the parking pull-out for The Dome, the highway goes through a rock cut that has isolated a large mass of rock on the north side. The northwest aspect of this outcrop has several popular top-rope routes. A steep dihedral immediately south of the steel footbridge is the best of the lot (8 or 9). More difficult ventures are found to either side.

ROCK ISLAND II

This mound of broken rock stands between a cut that was blasted for the contemporary roadway and an outside curve of an older road that followed the stream and is about 100 yards west of Rock Island I. A steel waterpipe crosses the creek on the north side of the area. Use a pull-out at 0.7 mile, beside the southwest corner of the island.

CANDELARIA'S CRACK 12A ★
FA: ROB CANDELARIA, C. 1975.

Locate a big overhang at the east side of the auto pull-out. Climb a beautiful finger crack through the roof. There is also an easier crack just to the right.

LITTLE CRAG

Little Crag is located about one mile up the canyon on the left side of the road and about 60 yards up the hillside. It is more easily seen when traveling down the canyon. The rock is excellent, but the pro is naught. Use an auto pull-out on the right at 0.9 mile.

1.   BELLADONNA 10
FA: DAN HARE, 1979.

Climb a left-angling crack and corner on the northwest side.

2.   SHORT BUT CUTE 10 VS
FA: CHARLIE FOWLER AND PAT AMENT, 1984.

Just right of the western nose of the rock is a small, right-facing corner.

3.   NOTHING TO FEAR 10C S
FA: PAT AMENT AND SHAWN WILSON, 1981.

Begin as for *Short* but move up and right passing a horn (that was lassoed on the first ascent).

4.   COOL OPERATOR 11D VS ★
FA: MARK ROLOFSON, HENRY LESTER, JOHN PAINE, 1985.

A short way around on the southwest side, climb a right-facing corner, then go up and right along seams (tiny wires). The route was rehearsed before it was led.

The following three routes are located on isolated features that do not have names or other routes.

TEFLON WALL A4
FA: KYLE COPELAND AND MARC HIRT, 1982.

This is the flat, overhanging wall that draws the eye of the climber as one drives up the canyon beyond Little Crag. It is on the south side of the highway, so close that a fall could drop you into the seat of a passing convertible. Climb a very thin diagonal crack out the upside-down slab, turn the lip, and continue to easier terrain.

RED LYIN' SLAB 8
FA: PAT AMENT AND TOM AVERY, 1971.

The route climbs a slab just up the highway from the Red Lion Inn and on the right.

SUGAR CRACK 10D
FA: LARRY DALKE, C. 1965 OR POSSIBLY GARY ISSACS, C. 1977.

Climb a flake/crack on the southwest side of a small buttress on the north side of the road, at the Sugarloaf Road junction.

BUMMERS ROCK

To reach Bummers Rock, turn north on Sugarloaf Road and follow it to an intersection at 0.8 mile. Turn right and follow the Betasso Preserve Road for 0.6 mile to the Bummers Rock parking area. A short trail leads to the top of the rock. Scramble down around either side of the rock to reach the bottom of the south face. I have listed all known routes, but be warned that most of them cannot be climbed safely until the fixed pro is restored.

Originally known to climbers as Sugarloaf Dome, Bummers Rock is an obscure south-facing buttress high on the north side of Boulder Canyon. It features good granite and an array of bolt-protected face climbs. It is unfortunately located within Boulder County Open Space and has become a target for anti-climber malice. The south face of the rock is not visible to hikers or tourists, and is not a nesting area for raptors, yet the fixed protection on most of the routes has been destroyed by park rangers. The only justification offered by county officials is that they don't like the idea of bolts in the rock. Note, however, that the bolts were not necessarily removed. Instead, the hangers have been smashed into useless junk (apparently with a sledge hammer) and left in place on the rock. Was it Mark Twain who quipped, "Beware of jobs requiring uniforms."?

1.   VECTOR 10C
This appears to be the farthest left route on the rock. Climb the rounded buttress just left of *The Simpsons* (10b) and belay on a ledge. Climb overhanging rock just left of an arête, then traverse left (10c) and back right to the top.

2.   THE SIMPSONS 11B ★
Climb the left side of the shield past four bolts.

3.   CENTER 10D ★
Climb to the first bolt on *The Simpsons*, then move right and up past two more bolts and a thin crack.

4.   MALAMUTE WITH AN ATTITUDE 9+ ★
Climb past three bolts along the right side of the shield.

5.   OLD ROUTE 8
Right of the shield, climb past two bolts and a pin and belay on a ledge with a two-bolt anchor. Climb a second pitch past a pin and a bolt.

6.   LOVE TO REGRET IT 9+ ★
Begin at a two-bolt anchor just down and right from the anchor midway on *Old Route*. Climb a right-facing dihedral with three bolts.

7.   O.J. FLAKE 9
FA: KURT GRAY AND CHARLY OLIVER, 1980.
In the middle of the buttress is a large roof. Climb the left of two shallow, right-facing dihedrals left of the roof. The corner has an abundance of orange lichen.

8.   SULTRY 10
FA: DAN HARE AND CHARLY OLIVER, 1980.
Climb the right of the two dihedrals just left of the roof in the middle of the wall.

9.   ROOF ROUTE 11A
In the middle of the buttress is a large roof. Begin near a pine tree and at the left side of a slab that runs across the right side of the buttress. Climb easy rock up to the roof, then follow a thin crack through the roof and continue in an easier crack to a ramp. Escape up and left or rappel.

10.   BROKEN CAMERA BLUES 11A S
Begin down and right from the roof described above, and follow a thin crack up and left to the roof. Two fixed pins.

11.   C'EST CHOUETTE 10
Begin from the top of a steep slab set in the right side of the buttress. Climb a large, right-facing dihedral (9+) and belay on a ramp with a bolt anchor. Climb an overhanging handcrack along the left side of an orange dike and gain the top of the buttress (crux).

12.   SUSPENDED MAN 12B ★
This route follows the right of two vertical orange dikes in the right side of the buttress. Begin about ten feet right of a big, right-facing dihedral. Climb around the right side of a flake, then straight up to a bolt belay on a ramp (9+). Climb past three bolts just right of the orange dike and just left of an arête (crux), and gain the top of the buttress.

13.   THANKS BILL LEFT 11A S- ★
Begin at the right side of the buttress and climb a short pitch to a bolt anchor (8). Follow bolts up and left past a difficult mantle, then veer right and climb more easily past three more bolts to the top of the buttress.

14.   THANKS BILL RIGHT 8 OR 10A ★
From the two-bolt anchor, move out right, then climb past five bolts to the top of the rounded buttress. It also is possible to climb straight up to the first bolt above the anchor and traverse right into the main line (10a).

ISLAND ROCK
Island Rock is located at 4.2 miles on the south side of the creek, across from a rock island between the main highway and an older stretch of unpaved road. The northwest-facing buttress is about 150 feet high and has two known routes. From the top, walk off to the west.

1.   CRACKS ARE FOR KIDS 8
FA: ? NAME IS FROM A 1988 ASCENT BY ELAINE AND ERIK CHANDLER. THIS ROUTE MAY FORMERLY HAVE BEEN CALLED *DOGGIE DOO BUTTRESS*, WHICH WAS CLIMBED C. 1982.
Climb a hand crack along the left side of a pillar, just left from the center of the face. Belay at a tree.

Nancy Pritchard of *The Owl*, The Dome. Photo by Richard Rossiter.

2.   LOST RING   7
FA: RICHARD AND JOYCE ROSSITER, 1983.

Climb a dihedral and crack system along the northwest side of the buttress.

THE BRICK WALL

At about 4.6 miles and on the north side of the canyon is an attractive and popular buttress of ideal proportions for top-roping. Most of the conceivable routes have been led at one time or other but are risky affairs on the sharp end. Some bolts are in place on the summit, which is reached by scrambling around on the east side. A few boulder problems will be found along the base.

1.   PERFECT ROUTE   9 OR 10C
FA: PAT AMENT AND JIM ERICKSON, 1970; OF DIRECT FINISH (HIGH EXPOSURE): ROB CANDELARIA AND JOE ZIMMERMAN, 1973.

Begin below the southwest corner of the face and climb a bowl for about 20 feet without protection, or traverse in from a slab on the right. Climb a crack and corner system just left of the arête. Escape to the left or diagonal up and right through a bulge via *High Exposure* (8+).

2.   LIVING ON THE EDGE   11B S ★
FA: DAN HARE AND SCOTT WOODRUFF, C. 1974.

Climb through the bowl as for the previous route, but go straight up through a small triangular roof (crux), and continue up the southwest arête.

3.   DIRECT   11
FA: ROB CANDELARIA (TR), 1974.

Climb straight up the blank wall along a vague yellow streak and a bit left of center.

4.   CREASE   11A
FA: PAT AMENT (TR), 1976.

Climb the wall just left of a faint crease and join *South Face*.

5.   SOUTH FACE   10C VS ★
FA: LAYTON KOR (TR), 1963. DUNCAN FERGUSON (LEAD), 1971. SOLOED BY ROB CANDELARIA, C. 1975.

Begin at a slab just right of the bowl and climb to a ledge about 30 feet up. Work up and left over the beautiful face and climb parallel cracks to a horizontal break (crux). Climb a hand crack through the bulge and arrive on the summit.

SPASMODIC ROCK

This feature lies just west of The Brick Wall and has one known route.

THE JOKER AND THE THIEF   11D
FA: MARK ROLOFSON AND FRANK STERN, 1980.

Begin from the right side of a ledge that angles up and left across the bottom of the south face. P1. Follow a crack up and left past a pin and through an overhang (11). P2. Climb double cracks up a short, overhanging wall (11d). P3. Finish with a short crack (8).

MENTAL ROCK

A short way past the Brick Wall (at 4.8 miles) and on the south side of the creek, is a small north-facing buttress. Cross the creek on a dilapidated foot bridge a short way east of the rock. Several very difficult routes have been led here, but they are more frequently top-roped.

THE BRICK WALL

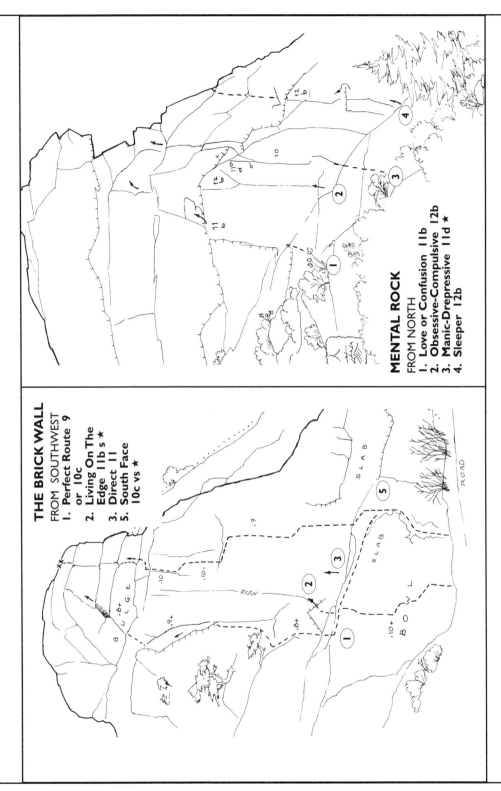

THE BRICK WALL

FROM SOUTHWEST
1. Perfect Route 9 or 10c
2. Living On The Edge 11b s ★
3. Direct 11
5. South Face 10c vs ★

MENTAL ROCK

FROM NORTH
1. Love or Confusion 11b
2. Obsessive-Compulsive 12b
3. Manic-Drepressive 11d ★
4. Sleeper 12b

29

1.   LOVE OR CONFUSION 11B
FA: MARK WILFORD AND SKIP GUERIN, 1979.
Climb a flake/crack and roof along the left side of the north face.

2.   OBSESSIVE-COMPULSIVE 12B
FA: ERIK GOUKAS, SCOTT REYNOLDS, HENRY LESTER, 1986.
Climb a very difficult seam and thin crack in the middle of the face.

3.   MANIC-DEPRESSIVE 11D ★
FA: MARK WILFORD AND SKIP GUERIN, 1979.
Climb a thin crack and roof (crux) with some fixed gear.

4.   SLEEPER 12B
FA: CHRIS PEISKER AND MARK ROLOFSON, 1980.
Climb through two roofs along the right side of the north face.

CANYON BLOCK

This giant boulder (also known as the Milk Dud) features several excellent short routes. It is located on the north side of the highway across from Mental Rock. Park at a gravel pull-out at 4.8 miles. Hike north up a gully, then break right along a faint path that leads east to the objective. Just down-slope to the west is a smaller rock with a bolt on top for top-roping.

1.   AMENT CRACK 11B/C
FA: PAT AMENT, 1975 (TR).
Climb a 5.10a overhang to get up on a ledge that runs across the west face (or climb in from either side). Take the incipient crack on the left.

2.   SEAM 11 A0
FA: DAN HARE AND HARVEY ARNOLD, 1983, WITH A BIT OF AID AT THE TOP.
Climb the seam a few feet right of *Ament Crack*.

3.   SCORCHER 9+
FA: DAN HARE AND HARVEY ARNOLD, 1983.
Climb the offset, left-leaning cracks in the center of the west face.

4.   WALLFLOWER 12B
FA: BOB HORAN AND DAN McQUADE, 1987.
Begin as for *Scorcher*, but follow a right-leaning flake to a bolt, then up and right to *Damaged Goods*.

5.   DAMAGED GOODS 13A ★
FA: SKIP GUERIN, 1985 (TR). MARK ROLOFSON AND BOB HORAN, 1987 (LEAD).
Begin at the bottom of the overhanging southwest arête. Boulder up to a good hold, and follow a left-leaning crack to the top.

6.   RUDE BOY 12B ★
FA: CHRISTIAN GRIFFITH AND HARRISON DEKKER, 1982 (TR?). REDPOINT (?): BOB HORAN AND DAN McQUADE, 1986.
Begin this awesome little route just right of *Damaged Goods*. Climb the out-leaning crack/corner, mantle past the roof, etc.

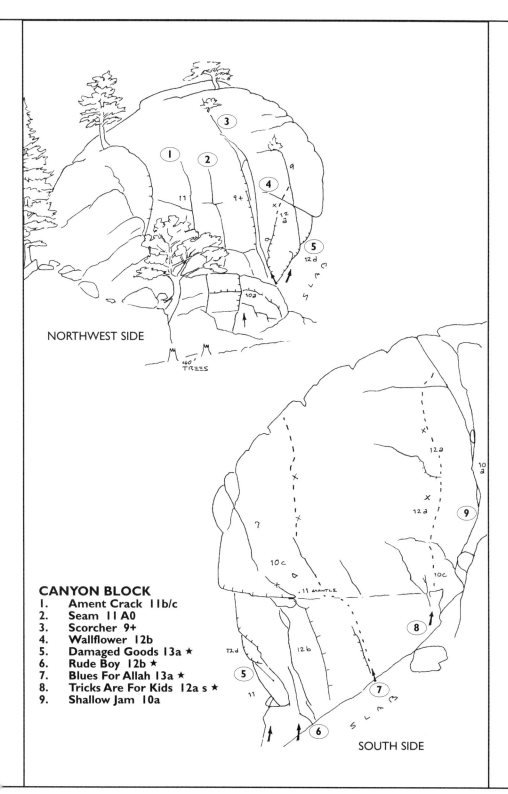

NORTHWEST SIDE

CANYON BLOCK
1. Ament Crack 11b/c
2. Seam 11 A0
3. Scorcher 9+
4. Wallflower 12b
5. Damaged Goods 13a ★
6. Rude Boy 12b ★
7. Blues For Allah 13a ★
8. Tricks Are For Kids 12a s ★
9. Shallow Jam 10a

SOUTH SIDE

7.   BLUES FOR ALLAH 13A ★
FA: Mark Rolofson, 1987.

Just up and right from *Rude Boy*, climb a left-angling ramp (RPs), mantle up to a crack, step left at a bolt, then climb straight up past a second bolt (crux). A 1.5 Friend may be placed near the top of the face. Rolofson claims the route may be led safely on sight.

8.   TRICKS ARE FOR KIDS 12A S ★
FA: Mark Rolofson, 1985.

This is a superb short pitch, but the clip-ins are difficult for someone less than six feet tall. Begin along the right side of the smooth south face and climb past two bolts.

9.   SHALLOW JAM 10A
Climb the crack at the right side of the south face.

LONG WALK ROCK

At about 4.1 miles up the highway, two small buttresses come into view, high on the ridge to the north. Approach as for Canyon Block, but continue up the long slope to the buttresses. The first five routes are on the lower buttress. All routes by Ted Anderson unless otherwise noted.

1.   OSTRICH IN BONDAGE 9
Begin around on the west side of the lower rock. This could be *Free The Ostriches*. Gear.

2.   FAT BIRD 10A
Begin a short way right of *Ostrich In Bondage*. Climb a right-angling crack to a gear belay. Gear, one bolt.

3.   TIGER PAW 11
Climb a curving crack and seam on the left side of the south face. Two bolts with chains at the top.

4.   FREE THE OSTRICHES 9
FA: Pat Ament, Shawn Wilson, Audrey Huerta, 1979.

Climb the obvious crack that splits the south side of the rock.

5.   THE CAT'S MEOW 9
Climb the crack and steep face just right of *Free The Ostriches*. One bolt, a fixed pin plus gear. Chains at the top.

This formation is located north and uphill from the lower rock.

1.   LITTER BOX 10A
This route is around on the left side of the formation. Make a fingertip traverse right, then climb a corner to the top. Two bolts plus a #2 Camalot. Chains at the top.

2.   BIG CAT CLUB 11
Begin near the right side of the west face behind a small pine tree. Climb past a bolt to a ledge, then continue up the face past another bolt to the top. Two bolts plus small to medium gear. Chains at the top.

3.   WELCOME TO TED'S WORLD 12A
Begin on the south side. Follow a finger and hand crack to a ledge, then climb an arête with bolts. Three bolts plus gear. Chains at the top.

THE ARENA

This clandestine wall is located about 6.3 miles up the canyon, just past Eagle Rock, high on the north side. The climbs range from 20 to 80 feet in length. The wall is dead vertical and flat as a board with tiny square-cut face holds. Use a pull-out on the right at 6.2 miles or a smaller pull-out directly below the wall. A steep, five minute hike leads to the objective. Bring a stick-clipper. See topo on page 32.

1.   SUCKER PUNCH 11D
FA: Dave Bangert and Dan Hare, 1995.

This line takes the upper left corner of the wall. Two bolts to a two-bolt anchor.

2.   STANDING EIGHT COUNT 11B
FA: Dan Hare and John Fort, 1995.

This route begins from a flat block and climbs the left side of the face. Three bolts to a two bolt anchor.

3.   CONTENDER DIRECT 11c ★
FA: Harris, Cardoza, Randy Spears.

Begin just left of a black streak in the middle of the wall. Climb up and right to join *Contender*. Four bolts to a two-bolt anchor.

4.   CONTENDER 12a ★
FA: Dave Cardoza, Scott Harris, Mick Fairchild, c. 1989.

Begin at the lower right section of the wall. Climb straight up past three bolts, left along a crack, and up to a block in a triangular recess. Hand traverse left, then straight up past two bolts to the top of the face. The crux is at the second bolt. Six bolts to a two-bolt anchor. A TCU or equivalent may be placed before reaching the third bolt.

5.   FIRST ROUND 10B
FA: Dan Hare and Susan Simpson, 1995.

Climb the right side of the steep face. Three bolts to a two-bolt anchor.

ONE SHOE MAKES IT MURDER

This is the long name given to the short wall just around the bend, west of The Arena. Park as for Cob Rock, then cross the road and gain a grassy ramp that leads east to the crag. See topo on page 33.

1.   DATING GAME 12a/b

Climb up and left to the end of a left-leaning seam, then traverse right across *Rockin' Horse* and turn the roof, topping out at a separate anchor. Six bolts to a two-bolt anchor.

2.   ROCKIN' HORSE 12a ★
FA: Kyle Copeland and Ray Reichert, 1983. FFA: Charlie Fowler, Mark Rolofson, Kyle Copeland, 1986. QDs plus stoppers and a #1.5 Friend.

Begin at a right-leaning, right-facing dihedral in the middle of the wall. Climb left past a jug, then straight up the face past several bolts and a difficult roof. Four bolts to a two-bolt anchor.

3.   PALE HORSE 11D
FA: Kyle Copeland 1983.

Climb the right-facing dihedral and traverse left at the roof to join the preceding line.

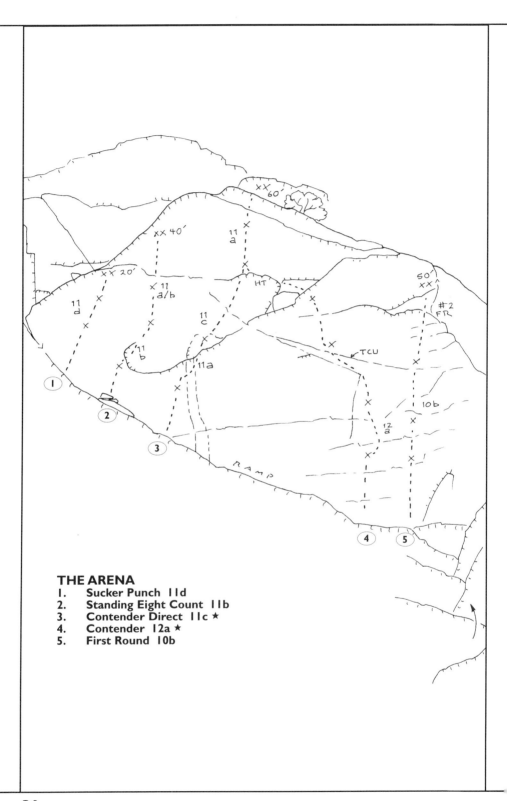

THE ARENA

1. Sucker Punch 11d
2. Standing Eight Count 11b
3. Contender Direct 11c ★
4. Contender 12a ★
5. First Round 10b

CASUAL VIEWING

Across from Cob Rock is a steep, southeast facing wall with some right-angling cracks. The top of this wall is just below Short Cliff With Three Cracks. The approach is steep and loose and directly above the highway.

1.   CARL'S OVERLOOK A2
FA: PAT AMENT, C. 1963.

Actual line of the route is not known.

2.   CASUAL VIEWING 11
FFA: RANDY LEAVITT AND DAN HARE, 1981.

Begin at a hanging left-facing corner, go up and left to a flake and to a thin crack in the middle of the face.

3.   HARE LOSS 10
FA: KURT GRAY AND CHARLY OLIVER, 1980.

Start to the right of *Casual Viewing* beneath a crack in the right side of the wall. Climb up to a ledge (9), do a difficult lieback (10), and continue in the same system to the top of the wall.

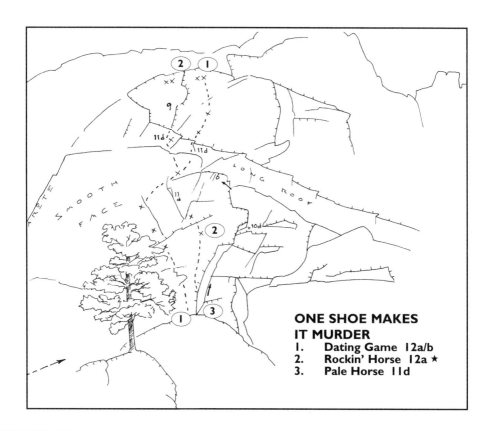

ONE SHOE MAKES IT MURDER
1.   **Dating Game 12a/b**
2.   **Rockin' Horse 12a ★**
3.   **Pale Horse 11d**

Moe Hershoff on *Ecstasy of the People*. Photo by Richard Rossiter.

Cob Rock Area

Cob Rock is the central feature in a series of impressive buttresses located on the south side of the canyon between the 6 and 7 mile marks. These crags offer a broad variety of terrain from easy "mountaineering" routes such as Great Dihedral on Eagle Rock to the difficult sport climbs on Sherwood Forest. The monolithic buttress of Cob Rock is one of the most popular features in Boulder Canyon. Each of these crags requires a crossing of Boulder Creek.

EAGLE ROCK

At 6.2 miles and on the left, the large west-facing buttress of Eagle Rock towers above the highway. The broad wall is somewhat irregular with several large roofs and an abundance of lichen. To approach, ford the creek and hike up the brushy slope to the base. To escape from the summit ridge, hike south, then cut down through the trees to the west.

1.   CHICKEN'S DELIGHT 8
FA: ROGER BRIGGS AND BILL BRUENER, 1967.

Climb the left side of the west face. The line is indistinct and the difficulty will vary according to one's wanderings.

2.   GROS VOGEL 8 A2
FA: PAT AMENT AND MIKE STANLEY, 1963.

This route ascends the middle of west face passing just right of some orange lichen streaks beneath a big roof. P1. Climb up and left across an easy slab to a tree on the steep part of the wall. Go behind the pine, then up and left to a steep crack that is aided to a belay stance. P2. Climb a slab up and right for 35 feet, then go up a vertical wall to the left. Traverse five feet left to a small, sloping ledge. P3. Go up and right for 15 feet to an awkward corner with a loose block, then climb a 25-foot dihedral to a ledge beneath a reddish overhang. P4. Climb the left side of the overhang (9 or aid) and belay near a big ledge. Scramble to the top.

3.   FREI VOGEL 9 s
FA: DAN HARE AND MASON FRICHETTE, 1980.

This would be the Lynnard Skynnard version of *Gros Vogel*, except that it appears to be a completely independent line. Scramble up to the low point, a bit left of center, and rope up near a tree. One may also begin a bit further to the right by scrambling up the ramp toward *Gros Vogel*.

4.   SCREAMING WAR EAGLE 10c
FA: CHRIS BRISLAWN AND JIM SWENSON, 1988. SR WITH EMPHASIS ON SMALL GEAR.

The relationship between this and the preceding route is not known, however they appear to have common terrain. This route begins near a small pine, then passes just right of the big roof in the center of the face. Three pitches (10a, 150 feet; 10b, 160 feet; 10c, 80 feet).

5.   GREAT DIHEDRAL 5 ★
Also known as *Right Center Face*. Scramble up as for the previous routes, but continue up a narrowing ramp to the right (south). Belay on a pedestal and climb up and left to gain the dihedral. Two pitches.

EAGLE ROCK
2. Gros Vogel 8 A2
5. Great Dihedral 5 ★
6. To The Sun 5

38

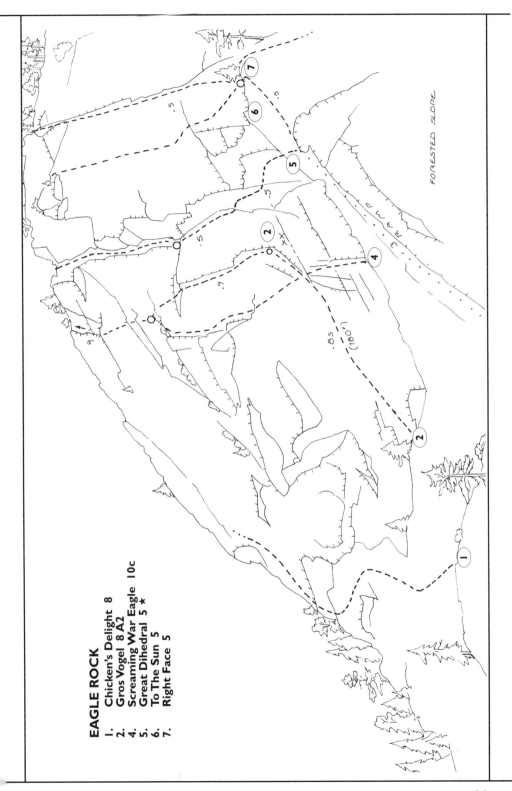

EAGLE ROCK

1. Chicken's Delight 8
2. Gros Vogel 8 A2
4. Screaming War Eagle 10c
5. Great Dihedral 5 ★
6. To The Sun 5
7. Right Face 5

FORESTED SLOPE

COB ROCK
7. Ms. Fanny Le Pump 11c ★
11. Huston Crack 8+ ★
14. East Edge 10a (9s) ★
15. North Face Left 8 ★
16. North Face Center 7 ★
17. Empor 7+ ★
19. Northwest Corner 8 ★
23. West Rib 8

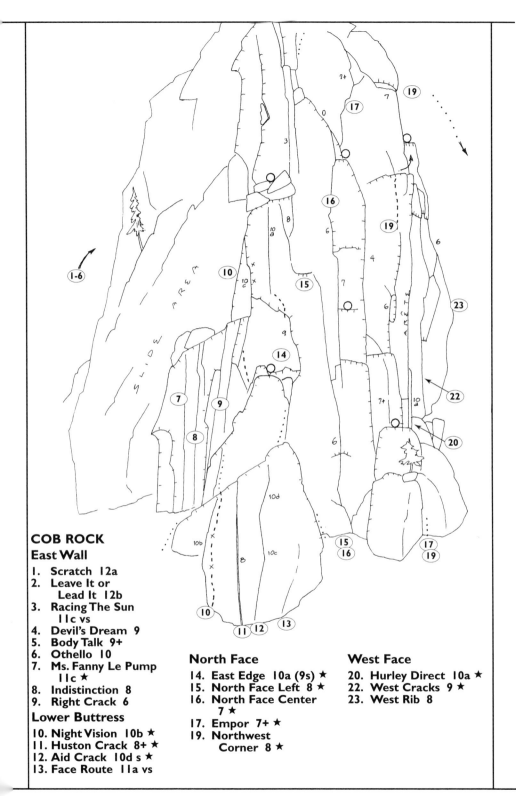

COB ROCK
East Wall

1. Scratch 12a
2. Leave It or
   Lead It 12b
3. Racing The Sun
   11c vs
4. Devil's Dream 9
5. Body Talk 9+
6. Othello 10
7. Ms. Fanny Le Pump
   11c ★
8. Indistinction 8
9. Right Crack 6

Lower Buttress

10. Night Vision 10b ★
11. Huston Crack 8+ ★
12. Aid Crack 10d s ★
13. Face Route 11a vs

North Face

14. East Edge 10a (9s) ★
15. North Face Left 8 ★
16. North Face Center
    7 ★
17. Empor 7+ ★
19. Northwest
    Corner 8 ★

West Face

20. Hurley Direct 10a ★
22. West Cracks 9 ★
23. West Rib 8

6. TO THE SUN 5
FA: RICHARD ROSSITER AND LYNN HOUSEHOLDER, 1979.

Approach as for *Great Dihedral*, then climb up and right past the pedestal, around a roof, and belay by a tree. Climb the middle of the broad buttress right of *Great Dihedral*.

7. RIGHT FACE 5
FA: CLEVE MCCARTY, TED ROUILLARD, JOHANNA BENNETT, 1956.

Begin from the forest slope about 80 feet right of *Great Dihedral*. Climb a crack and corner system along the right side of a broad buttress.

COB ROCK

At about 6.6 miles, the compact buttress of Cob Rock comes into view on the south side of the canyon. In fall and winter, Cob is a cold and shady place. That climbers may be seen on the rock during any season attests to the quality and great popularity of its routes. Park at a convenient pull-out on the left, beneath the rock. A convenient bridge across Boulder Creek, however, does not exist. Look for a tyrolean traverse just upstream, or as a last resort, brave the rapids. To descend from the top, scramble off to the south, then down through the trees along the west side.

East Wall

The following six routes ascend a long narrow wall that climbs the hillside just east of the main rock.

1. SCRATCH 12A
FA: DAN HARE AND ROB STANLEY, 1996.

This is the farthest left route on the East Wall. Climb past four bolts to a two-bolt anchor near the left side of this wall.

2. LEAVE IT OR LEAD IT 12B
FA: JOEL DYER AND DEREK HERSEY, (TR).

Begin 30 feet up and left from *Devil's Dream*, set a top rope from a tree. Climb a curving crack that fades at a headwall (10c). Climb the headwall just right of a small, left-facing corner.

3. RACING THE SUN 11C VS
FA: JOEL DYER AND TALLY O'DONNEL. RACK: #1 AND 4 FRIEND, RPS, AND ROCKS #1-4.

Begin ten feet uphill from *Devil's Dream*. Climb two left-leaning seams to some knobs (10c), then go straight up the wall (crux).

4. DEVIL'S DREAM 9
FA: JIM ERICKSON AND VICKI HODGE, 1979.

What's in a name? Begin about 100 feet up along the East Wall. Follow a thin crack up and slightly left, almost to a ledge, then step right and pull up over a bulge to a tree.

5. BODY TALK 9+
FA: DAN HARE AND ALAN BRADLEY, 1980.

To the right of *Devil's Dream*, climb up into a left-facing, left-leaning corner.

6. OTHELLO 10
FA: PAT AMENT AND DAVID BREASHEARS, 1975.

Toward the lower end of the East Wall, climb up and right, then follow a slightly left-leaning dihedral.

The following three routes are located on a short wall at the lower left side of the north face.

7. MS. FANNY LE PUMP 11c ★
FA: BRUCE MORRIS AND DAVE ROSENTHAL, 1977.
Climb the left and more difficult of the three cracks.

8. INDISTINCTION 8
FA: JIM ERICKSON, SOLO, 1978.
Climb the middle crack.

9. RIGHT CRACK 6
FA: R. ROSSITER, SOLO, 1980.
Climb the third crack from the left.

Lower Buttress

At the bottom of the north face is a 50-foot wall with the following three routes.

10. NIGHT VISION 10B ★
FA: DAN HARE AND STEVE MATOUS, 1986.
Begin at the left edge of the north face, above the Lower Buttress. Climb up the far left edge of the north face. Two pitches.

11. HUSTON CRACK 8+ ★
FA: CARY HUSTON, C. 1955.
Climb the prominent wide crack along the left side of the buttress.

12. AID CRACK 10D s ★
FFA: JIM ERICKSON AND DUNCAN FERGUSON, 1971.
Climb a thin finger crack up the middle of the buttress.

13. FACE ROUTE 11A vs
Climb the face to the right of the preceding route via top-rope.

North Face

The following routes ascend the narrow and classic north face of Cob Rock.

14. EAST EDGE 10A (9s) ★
FA: PAT AMENT AND LARRY DALKE, 1962. FFA: LARRY DALKE, 1966.
Climb around either side of the Lower Buttress and belay on a ledge below the steep part of the north face. From the right side of the ledge, climb a shallow and poorly protected left-facing corner and turn the roof at its top (9). Traverse up and left and climb a thin crack to a ledge with some blocks. Follow easy cracks to the summit.

15. NORTH FACE LEFT 8 ★
FA: LAYTON KOR AND CHUCK NAYLOR, 1959.
Begin at an alcove up and right from the Lower Buttress. Follow a prominent crack up and left to a narrow ledge, step left and climb to a ledge with blocks. Easy cracks lead to the top.

16. NORTH FACE CENTER 7 ★
FA: LAYTON KOR AND GEORGE HURLEY, 1959.
Begin in the alcove as for the preceding route. Climb the crack for about 50 feet, then move right into the next system and continue to a ledge. Continue up the crack to a stance on an arête above a V-slot. Climb up the slot or do the final pitch of *Empor*.

17. EMPOR 7+ ★
FA: George Lamb and Dallas Jackson, 1954.

Begin beneath a large boulder at the lower right corner of the north face. P1. Climb a dihedral on the main wall behind the boulder (8), or climb the west side and mantle to its top (6). P2. Make difficult moves up a vague crack (7+), then move left into a right-facing dihedral and belay in a V-slot at its top. P3. Climb a steep crack up and right across the steep headwall to the top of the rock (7+).

18. SCARY VARIANT 9 s
FA: Pat Ament and Lowell Green, 1980.

Begin with *Empor*, but where that route moves left, climb straight up the face until forced right onto the *Northwest Corner* route.

19. NORTHWEST CORNER 8 ★

Begin as for *Empor* or climb *Hurley Direct* around on the west side. In either case, gain a right-facing corner and follow it up the right side of the north face. Belay on a pedestal on the right side of the arête. Climb through a tricky roof and belay on the summit.

West Face

The following routes are located or at least begin on the west side of the main buttress.

20. HURLEY DIRECT 10A ★
FA: George Hurley, 1967.

Climb a difficult thin crack just right of the northwest arête and join *Northwest Corner*.

21. BROWNIES IN THE BASIN 9+ s+ ★
FA: Rob Candelaria, solo, 1974.

Rob is well-known for his bold ventures into the unknown. As a consequence, this excellent route is still largely unknown. Begin just up and right from *Hurley Direct* and follow a difficult crack system up the left side of the west face. Finish as for *Northwest Corner*.

22. WEST CRACKS 9 ★

Follow cracks up the left side of the west rib and join *Northwest Corner*.

23. WEST RIB 8

Climb a crack up the west rib and join *Northwest Corner* for its final pitch.

24. WEST DIHEDRAL 8

Climb the dihedral that forms the right margin of the west rib, and finish with *Northwest Corner*.

25. UPPER WEST FACE ?

There may be a route in the upper west face. Look for an old bolt.

LOST FLATIRON

A flatiron in Boulder Canyon? About 200 yards west of Cob Rock and 500 feet up the hillside is a 350-foot-high granite pinnacle with a sloping north face and a steep arête on the east side - the Lost Flatiron. A cairn in the notch behind the summit indicates that someone had at least been there, if not climbed one of several possible lines on the north face. The following routes were climbed by Richard Rossiter during 1996. The easiest approach is to ford the stream and hike directly up open forest to the bottom of the north face. One may also proceed up and right from the west side of Cob Rock. Descend from the summit by hiking down the steep gully on the west side of the pinnacle.

LOST FLATIRON
1. Arête 10c ★ (incomplete)
3. North Face Left 7 ★

1.   ARÊTE 10C ★ (INCOMPLETE)

Scramble up around the east side of the buttress to the bottom of a pronounced arête. Pull up and right toward a ledge with a juniper tree, then start up along the left edge of the arête. Follow bolts and occasional gear placements to the top of the arête. TR only at time of writing.

2.   RAMP 8

Begin just left of the northeast arête and scramble up to a grassy ledge where a six-foot tree arches out of a crack. Climb the crack to a bulge, then follow a thin crack up and right to a broken dihedral. Belay at its top on a grassy ledge. Climb a slot and left-facing dihedral on the right and belay on the summit. The best finish, however, is variation B.

2A.   VARIATION 9+

From the bulge on the first pitch, follow a hand and fist crack up and left and join *Arête*.

2B.   VARIATION 8

From the belay at the top of the first pitch, work up and left and join *Arête*.

3.   NORTH FACE LEFT 7 ★

Begin six feet right from east edge of the north face and continue very near the east edge all the way to the summit. On the upper face, one may climb right along the arête. The crux is in passing left of a small tree about 300 feet up. Two or three pitches.

4.   NORTH FACE RIGHT 6

Begin at the lower right side of the north face. Climb a slab to a ledge with a large tree, then continue up moderate terrain to the top.

WITCHES TOWER

Witches Tower is a steep buttress at the bottom of a long rock rib that climbs the forested slope across the canyon from The Bihedral. It comes into view on the south side of the creek at 6.8 miles. Several old routes have been climbed or at least attempted on the lower west side of the buttress.

SHERWOOD FOREST

Sherwood Forest is a steep northwest-facing wall on the same rib as Witches Tower and about 200 feet farther above the stream. The wall is on the upper right side of the buttress and features seven sport climbs (QDs only), most of which are good. Be watchful for loose rock on some of the roofs. Approach via tyrolean traverse about 100 yards upstream from the buttress. Follow a trail eastward along the stream until below the buttress, then hike up the steep slope along the base of the wall.

1.   MERRY MEN 11B ★

Begin just left of a large Douglas fir. Seven bolts to a two-bolt anchor.

2.   ROBBIN' THE HOOD 11D ★

This is perhaps the best route on the wall. Start just right of a large Douglas fir and follow bolts along a right-leaning, right-facing dihedral. Six bolts to a two-bolt anchor.

3.   PRINCE OF THIEVES 12B ★

Begin about 10 feet right of a large Douglas fir. Follow bolts over two roofs and along the right side of a V-slot. Eleven bolts to a two-bolt anchor.

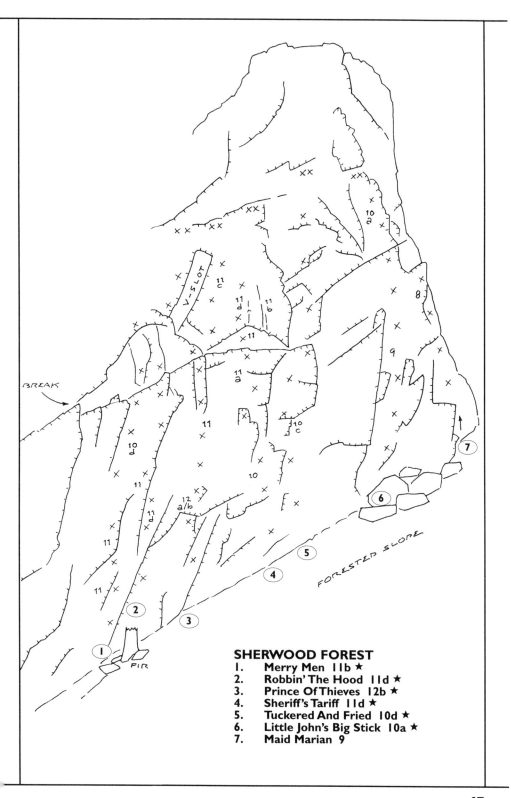

SHERWOOD FOREST

1. **Merry Men** 11b ★
2. **Robbin' The Hood** 11d ★
3. **Prince Of Thieves** 12b ★
4. **Sheriff's Tariff** 11d ★
5. **Tuckered And Fried** 10d ★
6. **Little John's Big Stick** 10a ★
7. **Maid Marian** 9

SHERWOOD FOREST
4.   Sheriff's Tariff 11d ★
GARDEN PARTY WALL
3.   Right Crack 10c ★

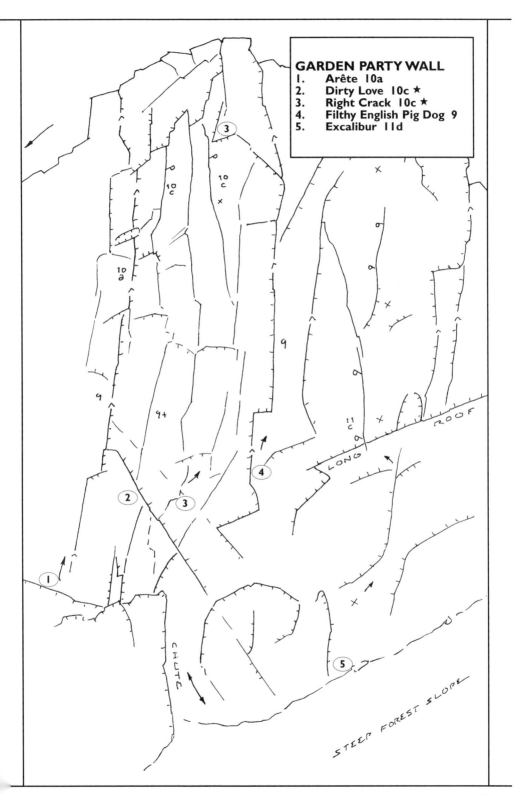

GARDEN PARTY WALL
1.   Arête 10a
2.   Dirty Love 10c ★
3.   Right Crack 10c ★
4.   Filthy English Pig Dog 9
5.   Excalibur 11d

4.   SHERIFF'S TARIFF 11D ★

Begin just right of a low roof in the middle of the wall. Climb past a white dike and over a roof. Nine bolts to a two-bolt anchor.

5.   TUCKERED AND FRIED 10D ★

Begin just right of the preceding route and follow bolts through a series of roofs. Eight bolts to a two-bolt anchor.

6.   LITTLE JOHN'S BIG STICK 10A ★

Climb along a right-facing dihedral near the right side of the wall. Nine bolts to a two-bolt anchor.

7.   MAID MARIAN 9

Follow bolts along the right margin of the wall. Six bolts to a two-bolt anchor.

GARDEN PARTY WALL

Garden Party Wall is located on a separate buttress, a short way uphill from Sherwood Forest. Follow a vague trail up to the base of the wall. To escape from the top of the wall, rappel from trees or scramble down a gully on the north. All known routes established by Dave Fortner, T. Collins, and Martin Burch.

1.   ARÊTE 10A

Scramble up a chute to start, then follow cracks up the left side of an arête.

2.   DIRTY LOVE 10C ★

Start up the chute, then follow a crack system up the main wall just right of the arête. One pin near the crux.

3.   RIGHT CRACK 10C ★

Begin as for the preceding route, but follow a crack out to the right and up the right side of the wall past some fixed gear.

4.   FILTHY ENGLISH PIG DOG 9

Climb a right-facing dihedral along the right side of the main wall. A large rat or the like was observed inside the crack on the first ascent.

5.   EXCALIBUR 11D

Follow a line of bolts and pins up the steep wall about 30 feet right of the preceding route.

Scott Reyonlds on *Hot Flyer*. Photo by Richard Rossiter.

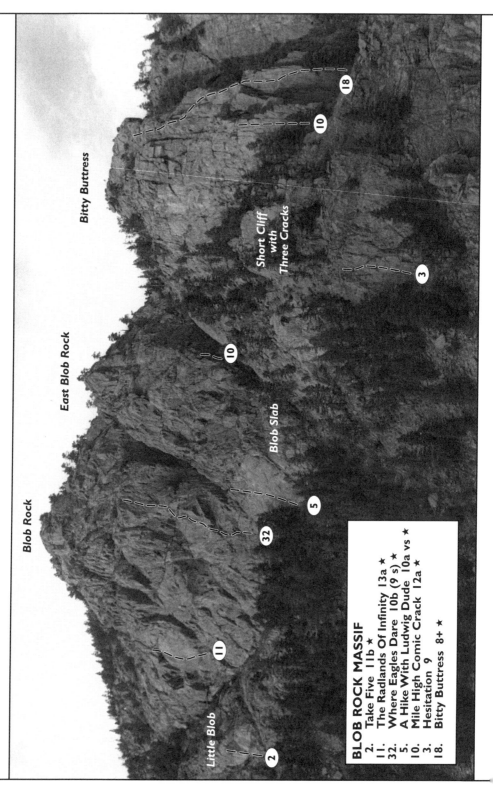

Blob Rock

East Blob Rock

Bitty Buttress

Little Blob

Blob Slab

Short Cliff
with
Three Cracks

BLOB ROCK MASSIF
2.   Take Five 11b ★
11. The Radlands Of Infinity 13a ★
32. Where Eagles Dare 10b (9 s) ★
5.   A Hike With Ludwig Dude 10a vs ★
10. Mile High Comic Crack 12a ★
3.   Hesitation 9
18. Bitty Buttress 8+ ★

Blob Rock Massif

On the north side of the canyon directly across from Cob Rock are three, large south-facing buttresses and their satellites. Due to proximity and common line of approach, they are described from west to east in the following manner: Little Blob, Blob Rock, East Blob, Bitty Buttress and Short Cliff with Three Cracks. All features face south and offer warm climbing even during winter.

Approach. Park at a small pull-out on the right, shortly after passing the Cob Rock pull-out. Follow a footpath northeast past a platform, then more directly up the slope to the bottom of Blob Rock. East Blob and Blob Slab (its lower apron) are just to the right (east). Bitty Buttress and Short Cliff With Three Cracks are reached by traversing south just below Blob Slab. Look for a right branch in the main trail.

LITTLE BLOB

Just below the west end of the main wall is a small buttress with three routes.

1.   UNNAMED 11c ★
Step off a block and follow a seam past four bolts. Lower off from chains.

2.   TAKE FIVE 11b ★
FA: Dave Bruebeck Quartet (unknown).
This route follows the arête about 15 feet right of *Unnamed*. Four bolts to a two-bolt anchor.

3.   SLOW DEATH 11b s
FA: John Baldwin and Dick Cilley, c. 1985.
Climb a slab to a big roof (fixed pin) and battle out around its left side.

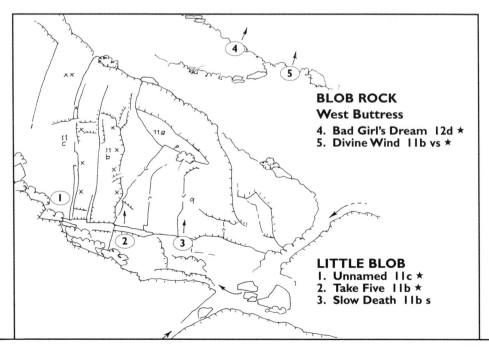

BLOB ROCK
West Buttress
4. Bad Girl's Dream 12d ★
5. Divine Wind 11b vs ★

LITTLE BLOB
1. Unnamed 11c ★
2. Take Five 11b ★
3. Slow Death 11b s

BLOB ROCK MASSIF

Little Blob

2.   Take Five 11b ★

Blob Rock

5.   Divine Wind 11b vs ★

Central Chimney Area

11. The Radlands Of Infinity 13a ★

Main Wall

21. On Ballet 9 ★
28A. Bolt Cola 10a ★
32. Where Eagles Dare 10b (9 s) ★

Right Gully Area

41. Vasodilator 13a ★

Blob Slab

5.   A Hike With Ludwig Dude 10a vs ★

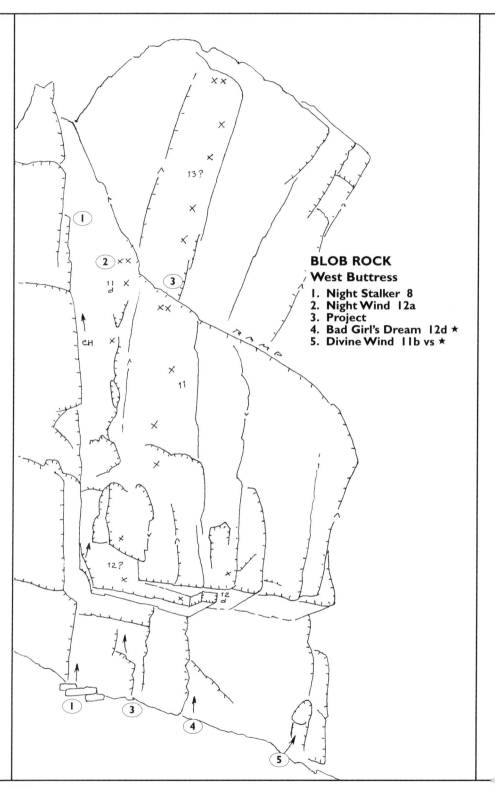

BLOB ROCK
West Buttress
1. Night Stalker 8
2. Night Wind 12a
3. Project
4. Bad Girl's Dream 12d ★
5. Divine Wind 11b vs ★

BLOB ROCK

This large, south-facing buttress features excellent rock and many great routes. The approach trail leads directly to the bottom of the face, a ten-minute hike. Descend from most routes by following a grassy ledge system to the west end of the rock. Beware of some exposed traverses (fourthclass) and a short down-climb at the end. Most of the newer routes have fixed anchors at the top from which one may lower off or rappel.

West Buttress

The following routes ascend the square-cut buttress at the far west end of the south face. A large roof cuts across the lower part of the buttress.

1.   NIGHT STALKER 8
FA: MARK (BUCK) NORDEN AND BRUCE ADAMS, 1974.
This route takes the left-facing dihedral along the left side of the west buttress.

2.   NIGHT WIND 12A
FA: DAN HARE AND FRED KNAPP, 1996. STOPPERS PLUS A #2 AND 3 FRIEND.
Climb the first 10 feet of *Night Stalker*, then climb a thin crack on the right and continue past two bolts to an anchor with coldshuts.

3.   PROJECT
Begin a few feet right of the arête at the left side of the West Buttress. Climb past a difficult roof (12), then work up and slightly right to an anchor with coldshuts. Six bolts. Lower off or continue up to a higher anchor beneath an overhanging head wall. A second pitch ascends the head wall past four bolts to a third anchor (13?).

4.   BAD GIRL'S DREAM 12D ★
FA: HARRISON DEKKER, 1984 (TR). REDPOINT: DEKKER AND TODD SKINNER, 1988.
Climb out along a spike and turn the big roof (two bolts), then continue in the right of two cracks.

5.   DIVINE WIND 11B VS ★
FA: ALEC SHARP AND RICHARD CAREY, 1979. SR PLUS EXTRA THIN STUFF.
Begin just below the right edge of the big roof. P1. Climb the fierce right-facing dihedral at the right side of the west buttress and belay at a bolt anchor atop a sloping bench (11b s). P2. Climb out left around a large roof (11b vs), then go up an overhanging dihedral (9) and belay on the walk-off ledge.

5A. DIVINE INTERVENTION 11D
Climb the first 20 feet of *Divine Wind*, then step left and climb the arête past 3 bolts.

6.   ROOF BYPASS 10A ★
FA: CHRIS REVELEY AND DUDLEY CHELTON, 1973.
The roof of the second pitch may be avoided by climbing a slot on the right with two pins.

Dike Wall

The following routes ascend the beautiful smooth wall between the West Buttress and the Central Chimney.

7.   WOUNDED KNEE 11B ★
FA: MICHAEL TOBIAS AND MURRAY CUNNINGHAM, 1971 (TAPESTRY 5.7 A3). FFA: CHRIS REVELEY AND JIM ERICKSON, 1974. SR PLUS A #4 FRIEND.
Begin with *Divine Wind* or take the original line about 40 feet to the right and arrive at a sloping ledge as for *Divine Wind*. Undercling/lieback up and right and belay from bolts beneath a crack that splits the big roof at the top of the wall (10). Jam the wide crack (crux). This crack may also be reached from *Bearcat Goes To Hollywood*.

7A. Variation 11b s
FA: Jeff Achey and Kent Lugbill, 1980.
Climb an overhanging corner with a thin crack before reaching the big roof.

8. Bearcat Goes To Hollywood 11d s ★
FA: Erik Eriksson and Mark Rolofson, 1982.
Begin with *Wounded Knee* and follow a quartz dike to a bolt anchor beneath the roof of *Wounded Knee* (11d, RPs). Rappel or climb the roof. One may also traverse around the right end of the roof (10b s). Another option is to climb the first pitch of *Divine Wind*, then from the bolt anchor, traverse right into the main line.

9. Eye Of The Storm 10c s ★
FA: Dan Hare and partner, c. 1985.
Begin as for *Wounded Knee* and *Bearcat*, but break right at a down-pointing spike (crux) and traverse to a bolt anchor on *The Radlands*. Climb about 15 feet up a seam, then break right again and join *Silent Running*.

Central Chimney Area
The following routes begin from the long diagonal chimney that splits the rock and forms the margin between the Dike Wall and the Main Wall.

10. Central Chimney 6 ★
This is the long diagonal chimney system that splits the left side of the south face of Blob Rock. It can be climbed in three or four pitches and is actually a pretty cool moderate route. The easiest exit on the last pitch is the right of three wide cracks and chimneys. One may also finish with last pitch of *On Ballet* (right wall, 7).

11. The Radlands Of Infinity 13a ★
FA: Richard and Joyce Rossiter and Rob Woolf, 1988. Redpoint: Joyce Rossiter, 1988. Bring assorted small stuff up to one inch and eight QDs, plus a #2 and 2.5 Friend for the initial anchor in the Central Chimney.
Scramble up the Central Chimney and belay on a platform below a large granite spike. P1. Climb a right-facing dihedral and turn the roof at its top (11b), then work up and left across a steep slab to a two-bolt anchor (13a, five bolts, QDs only). P2. Climb a thin crack (gear) followed by a seam with three bolts (12b), then traverse up and right and follow a ramp up and left to a ledge with a two bolt anchor.

12. Silent Running 11a vs ★
FA: Randy Leavitt, Rick Accomazzo, and Dan Hare, 1981. SR plus a #4 Friend for the first belay in the Central Chimney.
This is a great pitch, but its lack of protection has kept it from becoming popular. Begin just above a large spike of rock about 50 feet up the Central Chimney. Stem off the spike and pull over a difficult bulge, then follow left-angling grooves into the middle of the face. From the left end of the highest groove, climb straight up to a flake (crux), undercling up and right, and finish as for *The Radlands*.

13. Kamikaze 10c ★
FA: Richard and Joyce Rossiter, 1988.
Stem off the flake and gain a precarious stance above a bulge as for *Silent Running*. Make a difficult move up and right, then climb straight up to a dike that angles up to the left. Follow the dike for about 45 feet, then break right at a small, left-facing dihedral and continue to a sloping shelf near the top of the wall. Traverse left and belay from the bolt anchor at the top of *The Radlands*.

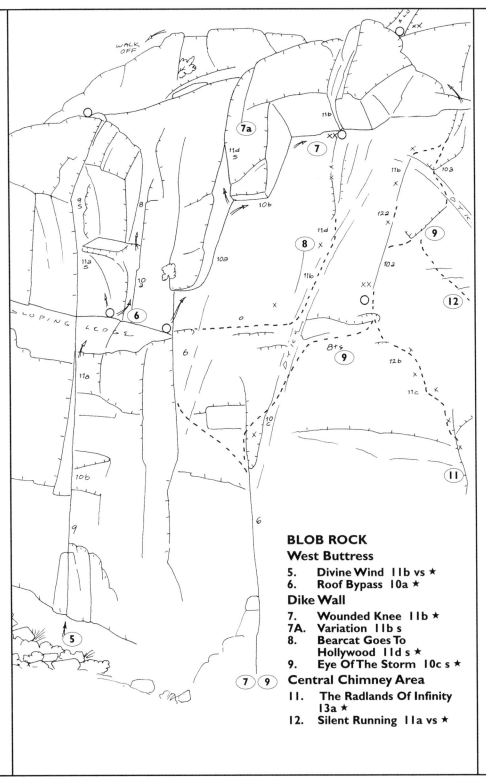

BLOB ROCK

West Buttress

5. Divine Wind 11b vs ★
6. Roof Bypass 10a ★

Dike Wall

7. Wounded Knee 11b ★
7A. Variation 11b s
8. Bearcat Goes To
    Hollywood 11d s ★
9. Eye Of The Storm 10c s ★

Central Chimney Area

11. The Radlands Of Infinity
     13a ★
12. Silent Running 11a vs ★

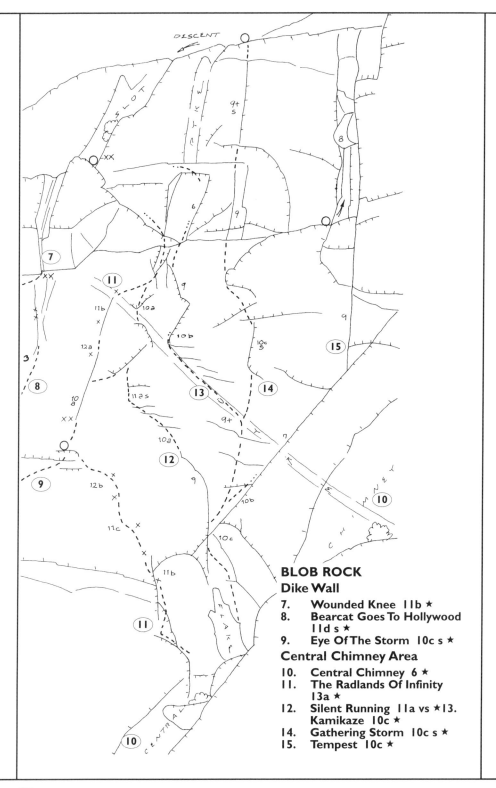

BLOB ROCK

Dike Wall

7. **Wounded Knee** 11b ★
8. **Bearcat Goes To Hollywood** 11d s ★
9. **Eye Of The Storm** 10c s ★

Central Chimney Area

10. **Central Chimney** 6 ★
11. **The Radlands Of Infinity** 13a ★
12. **Silent Running** 11a vs ★13. **Kamikaze** 10c ★
14. **Gathering Storm** 10c s ★
15. **Tempest** 10c ★

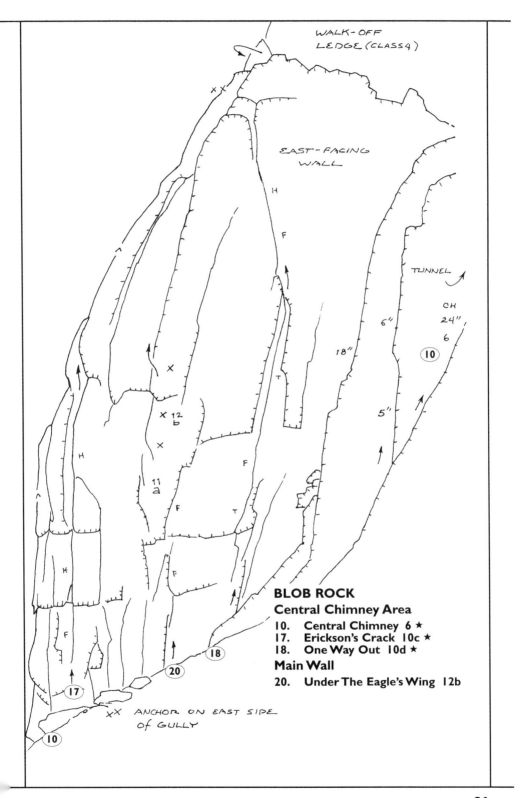

WALK-OFF
LEDGE (CLASS 4)

EAST-FACING
WALL

TUNNEL

BLOB ROCK
Central Chimney Area
10. Central Chimney 6 ★
17. Erickson's Crack 10c ★
18. One Way Out 10d ★
Main Wall
20. Under The Eagle's Wing 12b

ANCHOR ON EAST SIDE
OF GULLY

14. GATHERING STORM 10c s ★
FA: DAN HARE AND MIKE DOWNING, 1984.

Begin at the granite spike as for the preceding routes and climb to the precarious stance above the bulge. Continue up a thin crack as for *Silent Running*, then break right and head for a shallow, left-facing corner. Climb the corner, then work up and left and follow cracks to the top of the wall.

15. TEMPEST 10c ★
FA: STEVE MATOUS AND DAN HARE, 1980.

Begin from the spike as for the three preceding routes and gain the precarious stance above the bulge. Make a difficult move up and right and follow a steep ramp to a vertical crack. Climb the crack and corner system to the top of the wall.

16. FAR LEFT FACE 9
FA: CHRIS REVELEY AND DUDLEY CHELTON, 1974.

The exact location of this route is not known. Begin about 30 feet up a gully that leans to the right and merges with the original *Left Face* route. Angle left for 40 feet, then climb a long, left-facing dihedral.

17. ERICKSON'S CRACK 10c ★
FA: JIM ERICKSON AND ART HIGBEE, 1974.

About three-quarters of the way up to the walk-off ledge, the Central Chimney becomes a deep recess with a vertical left wall. Climb a hand crack near the left side of the wall.

Note: The crack system with three bolts (center) is the final pitch of *Under The Eagle's Wing* (route 20).

18. ONE WAY OUT 10D ★
FA: DAN HARE, DAVE BATTEN, KAREN SCHNEIDER, 1985.

Climb a difficult crack a short way up and right from the preceding line. Three wide crack finishes.

Main Wall

The following routes ascend the big rounded wall to the right of the Central Chimney.

19. COLD FUSION 10c
FA: DAN HARE AND SUSAN SIMPSON, 1995.

Begin a short way down and right from the bottom of the Central Chimney. Climb the wall past two bolts to a bolt anchor below the start to *Silent Running*. Small gear needed.

20. UNDER THE EAGLE'S WING 12B
FA: FRED KNAPP AND DAN HARE, 1997.

Begin just right of a large block, about 60 feet left of *On Ballet*. P1. Climb straight up, then veer left and climb two small, right-facing dihedrals (9). Belay on a ledge. P2. Climb through the right of two small dihedrals (10d), then gain the Central Gully and continue to a belay beneath a right-facing dihedral. P3. Climb the dihedral and continue past three bolts (12b), then move left and follow a hand crack to the walk-off ledge.

21. ON BALLET 9 ★
FA: RICHARD AND JOYCE ROSSITER, 1983.

Begin about 75 feet up and left from the low point of the face. Scramble up a ramp and belay at the bottom of a thin crack. P1. Follow the crack up and left and climb a short, right-facing dihedral (8). Move up left and belay. P2. Climb up a short way, then stretch right (9) to a crack in a right-facing dihedral and climb to a small sloping ledge (8). P3. Climb up and left over a slab (8) and step around into the Central Chimney. Climb a crack in the buttress on the right (7) and continue more easily to the walk-off ledge.

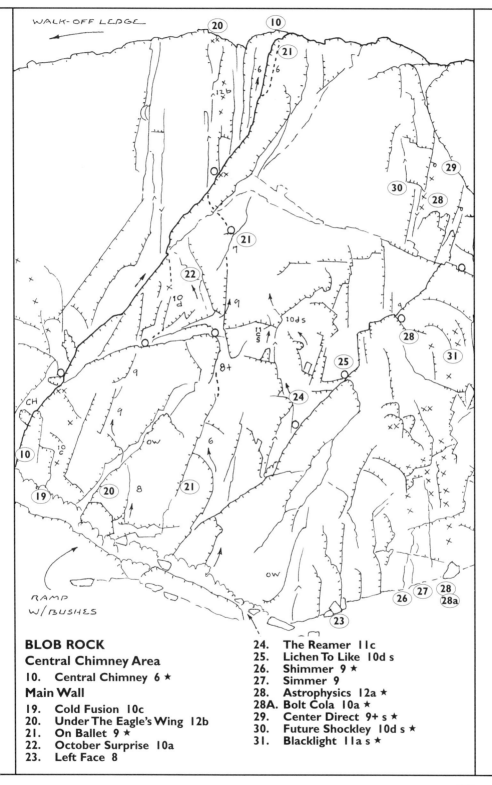

BLOB ROCK

Central Chimney Area

10.   Central Chimney 6 ★

Main Wall

19.   Cold Fusion 10c
20.   Under The Eagle's Wing 12b
21.   On Ballet 9 ★
22.   October Surprise 10a
23.   Left Face 8

24.   The Reamer 11c
25.   Lichen To Like 10d s
26.   Shimmer 9 ★
27.   Simmer 9
28.   Astrophysics 12a ★
28A. Bolt Cola 10a ★
29.   Center Direct 9+ s ★
30.   Future Shockley 10d s ★
31.   Blacklight 11a s ★

22. OCTOBER SURPRISE 10A
FA: MICHAEL YOKELL AND JIM WALSH, 1992.

From the top of the first pitch of *On Ballet*, angle up and left along a left-leaning, left-facing dihedral that leads into the Central Chimney.

23. LEFT FACE 8
FA: RICK HORN AND TEX BOSSIER, 1962.

From the low point of the face climb up and left to a ledge beneath an overhanging wall. Work up and left into the Central Chimney and continue to the walk-off ledge. The Central Chimney continues in the upper buttress as a steep, right-facing dihedral and crack system. Follow this system to the top of Blob Rock.

23A. VARSITY CRACK 9
FA: JIM ERICKSON AND ART HIGBEE, 1974.

From the walk-off ledge, climb a V-groove about 15 feet right of upper *Left Face*.

24. THE REAMER 11C
FA: STRAPPO AND SIMON PECK, 1988.

Begin as for *Lichen To Like*, but belay a bit sooner beneath a prominent spike of rock. Gain the top of the spike and place a #4 Rock high on the right. Start up the overhanging wall, then crank left and finish as for *Lichen To Like*.

25. LICHEN TO LIKE 10D S
FA: CHRIS REVELEY AND DUDLEY CHELTON, 1974.

From the low point of the face, ascend easy slabs and belay in a right-angling groove/ledge that runs all the way from the beginning of *On Ballet* to the old eagle's nest on *Where Eagles Dare*. Work up and left across an overhanging wall and pull around onto a slab, then continue up a slab to the walk-off ledge. Climb the upper wall to the left of *Left Face*.

26. SHIMMER 9 ★
FA: DAN HARE AND SUSAN SIMPSON, 1996.

Begin about 50 feet up and right from the low point of the wall and climb the face past 5 or 6 bolts to a bolt anchor. A #2 Friend or the like may be placed before reaching the first bolt.

27. SIMMER 9
FA: HARE AND SIMPSON, 1996.

Begin 5 feet left of the pointed flake at the start to *Astrophysics*. Follow a thin crack (gear) and continue past three bolts past a bulge, then veer left (more gear) to the bolt anchor of the previous route.

28. ASTROPHYSICS 12A ★
FA: DAN HARE AND MIKE DOWNING, 1987. SR WITH EXTRA SMALL STUFF. BOLTS ON THE FIRST PITCH WERE PLACED BY A SUBSEQUENT PARTY.

Begin at a pointed flake about 75 feet up and right from the low point of the face. P1. Step off the flake and climb straight up past six bolts to a bulge. Pull right and up over the bulge past a seventh bolt and continue up an easy slab to a bolt anchor. Continue

BLOB ROCK
(ON RIGHT PAGE)
Main Wall
26. Shimmer 9 ★
27. Simmer 9
28. Astrophysics 12a ★
28A. Bolt Cola 10a ★
29. Center Direct 9+ s ★
30. Future Shockley 10d s ★
31. Blacklight 11a s ★
32. Where Eagles Dare 10b (9 s) ★

Right Gully Area
33. Respite 11d ★
34. Jolt Cola 11c or 12a ★
35. Ginseng Rush 12a ★
37. Little Juke 10a
38. Decade Dance 11a ★
39. Aging Time 11c ★
40. Limits Of Power 12a s+ ★
41. Vasodilator 13a ★

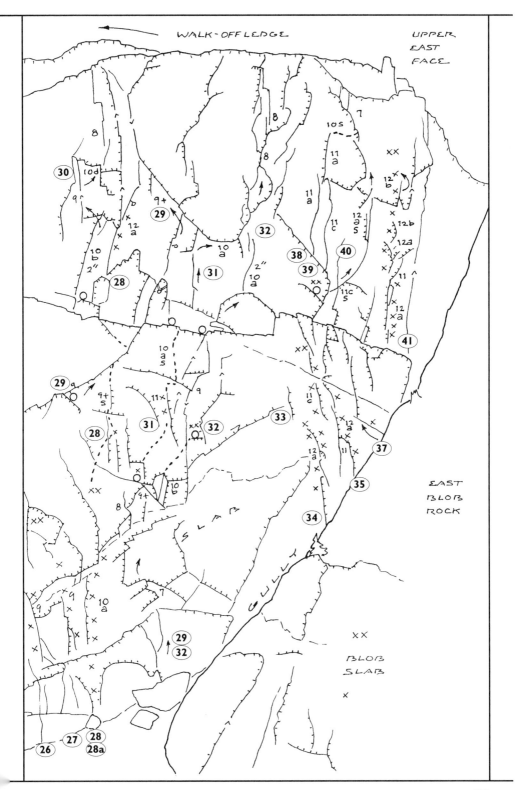

Mark Rolofson on *The Ticket*. Photo by Richard Rossiter.

up and left and belay on a ledge. P2. Traverse up and right across the slab to an old bolt, then go straight up past a small roof to a big ledge (9+ s). Belay up and left at the bottom of a right-leaning, right-facing dihedral. P3. Climb the dihedral past three bolts (12a) and a fixed pin and finish with the last few moves of *Center Direct*.

28A. BOLT COLA 10A ★

Climb the first 80 feet of *Astrophysics* and lower off from a bolt anchor. Seven bolts.

29. CENTER DIRECT 9+ s ★
FA: DEAN MOORE AND CHARLES ALEXANDER, 1962. FFA: CHRIS REVELEY AND JIM ERICKSON, 1974.

Begin behind a huge boulder about 100 feet up and right from the low-point of the wall. Proceed as shown in the topo. The crux of the climb is an awkward hand traverse out left along a roof band, about 90 feet off the ground. Three or four pitches.

29A. VARIATION 8+ ★
FA: RICHARD ROSSITER, JOYCE ROSSITER, RAOUL DE ROSSITER, 1984.

The crux can be avoided by climbing a steep, clean corner on the left before reaching the hand traverse.

30. FUTURE SHOCKLEY 10D s ★
FA: RANDY LEAVITT AND DICK SHOCKLEY, 1981.

Climb *Center Direct*, or any route that leads to the big ledge in the upper wall, and belay at the left end of the ledge beneath a two-inch crack. Climb the crack up and over a bulge (10b), then traverse left until it is possible to climb up under a roof. Move boldly out to the right and turn the roof (crux).

31. BLACKLIGHT 11A s ★
FA: DAN HARE, SCOTT WOODRUFF, AND JEFF WHEELER, 1985.

Begin with *Center Direct* and belay at a bolt above the crux roof. Climb directly up the slab past two bolts (11a s), around the right side of a roof and up to a big ledge (10a s). Climb a crack to the right of *Center Direct*, undercling right beneath the roof (10a), and join the last pitch of *Where Eagles Dare*.

32. WHERE EAGLES DARE 10B (9 s) ★
FA: SCOTT WOODRUFF, DAN HARE, BRAD GILBERT, 1975.

Begin behind the big talus block. P1. Follow *Center Direct* to its crux hand traverse about 90 feet up and climb through a fierce overhanging corner just to the right (crux). Go up and right across a slab and belay at the bottom of a right-facing dihedral. P2. Climb the foxy dihedral and belay on the big ledge with the eagle's nest (9 s). P3. Monkey out right along a big flake and jam a short hand crack, then follow cracks up beautiful rock to the walk-off ledge.

Right Gully Area

The following routes begin about 150 feet up the gully between Blob Rock and East Blob.

33. RESPITE 11D ★
FA: DAN HARE, MOE HERSHOFF, DIANE CONNALLY, 1997.

Climb to the second bolt on *Jolt Cola*, then break left and continue up the wall to a two-bolt anchor out left from the start to *Decade Dance* (90 feet, 14 bolts). A 2.5 to 3-inch cam may be useful.

34. JOLT COLA 11c OR 12a ★
FA: KEN TROUT AND RICK LEITNER.

Look for a shallow left-facing dihedral and a line of bolts where the gully narrows. The crux can be avoided by climbing out to the right between the third and fourth bolts (11b). Seven bolts to a bolt anchor with chains.

35. GINSENG RUSH 12a ★
FA: MARK ROLOFSON AND BOB D'ANTONIO, 1985. RETRO-BOLTED BY ROLOFSON, 1993.

Begin about ten feet up and right from *Jolt Cola* at another shallow left-facing dihedral. Climb past four bolts, then veer left to the last bolt on *Jolt* and lower off from the same anchor.

36. DIRECT 11 s
FA: ERIK BADER AND MARK HONHART, 1981.

This route climbs to the ledge at the beginning of *Decade Dance*, however, its location is not known.

37. LITTLE JUKE 10a
FA: STEVEN DIECKHOFF, MARTY HAMBACHER, STRAPPO, 1990.

Begin just below a big chockstone a short way up the gully from *Ginseng Rush*. Start left and clip a bolt, then hand traverse left to a vertical crack that is followed to the ledge at the beginning to *Decade Dance*.

The following four routes begin from a ledge that runs out to the left about 200 feet up the gully between Blob Rock and East Blob.

38. DECADE DANCE 11a ★
FA: DAN HARE AND CHRIS WOOD ON NEW YEAR'S EVE, 1980. SR UP TO #4 FRIEND.

Walk left across the ledge, then climb an awkward (9) corner to a sloping ramp and belay. Climb the left of two cracks to where it fades, then traverse to the crack on the right. Climb a difficult dihedral, then make a scary traverse right to another crack and climb more easily to the walk-off ledge.

39. AGING TIME 11c ★
FA: MARK ROLOFSON AND SANDY MAH, 1981. SR TO A #4 FRIEND.

This route is the same as *Decade Dance* except that the second pitch begins with the crack on the right.

40. LIMITS OF POWER 12a s+ ★
FA: RANDY LEAVITT AND RICK ACCOMAZZO, 1981.

Start up the awkward initial corner of *Decade Dance*, then hand traverse out right and mantle onto a stance beneath an overhanging crack. Climb the crack, pass a small roof, and continue to the walk-off ledge.

41. VASODILATOR 13a ★
FA: MARK ROLOFSON.

Follow a line of bolts up the awesome, overhanging wall to the right of *Limits of Power*. Eleven bolts to a bolt anchor with chains.

Upper East Face

The following routes are located on the steep, east-facing wall at the top of the gully between Blob Rock and East Blob. There are four ways to reach these routes. 1. Gain the west end of the walk-off ledge and traverse all the way to the east end, which is near the route Perspective. 2. Scramble up the gully between Blob Rock and East Blob and climb a short pitch past some chockstones (7) to gain a bench below the routes. 3. Climb most of the Down Route on East Blob, then traverse

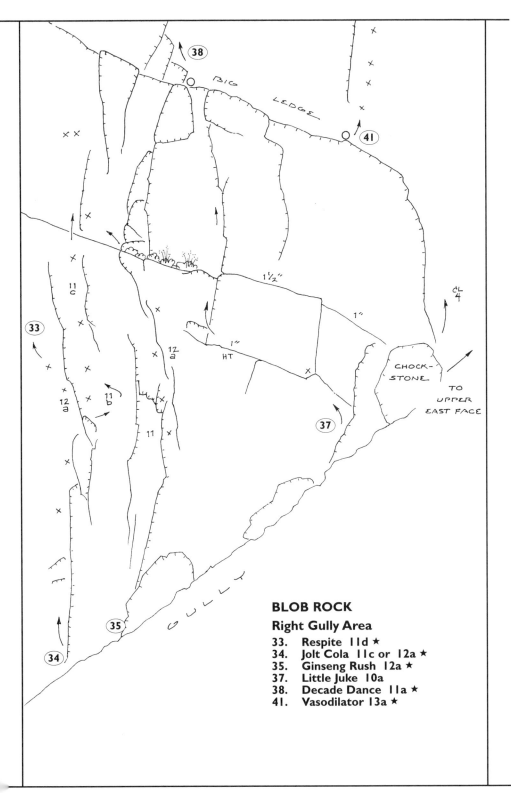

BLOB ROCK

Right Gully Area

33. **Respite** 11d ★
34. **Jolt Cola** 11c or 12a ★
35. **Ginseng Rush** 12a ★
37. **Little Juke** 10a
38. **Decade Dance** 11a ★
41. **Vasodilator** 13a ★

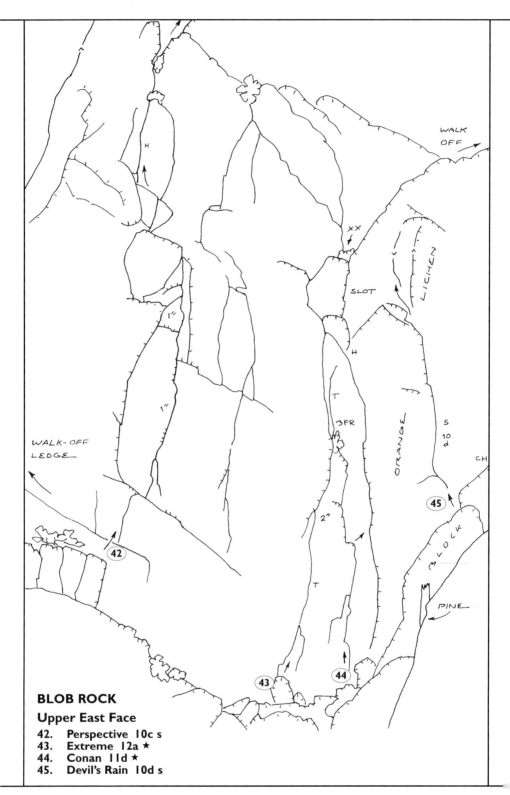

BLOB ROCK

Upper East Face

42. Perspective 10c s
43. Extreme 12a ★
44. Conan 11d ★
45. Devil's Rain 10d s

left to the bench (cl4). 4. Scramble up the gully on the east side of East Blob and traverse around to the notch on the west side, then scramble down to the bench at the bottom of the routes. The routes *Extreme*, *Conan*, and *Devil's Rain* can be top-roped from a bolt anchor above *Conan*. A belay is advisable to reach the anchor from above.

42. PERSPECTIVE 10C S
FA: ERIK BADER AND MARK HONHART, 1980.

Begin from a flake below the left side of the wall. Climb a short thin crack, step right, then climb a left-facing dihedral and turn a roof at its top. Follow a hand crack up and left, then straight up to easier ground. Scramble off to the north.

43. EXTREME 12A ★
FA: ERIC BADER AND STEVE MOSTAGH, 1980. SR TO A #3 FRIEND WITH EXTRA STUFF FROM RPS TO ONE INCH.

Begin above a big wedged block at the low-point of the wall. Step off a boulder and climb the left of two thin cracks to an anchor about 80 feet up.

44. CONAN 11D ★
FA: SKIP GUERIN, 1981. SR TO A #2 FRIEND WITH EXTRA GEAR UP TO ONE INCH.

Begin about 10 feet right of *Extreme*. Step off a block and climb a flake/crack to a jug, then pull across to the long crack on the right and climb to a bolt anchor.

45. DEVIL'S RAIN 10D S
FA: SKIP GUERIN, 1981. SR TO A #2 FRIEND.

Begin from a big block about 20 feet right of *Conan* and below a bright orange lichen streak. Climb a short flake/crack, then stretch up to a right-facing dihedral. Step around into a left-facing dihedral and climb to the chain anchor.

EAST BLOB ROCK

This is the large buttress between Blob Rock and Bitty Buttress. It has no summit routes of any merit, but is redeemed by a handful of short routes on its lower apron (Blob Slab) and another group of routes on the upper east face. To escape from the summit, should you find yourself there for any reason, down-climb the *Down Route*, or hike around to the grassy gully that drops down along the east side of the crag.

1. WEST FACE 6
Scramble 150 feet or so up the gully between Blob Rock and East Blob to where a ledge allows access to the west face. Follow a series of discontinuous cracks and corners up and left to the summit.

2. DOWN ROUTE CLASS 4
From the summit of the crag, drop down onto the south face, go east a bit at some ledges, then straight down for about 100 feet to a big ledge with trees. Traverse west, then go down corner/grooves to slabs that face Blob Rock. Look for an easy traverse into the gully.

Blob Slab

The following routes are located on the splendid granite apron at the lower left aspect of East Blob Rock. These routes may be led, but pro is pretty lean. A two-bolt anchor is located near the top of the slab above the route *A Hike With Ludwig Dude*. It is also possible to continue left of the anchor and gain a ledge, whence one may scramble off into the gully between Blob Rock and East Blob.

3.   LEFT ROOF 8 VS ★
FA: JIM WALSH AND JIM ERICKSON, 1971.

Begin about six feet right of a large, right-facing dihedral. Climb an insipient crack, a shallow left-facing dihedral, and pass the right side of a small roof.

4.   OLD ROUTE 8 VS ★

Begin from a small block a few feet right of the preceding route. Climb up to a crack that veers left, but veer right to a small roof. Turn the roof at a groove and continue up and right to the anchor at the top of the slab.

5.   A HIKE WITH LUDWIG DUDE 10A VS ★
FA: BOB POLING AND DICK DONOFRIO, 1970.

Begin about twelve feet right of *Old Route*. Make thin face moves up and left into a small left-facing corner, then friction more or less straight up past an old bolt to the top of the slab.

6.   OUT OF LIMITS 10D VS ★
FA: DUNCAN FERGUSON AND STEVE WOOD, 1971.

Start up a tiny crease as for *Crack Tack*, but pull left at the top and climb straight up the blank slab.

7.   CRACK TACK 10A VS ★
FA: PAT AMENT AND FRED PFAHLER, 1964. FFA: JIM ERICKSON AND JIM WALSH, 1971.

Begin at a tiny crease about ten feet right of *Ludwig Dude*. Climb straight up (crux) past an old bolt, then up and left over beautiful rock to the anchor at the top of the slab. The original ascent may have continued to the top of the rock, but the line is not known. A left-leaning crack to the right affords a safer and easier start.

8.   OF HUMAN BONDAGE 10B S
FA: DAN HARE AND STEVE MATOUS, 1984.

This is a summit route, but one may scramble off from the top of the first pitch. Begin with the easier start to *Crack Tack*, then head straight up before reaching the bolt. See topo.

Upper East Face

The following routes are located on the upper east face of East Blob, well up the grassy gully between East Blob and Bitty Buttress.

9.   NIGHT HAWK 10
FA: DAN MICHAEL AND DAN HARE, 1979.

Hike about 200 feet up the gully and look for a right-leaning, right-facing corner with a wide crack.

10.   MILE HIGH COMIC CRACK 12A ★
FA: ALEC SHARP AND DAN HARE, 1980. SR.

Classic. A short way right of the preceding route is an impressive, 25-foot overhanging finger and hand crack. Crux is early on. Lower off from two pins.

11.   THE ENLIGHTENMENT 13B/C ★
FA: MARK ROLOFSON. REDPOINT: ALAN LESTER, 1997.

Locate a series of seams on the overhanging wall a short way right of *Mile High Comic Crack*. Seven bolts to a two-bolt anchor. Crux is at the third bolt (but don't assume victory too soon).

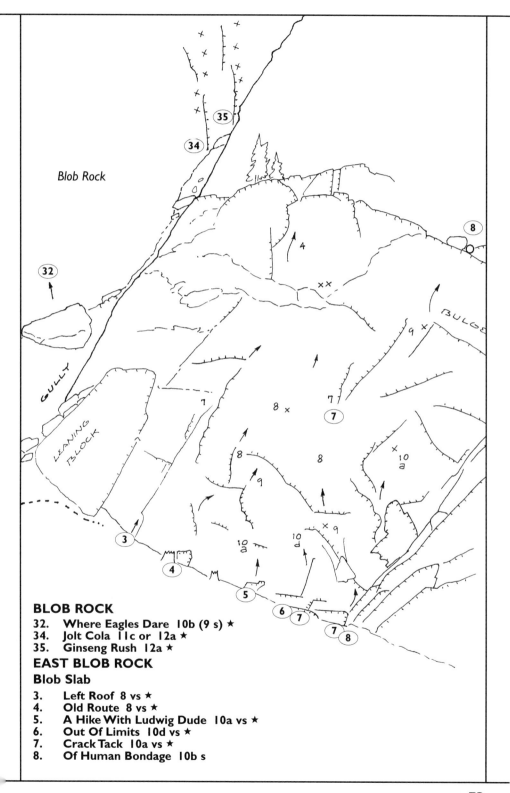

Blob Rock

BLOB ROCK
32. **Where Eagles Dare** 10b (9 s) ★
34. **Jolt Cola** 11c or 12a ★
35. **Ginseng Rush** 12a ★

EAST BLOB ROCK
Blob Slab

3. **Left Roof** 8 vs ★
4. **Old Route** 8 vs ★
5. **A Hike With Ludwig Dude** 10a vs ★
6. **Out Of Limits** 10d vs ★
7. **Crack Tack** 10a vs ★
8. **Of Human Bondage** 10b s

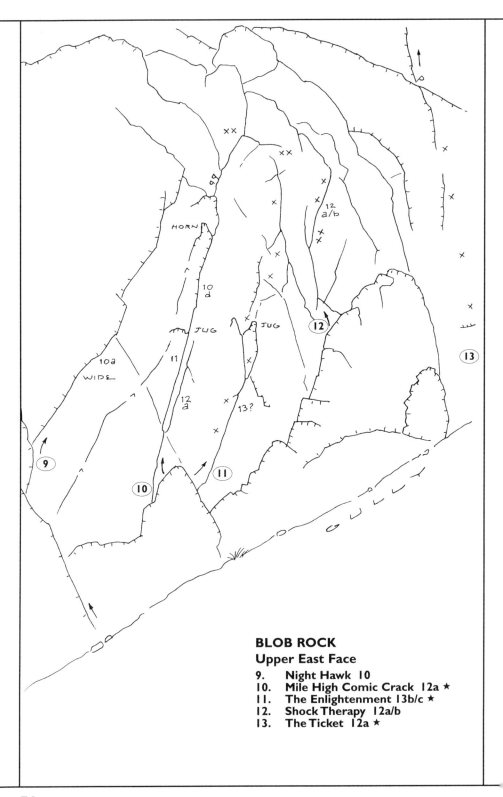

BLOB ROCK

Upper East Face

9. Night Hawk 10
10. Mile High Comic Crack 12a ★
11. The Enlightenment 13b/c ★
12. Shock Therapy 12a/b
13. The Ticket 12a ★

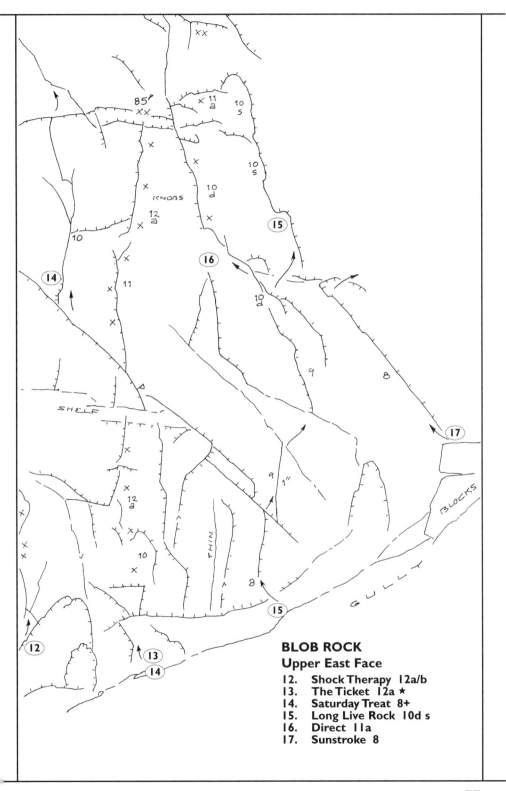

BLOB ROCK
Upper East Face

12. Shock Therapy 12a/b
13. The Ticket 12a ★
14. Saturday Treat 8+
15. Long Live Rock 10d s
16. Direct 11a
17. Sunstroke 8

Dan Hare on *Time Traveler*. Photo by Richard Rossiter.

12. SHOCK THERAPY 12A/B
FA: DAN HARE.

Begin about 30 feet up and right from *Mile High*. Start up a stepped left-facing corner, then undercling left to an overhanging seam that leads to a ledge (three bolts plus SR, 50 feet). Belay at a two-bolt anchor. Step right into a right-facing dihedral and climb to where the crack fades, then angle right along a white dike with a bolt. Climb straight up to easier ground. Walk off to the right (11d, 60 feet).

13. THE TICKET 12A ★
FA: TIM HUDGEL, DAN HARE, MARC HIRT, 1987.

This is a new and improved version of the original route. Begin about 60 feet up and right from *Mile High Comic Crack*, below a small triangular roof. Turn the roof and climb past four bolts to the ramp of *Saturday Treat*. Climb up and slightly right past a pin and six more bolts to a bolt anchor with chains. Lower off 85 feet.

14. SATURDAY TREAT 8+
FA: ALEC SHARP, 1979.

Begin at the bottom of *The Ticket*. Climb up and right through a left-facing dihedral and gain a crack/ramp that climbs up and left. Follow the ramp across *The Ticket*, then climb a crack system straight up to a big shelf. Traverse off to the northeast.

15. LONG LIVE ROCK 10D S
FA: ALEC SHARP, 1979.

A short way further up the gully, climb a small corner to an area of brown rock, take a finger crack up a short dihedral, pull right to some flakes, then go up and back left to the top of the wall.

16. DIRECT 11A
FA: BOB D'ANTONIO.

Climb about 60 feet up *Long Live Rock*, then follow three bolts along a shallow, right-facing corner and gain a two-bolt anchor with chains. Lower off or rappel 100 feet.

17. SUNSTROKE 8
FA: ALEC AND MURIEL SHARP, 1979.

Begin on a boulder near the top of the gully and climb the higher of two parallel cracks to a belay. Go left to a tree and up a V-slot.

BITTY BUTTRESS

Bitty Buttress is the farthest east feature of the Blob Rock Massif. It has a good assortment of crack climbs as well as bolt-protected face climbs. To descend from the summit area, walk west and scramble down the southwest shoulder of the buttress. One may also descend the gully between East Blob and Bitty Buttress.

1. LEAPING LIZARDS 11D S
FA: ERIC GOUKAS AND HENRY LESTER, 1986.

Locate a large, left-facing dihedral on the upper west side of the south face. Start up the dihedral, then move out left into a smaller corner that terminates at a roof. Turn the roof and continue up past two bolts.

Peapod Buttress

Below the middle of the south face is a 60-foot buttress with several routes.

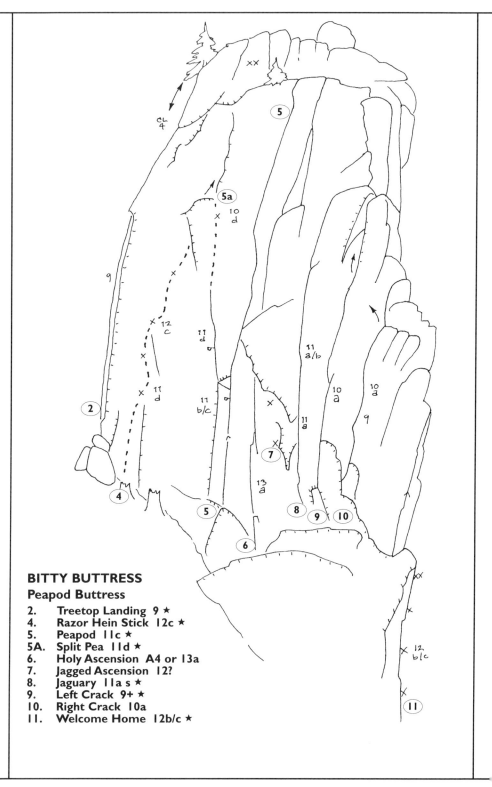

BITTY BUTTRESS
Peapod Buttress

2. Treetop Landing 9 ★
4. Razor Hein Stick 12c ★
5. Peapod 11c ★
5A. Split Pea 11d ★
6. Holy Ascension A4 or 13a
7. Jagged Ascension 12?
8. Jaguary 11a s ★
9. Left Crack 9+ ★
10. Right Crack 10a
11. Welcome Home 12b/c ★

2. TREETOP LANDING 9 ★
FA: Mark Rolofson and Wendy Sumner, 1981.
Climb a thin crack along the west edge of the buttress.

3. PALM SATURDAY 12c
FA: Joel Dyer and Tally O'Donnel.
Top-rope the the smooth wall just right of *Treetop Landing* and join *Razor Hein Stick* at its last bolt.

4. RAZOR HEIN STICK 12c ★
FA: led by Mark Rolofson, 1985.
Climb the bolt-protected face behind a tree. Four bolts to coldshuts. Bring a #1 Friend.

5. PEAPOD 11c ★
FA: Chris Peisker and Scott Woodruff, 1980. SR.
Climb a very clean, V-shaped corner capped by a small, triangular roof, then take the crack on the right.

5A. SPLIT PEA 11d ★
FA: Bret Ruckman and Bob Rotert, 1988. SR..
Climb the crack that goes left from the top of the pod (fixed pin and a bolt).

6. HOLY ASCENSION A4 OR 13A
FA: Tim Hudgel, 1985. FFA: John Arron, 1987 (TR).
Top-rope the thin crack about 8 feet right of *Peapod*.

7. JAGGED ASCENSION 12?
Begin with *Jaguary*, then work up and left via flakes (two bolts) and join *Holy Ascension*.

8. JAGUARY 11A S ★
FA: Kent Lugbill, Greg Hand, Mark Rolofson, 1981.
This is the left of three cracks on the right side of Peapod Buttress. Climb into a little A-shaped roof and continue up the crack.

9. LEFT CRACK 9+ ★
Climb the hand crack right of *Jaguary*.

10. RIGHT CRACK 10A
Climb the hand crack along the right side of the buttress. Near the top of the crack, step left into *Left Crack*.

11. WELCOME HOME 12B/C ★
FA: Jimmy Ratzlaff.
This route ascends the east end of the Peapod Buttress. Four bolts to a coldshut anchor.

12. ELECTRICITY 11D ★
FA: Dan Hare and Clay Wadman, 1992. SR.
This route ascends the upper east wall of Peapod Buttress. Scramble up a steep gully a short way right of *Welcome Home* and step left to a diagonal crack. Climb the crack up and left (#2 Friend and wires), then follow bolts up and right along a seam (11d) and up a small dihedral. Work up and right to a sling belay from three bolts. Step right past a bolt to a thin crack in a dihedral and jam it to the top of the buttress (11a). Scramble off to the west.

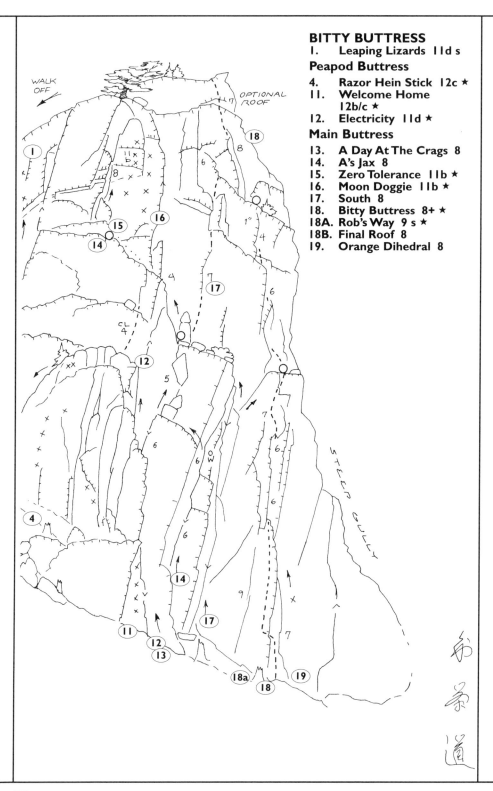

BITTY BUTTRESS
1. Leaping Lizards 11d s

Peapod Buttress

4. Razor Hein Stick 12c ★
11. Welcome Home
    12b/c ★
12. Electricity 11d ★

Main Buttress

13. A Day At The Crags 8
14. A's Jax 8
15. Zero Tolerance 11b ★
16. Moon Doggie 11b ★
17. South 8
18. Bitty Buttress 8+ ★
18A. Rob's Way 9 s ★
18B. Final Roof 8
19. Orange Dihedral 8

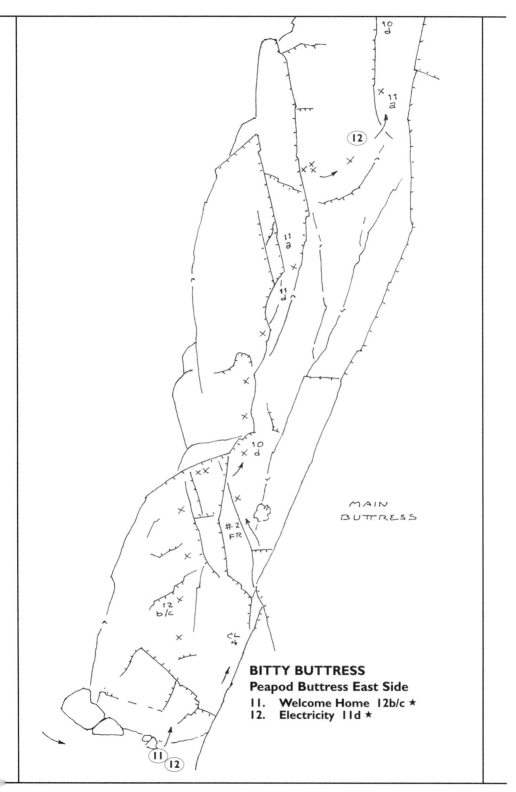

BITTY BUTTRESS
Peapod Buttress East Side
11.   Welcome Home 12b/c ★
12.   Electricity 11d ★

Main Buttress

13.   A Day At The Crags 8
FA: Carl Harrison and Jim Stuberg, 1981.

Begin in a large dihedral west of South, join A's Jax, then branch off right and lieback a hanging flake.

14.   A's Jax 8
FA: Pat Ament and Steve Komito, 1964.

Begin in the same large dihedral as *South*, but where the main dihedral begins to lean right, go left to a big ledge. Climb the corner above, then work up and left to a bench beneath some roofs. Climb a right-facing dihedral through the left side of the roofs (8), and continue to a ledge below the summit. Walk off to the west.

Reach the following two routes as well as the last pitch of *A's Jax* by scrambling up and right to a bench above Peapod Buttress.

15.   Zero Tolerance 11b ★
FA: Marc Hirt and Tim Hudgel.

Climb through the right side of the roofs in the upper wall, just right of A's Jax. Five bolts. Bring mid-range stoppers.

16.   Moon Doggie 11b ★
FA: Marc Hirt.

Climb a right-facing dihedral just right of the roofs in the upper wall. Four bolts. Bring mid-range stoppers.

17.   South 8
FA: Layton Kor and Charles Alexander, 1959.

Climb a large, brushy dihedral to the left of Bitty Buttress, presumably the right of two, and devise a line on the upper buttress.

18.   Bitty Buttress 8+ ★
FA: Paul Mayrose and Pat Ament, 1964.

Begin at the foot of the buttress, down and right from the preceding routes. P1. Make some weird moves to get started, then stretch the lead to a good ledge (8+, 165 feet). P2. Climb up and right via right-facing corners and belay on a ledge with a small tree (6). P3. Climb into a clean dihedral with a tapering crack, and from the last good nut placement, crank up and left through the crux. Walk off to the left or climb a short pitch past the left end of a roof (7) to reach the summit.

18A. Rob's Way 9 s ★
FA: Rob Candelaria, 1973.

Follow a vague crack system up the steep wall to the left of the first pitch.

18B. Final Roof 8
FA: Carl Harrison and Jim Stuberg, 1981.

Climb through the roof on the final short pitch to the summit.

19.   Orange Dihedral 8

Around to the right from Bitty Buttress is a large, lichenous right-facing dihedral with an old bolt about 60 feet up. Climb the dihedral and eventually join *Bitty Buttress*.

20. BIG ROOF A3?

Hike up the grassy gully along the east side of the Bitty Buttress until beneath a right-facing dihedral with two bolts and a gigantic roof pierced by a thin crack. No information is available on this route.

SHORT CLIFF WITH THREE CRACKS

This small-but-fun cliff is located along the approach path, about 60 yards before reaching Bitty Buttress. All routes can be safely led, but are also easy to top-rope.

1. FAR LEFT 9
FA: ERIC STROMSWOLD AND ANDREA HAZARD, 1994.

Climb the dihedral/crack on the left side of the buttress, passing just right of a tree.

2. CATALYST 9+
FA: ALAN BRADLEY AND DAN HARE, 1979.

Climb a steep finger crack just right of the preceding route.

3. HESITATION 9
FA: DAN HARE AND CHRIS WOOD, 1980.

Climb the middle of three cracks.

4. MIRAGE 9
FA: DAN HARE AND ALAN BRADLEY, 1979.

Climb the right of three cracks.

Additional top-rope lines of varying difficulty will be found to the right along the same cliff.

STONER SLAB

A large, broken buttress stands at the east end of the Blob Rock massif. Below and slightly east of this buttress is a narrow slab with a single known route. Approach as for Bitty Buttress and continue east, or scramble directly up to the slab from the highway (steep).

INAGODADAVIDA 5
FA: RICHARD ROSSITER, 1996.

Begin at the bottom of the slab just left of a large pine. Climb straight up to a ledge with a couple of pines and belay (5, 90 feet). From the left pine, climb up to a series of cracks that leads to the top of the slab (5, 120 feet).

Steve Ilg on *Country Club Crack*. Photo by Richard Rossiter.

Security Risk Area

Just beyond the Blob Rock Area and on the same side of the canyon, is a very popular group of crags. Nearest to the highway is Happy Hour Crag, a classic for moderate crack climbs with a few sport routes thrown in to the mix. An athletic hike leads farther up the slope to Security Risk Crag, which originally featured difficult cracks, but has more recently become host to a wide selection of challenging sport climbs. Still farther up the hill is The Lighthouse with more sport routes.

HAPPY HOUR CRAG

This popular little buttress is at the 6.8 mile mark on the north side of the highway. It is easily seen from the road a short way past the Blob Rock pull-out. Park on the south side of the highway across from the buttress, and climb a steep, loose trail to the base. Descend from the top by walking down around the west side or lower off from bolt anchors where provided.

1.   I, ROBOT 7
FA: KURT GRAY AND CHARLY OLIVER, 1979.

Begin in a shallow right-facing corner, then continue up the first workable crack on the west side of the rock.

2.   ARE WE NOT MEN 7
FA: CHARLY OLIVER AND STUART SCHNEIDER, 1979.

Start behind a tree a very short way right of the preceding route. Climb a right-facing corner through a roof and onward.

3.   TWOFERS 8
FA: ALLEN WOOD AND DAN HARE, 1979.

Climb up into a conspicuous right-facing system, then out left around a roof.

4.   TWOFERS BYPASS 8
FA: KURT GRAY AND CHRIS TAYLOR, 1980.

Continue up and right, then climb left through the next little roof.

5.   THE BIG SPIT 9
FA: KURT GRAY AND ALLEN WOOD, 1979.

Climb a shallow, right-facing corner up through the left end of the *Rush Hour* roof, then navigate a crack.

6.   RUSH HOUR 12 s ?
FA: DAN HARE AND SCOTT WOODRUFF, 1978.

Just right of *Twofers* is a broken gully and then a roof about 20 feet above the ground. Climb through the roof at a crystalline solution hole (crux), then follow vague cracks to the top of the wall. A key hold at the crux has broken off making the route much harder (original rating 10c).

7.   LAST CALL 9
FA: KURT GRAY AND LARRY SHUBARTH, 1979.

Begin about a few feet right of *Rush Hour* and climb into the bottom of the *Dementia* dihedral. Move out left and follow thin cracks to the top.

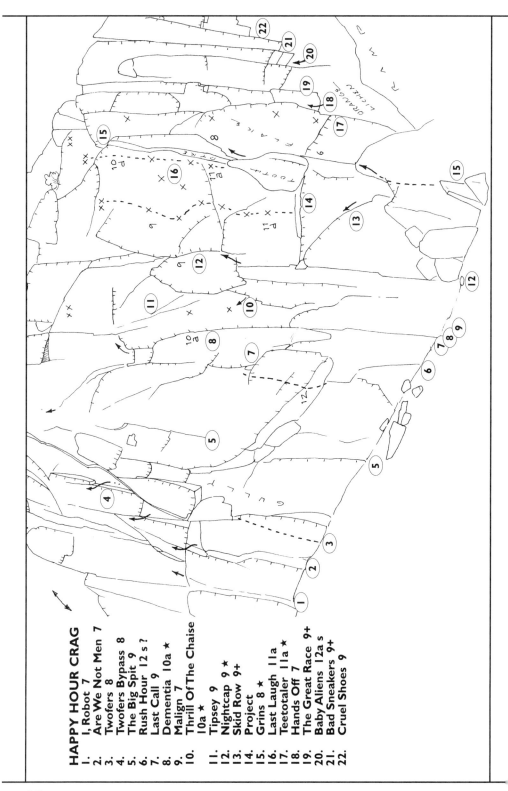

HAPPY HOUR CRAG

1. I, Robot 7
2. Are We Not Men 7
3. Twofers 8
4. Twofers Bypass 8
5. The Big Spit 9
6. Rush Hour 12 s ?
7. Last Call 9
8. Dementia 10a ★
9. Malign 7
10. Thrill Of The Chaise
    10a ★
11. Tipsey 9
12. Nightcap 9 ★
13. Skid Row 9+
14. Project
15. Grins 8 ★
16. Last Laugh 11a
17. Teetotaler 11a ★
18. Hands Off 7
19. The Great Race 9+
20. Baby Aliens 12a s
21. Bad Sneakers 9+
22. Cruel Shoes 9

8.   DEMENTIA 10A ★
FA: CHRIS SCANLON AND DAVE RICE, C. 1974.

Classic. Begin a few feet right of *Rush Hour*. Climb up and left into an obvious left-facing, left-arching flake/dihedral. Exit up and right at the top.

9.   MALIGN 7

Begin with *Dementia*, then break right and climb a nondescript left-facing corner system to the top of the wall.

10.   THRILL OF THE CHAISE 10A ★
FA: DAVE RICE AND ERIK JOHNSON, 1988.

Also known as *Cheers*. Begin with *Malign*, then break left and climb the beautiful knobby face past two bolts, et cetera. Bolts placed by a later party.

11.   TIPSEY 9
FA: DAN HARE AND CHARLY OLIVER, 1979.

Climb the first 50 feet of *Malign*, then break off to the left and follow a crack to the top.

12.   NIGHTCAP 9 ★
FA: DAN HARE AND ALLEN WOOD, 1979.

Begin about 12 feet right of *Dementia*. Follow a crack and corner system up through a left-leaning, left-facing dihedral (crux), and on to the top of the wall.

13.   SKID ROW 9+
FA: DAN HARE AND BOB HANSON, 1979.

Step off the spike as for *Grins*, but angle up and left through some improbable terrain.

14.   PROJECT
FA: DAN HARE..

Follow bolts up the wall between *Skid Row* and *Last Laugh*.

15.   GRINS 8 ★
FA: ALLEN WOOD AND DAN HARE, 1979.

Begin from a spike of rock at the low point of the Buttress. Climb about 50 feet up to the right side of a "tooth," then go up and right along a flake. Finish on a small ledge with a two-bolt anchor just below the top.

16.   LAST LAUGH 11A
FA: DAN HARE, 1995. GEAR SHOULD INCLUDE LARGE RPS.

Climb to the tooth on *Grins* and step left at a bolt, then work straight up past two more bolts and lower off from a two-bolt anchor.

17.   TEETOTALER 11A ★
FA: BRIAN HANSEN AND RICK LEITNER, 1989.

Follow four bolts along the right side of a flake/arête to the right of *Grins*.

18.   HANDS OFF 7
FA: CHARLY OLIVER AND MATT SLATER, 1979.

Climb a large, right-facing dihedral around to the right from *Teetotaler*.

19. THE GREAT RACE 9+
FA: PAT CLUBINE, KURT GRAY, ALLEN WOOD, ALAN BRADLEY, DAN HARE, 1979.

Climb the next right-facing dihedral to the right of *Hands Off.* It may be identified by a small stepped roof about halfway up.

20. BABY ALIENS 12A S
FA: MARK ROLOFSON AND ELAINE CHANDLER, 1987.

Climb a difficult seam up the wall just right of *The Great Race.*

21. BAD SNEAKERS 9+
FA: CHARLY OLIVER AND CHRIS TAYLOR, 1979.

Climb the penultimate right-facing dihedral along the right side of the buttress.

22. CRUEL SHOES 9
FA: LARRY SHUBARTH AND ALLEN WOOD, 1979.

Climb the farthest right dihedral on Happy Hour Crag.

23. BENT FAITH 7
FA: CHARLY OLIVER AND MATT SLATER, 1979.

Curious name. Climb a right-arching crack on a small buttress below the right side of Happy Hour Crag.

THE LIGHTHOUSE

This recently developed crag sits high on the ridge, several hundred yards up and left (west) from Higher Security Risk. It features some 14 routes ranging in difficulty from 9 to 12c. The hardest route actually ascends the overhanging arête of a nearby giant boulder. Perhaps the best route on the crag is Lady Of Light (12a, seven bolts, 55 feet). Approach via Security Risk.

SECURITY RISK CRAG

Security Risk consists of three buttresses separated by steep gullies. The highest and farthest north of the three has just a few routes on its southwest side. The middle buttress is larger and cleaner, characterized by bolt-protected face climbs. The lower buttress has a number of crack climbs as well as excellent bolted routes. Security Risk is located about 200 yards west of Blob Rock and several hundred yards above the road. It is most easily reached by hiking up a footpath a short way east of the trail leading to Happy Hour Crag.

Higher Security Risk

This is the upper and farthest north buttress, most of which is broken and undocumented. Several short routes have been established on a steep wall at the right side of the buttress.

1. GIMME THREE STEPS 11A/B
FA: TOM HAYES AND STEVE ANNECONE, 1993.

Follow discontinuous cracks up the left side of the wall. Two bolts and a fixed nut with a bolt anchor at the top. Bring a #2 Rock, #1 TCU, and appropriate QDs.

2. GIMME BACK MY BULLETS 11B/C
FA: ANNECONE AND HAYES, 1993 (TR).

Begin about ten feet right of the preceding route. Follow a seam past a flake, etc.

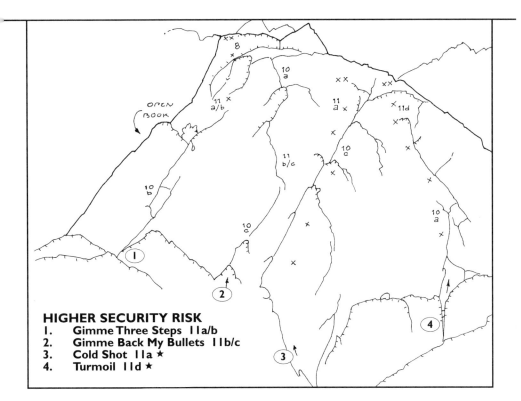

HIGHER SECURITY RISK
1.   **Gimme Three Steps 11a/b**
2.   **Gimme Back My Bullets 11b/c**
3.   **Cold Shot 11a ★**
4.   **Turmoil 11d ★**

3.   COLD SHOT 11A ★
FA: RICK LEITNER.

Climb along a steep crack/seam that angles up to the right from the low-point of the wall. Five bolts to a two-bolt anchor.

4.   TURMOIL 11D ★
FA: DAN HARE AND MIKE SMITH, 1996.

Begin about 25 feet up and right from *Cold Shot*. Follow five bolts along seams to a two-bolt anchor.

Upper Security Risk

This is the large central buttress, characterized by steep and difficult sport routes. Lower off or rappel from most routes; otherwise scramble down the gullies on either side of the buttress.

5.   S BUTTRESS 9+
FA: ANNECONE AND HAYES, 1993. SR.

Begin by the farthest left dike on the buttress. Climb a steep hand crack, go right under a roof, then up and right to the bolt anchor on *Pup*. All bolts placed by a subsequent party.

6.   PUP 9 ★
FA: RICK LEITNER.

Climb along the left of two quartz dikes at the left edge of the southwest face, pass the left end of a big roof, then go up and right to a bolt anchor. Nine bolts.

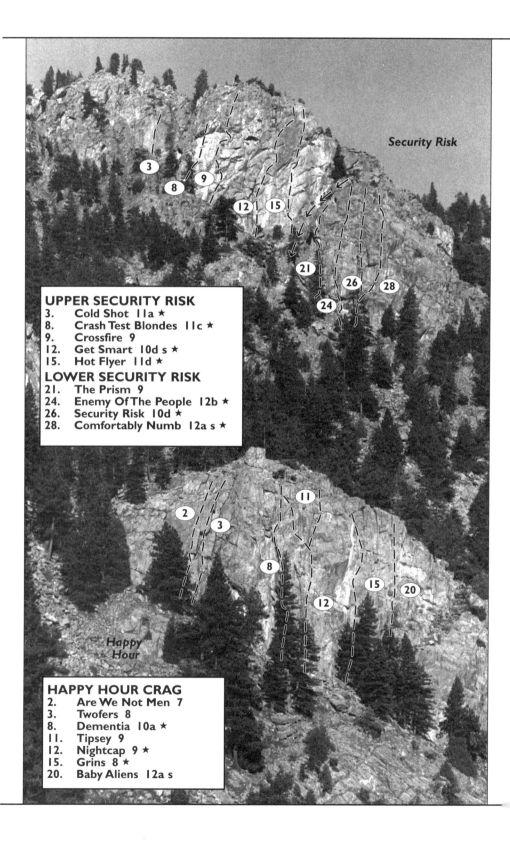

Security Risk

UPPER SECURITY RISK
3. Cold Shot 11a ★
8. Crash Test Blondes 11c ★
9. Crossfire 9
12. Get Smart 10d s ★
15. Hot Flyer 11d ★

LOWER SECURITY RISK
21. The Prism 9
24. Enemy Of The People 12b ★
26. Security Risk 10d ★
28. Comfortably Numb 12a s ★

Happy Hour

HAPPY HOUR CRAG
2. Are We Not Men 7
3. Twofers 8
8. Dementia 10a ★
11. Tipsey 9
12. Nightcap 9 ★
15. Grins 8 ★
20. Baby Aliens 12a s

7.   S BUTTRESS DIRECT 10B
FA: HAYES AND ANNECONE. (TR).

Begin just left of *Crash Test Blondes*. Climb up to a small roof, go left, then climb straight up past the left side of a big roof.

8.   CRASH TEST BLONDES 11C ★
FA: RICK LEITNER.

Follow five bolts up the wall between two prominent white dikes, turn a big roof with two more bolts, and lower off from a two-bolt anchor.

9.   CROSSFIRE 9
FA: DAN HARE AND ALAN BRADLEY, 1979.

Climb out onto a large pointed flake, then work up through roofs and continue up a right-leaning, right-facing dihedral. Step left and belay at its top. Follow a crack system up and slightly right to the top of the wall.

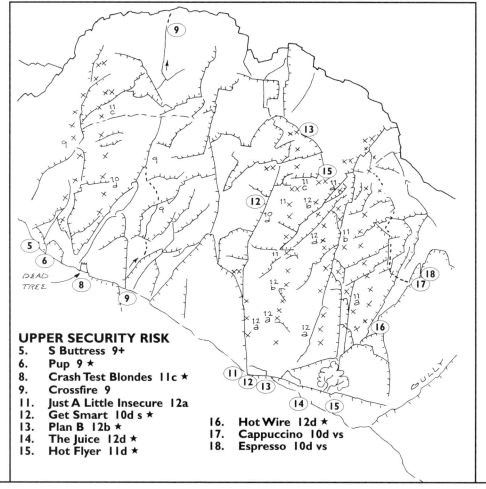

UPPER SECURITY RISK

5.   S Buttress 9+
6.   Pup 9 ★
8.   Crash Test Blondes 11c ★
9.   Crossfire 9
11.   Just A Little Insecure 12a
12.   Get Smart 10d s ★
13.   Plan B 12b ★
14.   The Juice 12d ★
15.   Hot Flyer 11d ★

16.   Hot Wire 12d ★
17.   Cappuccino 10d vs
18.   Espresso 10d vs

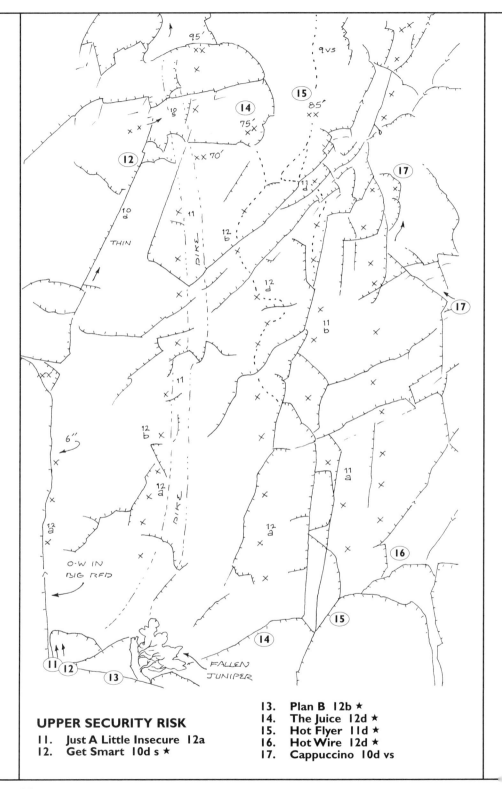

UPPER SECURITY RISK

11. Just A Little Insecure 12a
12. Get Smart 10d s ★
13. Plan B 12b ★
14. The Juice 12d ★
15. Hot Flyer 11d ★
16. Hot Wire 12d ★
17. Cappuccino 10d vs

10. CRACKING THE CODE 11B
FA: DAN HARE., FRED KNAPP, ROB STANLEY, 1998. ALL BOLTS, BUT THE SECOND PITCH CAN BE BACKED UP WITH GEAR FROM 0.5 TO 2 INCHES.

1. Begin just left of the following route in a small right-facing dihedral. Climb past a couple of bulges to a good ledge (11b). 2. Climb a short right-facing dihedral to a roof and turn it on the left, then go up a slab and right around another roof (10b) to a belay on a small stance. 3. Climb a right-facing dihedral and finish with a short arête (9+).

11. JUST A LITTLE INSECURE 12A
FA: KEN TROUT. REDPOINT: HENRY LESTER.

Climb the right side of a short arête, just left of the wide crack of *Get Smart*. Three bolts to a two-bolt anchor.

12. GET SMART 10D S ★
FA: RANDY LEAVITT, DAN HARE, JOEL SCHIAVONE, 1981.

Begin at the bottom of a large, right-facing dihedral with a wide crack. Climb the wide crack, pass a small roof on the right and follow a shallow dihedral with a thin crack (10d) to a two-bolt anchor beneath a roof. Turn the roof to the right and follow a right-leaning crack to a ledge (10d s). Rappel or continue up and right to the top of the buttress.

13. PLAN B 12B ★
FA: KEN TROUT. REDPOINT: HENRY LESTER. UPPER SECTION: MARK ROLOFSON.

Follow a line of bolts up the steep wall just left of a white dike. Lower off from coldshuts at 75 feet or continue to a higher anchor at 100 feet. Bring 14 QDs.

14. THE JUICE 12D ★
FA: MARK ROLOFSON.

Begin a short way right of the white dike at a shallow left-facing, right-leaning dihedral. Follow a line of bolts up the steep wall, past a roof, to a bolt anchor. Lower off 75 feet.

14A. JUICED FLYER 12A ★
Climb *The Juice* to a rest just right of the fourth bolt and finish with **Hot Flyer**. Bring ten QDs.

15. HOT FLYER 11D ★
FA: RANDY LEAVITT AND RICK ACCOMAZZO, 1981.

This excellent route was originally led with a single fixed pin and scant other pro. It was subsequently bolted with the consent of the first ascent party. Follow bolts along a shallow right-facing dihedral system at the southwest corner of the buttress. Nine bolts to a two-bolt anchor.

16. HOT WIRE 12D ★
FA: RICK LEITNER AND MARK ROLOFSON. REDPOINT: CHRIS ALBER.

Follow bolts up the steep wall just right of *Hot Flyer*. 13 bolts to a two-bolt anchor.

17. CAPPUCCINO 10D VS
FA: HARRISON DEKKER AND RANDY LEAVITT, 1981.

Begin at a perched block about 50 feet up and right from *Hot Flyer*. Climb up and left to a bolt, then climb up to a roof that is turned on the left. Climb straight up again to a fixed copperhead in an overhanging crack, then traverse down and left through the roofs, and gain the bolt and chain anchor on *Hot Flyer*.

18. ESPRESSO 10D VS
FA: RANDY LEAVITT AND RICK ACCOMAZZO, 1981.

Climb past the bolt as for *Cappuccino*, but turn the roof on the right. Work up and left along a flake/crack and gain a ledge. Turn the roof and continue up a slab to the top of the buttress.

Lower Security Risk

This is the lower of the three buttresses, characterized by steep crack climbs, including the route Security Risk for which the crag is named. Newer bolt routes have been completed on some of the narrow faces and arêtes between crack systems. To descend from the top, scramble down a steep gully on the north side or lower off as appropriate.

19. SCRAPING BY 10A
FA: JIM ERICKSON, SOLO, 1979.
Climb the big left-facing dihedral at the far north side of the buttress.

20. ELDO OF THE PEOPLE 12A/B
FA: MARK ROLOFSON AND. . . .
Begin with the opening moves of *Scraping By*, then follow bolts up and right.

21. THE PRISM 9
FA: DAN HARE AND ALAN BRADLEY, 1979.
Climb the big left-facing dihedral just right of *Scraping By*.

22. MAXIMUM SECURITY 9+ ★
FA: ALEC SHARP AND DAN HARE, 1980..SR WITH EXTRA MID-RANGE STOPPERS.
Begin with *The Prism*, then break right at a flake and follow a steep crack to the top of the wall.

23. ECSTACY OF THE PEOPLE 12D ★
FA: MARK ROLOFSON.
Start from a ledge at the bottom of *The Prism*. Stretch up and right to clip the first bolt, then traverse right past another bolt to the arête. Follow bolts up the right side of the arête. Seven bolts to a two-bolt anchor.

23A. DIRECT START (PROJECT)
Three bolts protect a direct start to the arête that was not red-pointed at time of writing.

24. ENEMY OF THE PEOPLE 12B ★
FA: RANDY LEAVITT, 1981. SR TO A #2.5 FRIEND WITH EXTRA THIN STUFF.
Begin about 30 feet down and right from *The Prism*. Turn a bulge at two bolts, and stem up a shallow inset (12b, #0.5 and 1.5 Friends). Follow a hand crack up a left-facing dihedral, then step left and climb shallow corners with a fixed pin.

25. CENTRAL INSECURITY 12C/D ★
FA: MARK ROLOFSON AND BOB D'ANTONIO.
Climb the steep wall between *Enemy Of The People* and *Security Risk*. Nine bolts to a two bolt anchor.

26. SECURITY RISK 10D ★
FA: SCOTT WOODRUFF AND DAN HARE, 1978; ALTERNATE START (10A): JIM ERICKSON AND ART HIGBEE, 1979. SR TO A #4 FRIEND.
Locate a steep left-facing dihedral that leads to a long crack system in the middle of the buttress. Climb the intimidating dihedral with an awkward bulge and belay on a good ledge. Two other cracks around to the right may be used to reach this ledge (7 or 10). Climb straight up a chimney, over a bulge via double cracks, and up a good hand crack to the top.

26A. SOFTWARE RELIABILITY 10 ★
FA: ALEC SHARP AND DAN HARE, 1980.
Just before the bulge on the second pitch, traverse about 25 feet left to join *Enemy Of The People*.

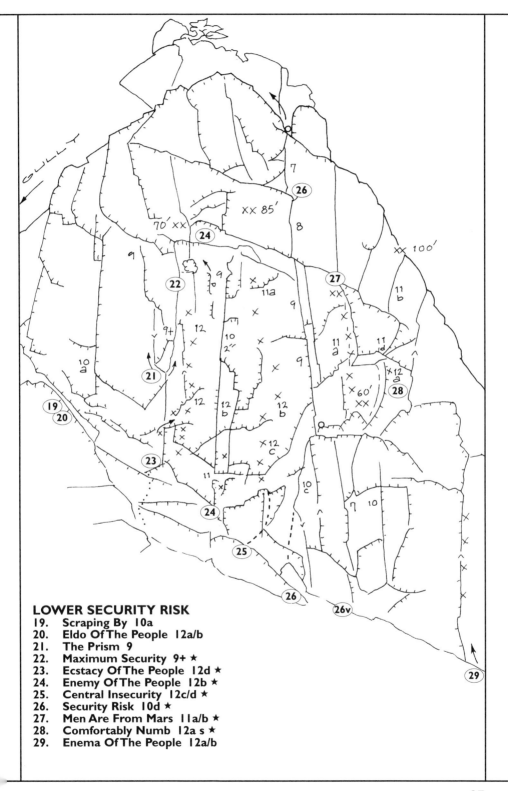

LOWER SECURITY RISK

19. **Scraping By** 10a
20. **Eldo Of The People** 12a/b
21. **The Prism** 9
22. **Maximum Security** 9+ ★
23. **Ecstacy Of The People** 12d ★
24. **Enemy Of The People** 12b ★
25. **Central Insecurity** 12c/d ★
26. **Security Risk** 10d ★
27. **Men Are From Mars** 11a/b ★
28. **Comfortably Numb** 12a s ★
29. **Enema Of The People** 12a/b

26B. SOCIAL SECURITY 10 S
FA: DAN HARE AND HARRISON DEKKER, 1981.

Start up the second pitch of *Security Risk*, then break right at a small roof and climb a steep, left fac-ing dihedral (crux). Finish in an easier crack above.

27. MEN ARE FROM MARS 11A/B ★
FA: DIANNE BARROW AND MARK ROLOFSON.

Gain the ledge atop the first pitch of *Security Risk* and belay from two bolts. Follow five bolts up a left-facing dihedral (the same as *Social Security*) and lower off from a two-bolt anchor (85 feet).

28. COMFORTABLY NUMB 12A S ★
FA: MARK ROLOFSON AND ERIK ERIKSSON, 1982. SR TO A #2.5 FRIEND.

Climb the first pitch of *Security Risk*, move right on the ledge and belay at two bolts. Climb a shallow left-facing corner to a bolt, turn a difficult roof, and follow a continuously difficult crack to a ledge with a two-pin and bolt anchor. Lower off (60 feet to the ledge or 110 feet to the ground).

29. ENEMA OF THE PEOPLE 12A/B
FA: BOB D'ANTONIO.

Climb a short, steep southeast-facing wall around to the right from *Security Risk*. Five bolts to a two-bolt anchor.

THE BIHEDRAL

The Bihedral is located on the north side of the highway at the seven mile mark, a short way beyond Happy Hour Crag. It is a large south-facing buttress with a variety of routes both old and new. Most of the older routes ascend the upper, central section of the crag, but several sport routes have been completed here as well. The lower-right aspect of the rock is called The Riviera and features an array of interesting sport climbs. To descend from the summit, hike off to the east.

1. GEOMETRICS 9
FA: MASON FRICHETTE AND DAN HARE.

Begin well up in the gully at the far west side of The Bihedral. Climb a left-facing corner, then work up and left along a ramp and belay beneath a roof. Climb through the right side of the roof and scram-ble to hiking terrain. Can be done as one pitch.

Main Wall

The following routes begin from a ledge system that runs across the bottom of the upper wall. To reach the ledges, scramble up the left side of a broken buttress from the lower left side of the south face.

2. EDGE OF REALITY 12A/B
FA: DAN HARE AND ROB STANLEY, 1997.

Climb the southeast arête of the West Tower (a small pinnacle at the west side of the upper face). Five bolts to a two-bolt anchor. This tower is easily reached from the gully at the far west side of The Bihedral.

3. HETEROHEDRAL 9
FA: BOB HANSON, ALAN BRADLEY, DAN HARE, 1979.

Begin down and right from the preceding route, along a ramp. Work up and right beneath a diagonal roof and belay on a ledge. Move right into a right-facing dihedral and finish in a thin crack just left of the second pitch of *Bihedral*.

4.   FACE 9 ★
Climb the slab just left from the first pitch of *Bihedral*. Eight bolts to a two-bolt anchor.

5.   BIHEDRAL 8+ ★
FA: LARRY DALKE AND CLIFF JENNINGS, 1967.

This route, something of a classic, ascends the big left-facing dihedral system in the middle of the wall. Two pitches.

6.   CRACK VARIATION 9
FA: CHRIS REVELEY AND DIANA HUNTER, 1975.

From the second belay, halfway up the route, step right and climb a shallow, left-facing flake/corner to join *Thumb Tack*.

7.   DIHEDRAL VARIATION 9 ★
FA: JIM ERICKSON AND CHRIS REVELEY, 1979.

This is really a separate route. From the initial belay at the start to *Bihedral*, branch right in a steep dihedral with a thin crack and join *Thumb Tack* below the final headwall.

8.   THUMB TACK 11D ★
FA: LARRY DALKE AND CLIFF JENNINGS, 1965. FFA: ALAN BRADLEY AND DAN HARE, 1984.

Begin down and right of *Bihedral*, and right of a tree. Climb a steep wall (8 s), then proceed more easily to a ramp beneath an overhanging headwall. Climb up into a recess, then follow a thin crack to the top (crux). An easier alternative is to continue up and left along the ramp.

9.   PARIAH 12B ★
This route may be reached via rappel from bolts on the summit or via *Thumb Tack*. Bring long slings to rappel from the bolts. Climb the overhanging headwall just right of *Thumb Tack*. Six bolts.

10.   ACID ROCK 6
FA: MICHAEL TOBIAS AND BILL PIERCE, 1970.

From the right side of the crag, scramble up and left along a sloping ramp, and climb a face for 30 feet. Go left along a ramp to a smooth inside corner and climb it to a ledge with a pine tree. Climb moderate rock along the right side of an overhanging arête and gain the top of the rock.

The Riviera

The following routes ascend a steep wall of excellent rock at the lower right side of The Bihedral. There are four two-bolt anchors near the top of the wall. A good path leads up to the bottom of the wall from a cement post with the number 430 on it.

11.   SEA BREEZE 11A ★
FA: DAN HARE AND SUSAN SIMPSON.

Follow a line of five bolts just left of a shallow, left-facing dihedral.

12.   MISTRAL 11A
FA: HARE AND SIMPSON.

Climb past four bolts just right of a shallow, left-facing dihedral.

13.   AU NATURAL 7
FA: HARE AND SIMPSON.

Climb the buttress just left of *Devil's Dihedral*.

THE BIHEDRAL
Main Wall

1. Geometrics 9
2. Edge Of Reality 12a/b
3. Heterohedral 9
4. Face 9 ★
5. Bihedral 8+ ★
8. Thumb Tack 11d ★
9. Pariah 12b ★

The Riviera

15. Devil's Dihedral 9+ ★
19. Le Nouveau Riche 10b
★

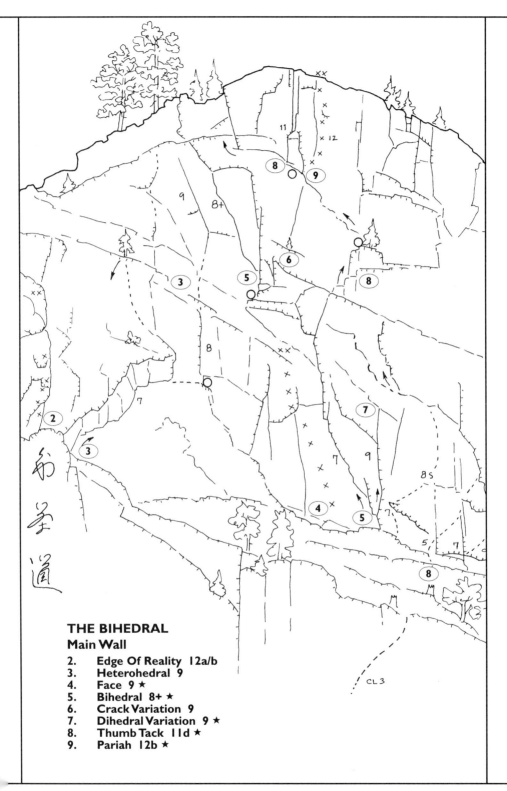

THE BIHEDRAL
Main Wall

2. **Edge Of Reality** 12a/b
3. **Heterohedral** 9
4. **Face** 9 ★
5. **Bihedral** 8+ ★
6. **Crack Variation** 9
7. **Dihedral Variation** 9 ★
8. **Thumb Tack** 11d ★
9. **Pariah** 12b ★

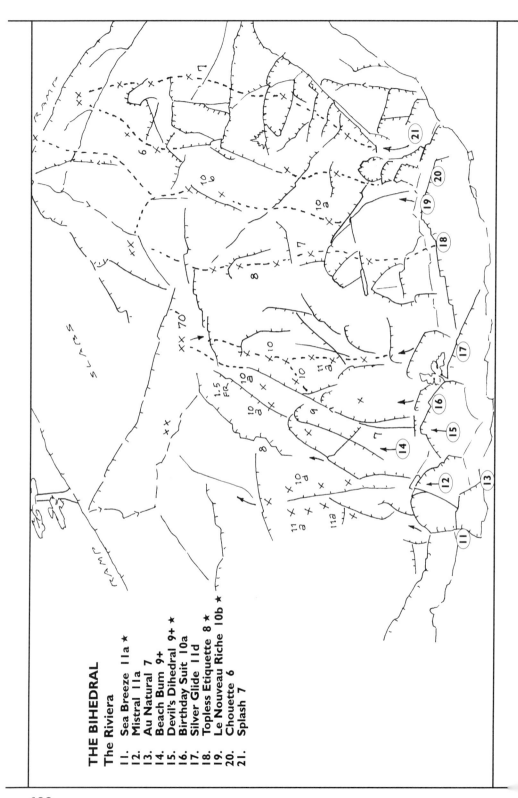

THE BIHEDRAL
The Riviera

11. Sea Breeze 11a ★
12. Mistral 11a
13. Au Natural 7
14. Beach Bum 9+
15. Devil's Dihedral 9+ ★
16. Birthday Suit 10a
17. Silver Glide 11d
18. Topless Etiquette 8 ★
19. Le Nouveau Riche 10b ★
20. Chouette 6
21. Splash 7

14. BEACH BUM 9+
FA: HARE AND SIMPSON.

Climb the arête just left of *Devil's Dihedral*. One bolt.

15. DEVIL'S DIHEDRAL 9+ ★
FA: GEORGE WATSON, STEVE ILG, RICHARD ROSSITER 1987. SR.

Scramble up onto a boulder and climb a smooth, black, open-book dihedral. A useful bolt has been placed on the left wall of the dihedral, apparently for the route *Beach Bum*.

16. BIRTHDAY SUIT 10A
FA: HARE AND SIMPSON.

Climb the arête just right of *Devil's Dihedral*. Five bolts.

17. SILVER GLIDE 11D

Climb through a bulge and join the preceding route near its third bolt. Five bolts.

18. TOPLESS ETIQUETTE 8 ★
FA: HARE AND SIMPSON.

Begin from a ledge about 60 feet right of *Devil's Dihedral* and follow a line of five bolts to the top of the face.

19. LE NOUVEAU RICHE 10B ★
FA: RICHARD ROSSITER AND STEVE ILG, 1987. SR TO A #2 FRIEND.

Begin from a ledge along the right side of the wall. Climb a steep slab past three bolts, then veer left and lower off from a two-bolt anchor. The original line continued straight up to the top of the wall.

20. CHOUETTE 6
FA: STEF STREICH AND ROB STANLEY, 1997. SR TO A #2 FRIEND.

Climb a left-facing corner system about 15 feet right of the preceding route. Four bolts.

21. SPLASH 7
FA: STEF STREICH AND ROB STANLEY, 1997. TCUS TO A #2 FRIEND.

Follow short cracks and ledges up the wall about 15 feet right of *Chouette*. Five bolts.

INCA STONE

This small buttress, also known as Truth Or Consequences, is easily seen about 200 feet above the north side of the highway, across from a gravel pull-out at 7.3 miles. Though most of the routes are short, several are of excellent quality and can be led or toproped. The first two routes are on a flat south-facing wall just left of the main buttress.

1. LEFT SIDE 10 S

Climb the left side of the steep wall past a bolt. A second bolt has been placed on a short step above a ledge. A bolt would be useful on the wall below the first bolt, which is about 25 feet off the deck.

2. THE TREADMILL 10C
FA: DAN HARE, KURT GRAY, CHARLY OLIVER, 1981.

Climb a thin crack up the middle of the wall and through a roof.

Main Wall

The following routes ascend the main buttress, which has two facets divided by a blunt prow. The ledge below the right side of the buttress is recessed behind a peculiar stone wall with a "window" through its middle.

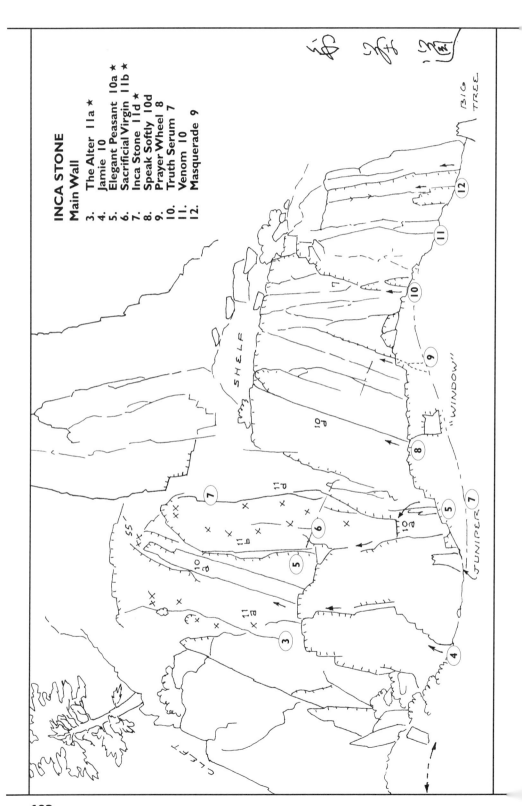

INCA STONE
Main Wall

3. The Alter 11a ★
4. Jamie 10
5. Elegant Peasant 10a ★
6. Sacrificial Virgin 11b ★
7. Inca Stone 11d ★
8. Speak Softly 10d
9. Prayer Wheel 8
10. Truth Serum 7
11. Venom 10
12. Masquerade 9

3. THE ALTER 11A ★
FA: DAN HARE AND ROB STANLEY, 1996.

Begin as for the following route or scramble up from the left. Follow four bolts along thin cracks in the left side of the main wall.

4. JAMIE 10
FA: DAN HARE AND RICH PERCH, 1981.

Begin just left of a juniper tree below the prow of the buttress. Climb a small, left-facing corner to a ledge and continue up the left of two right-leaning cracks.

5. ELEGANT PEASANT 10A ★
FA: DAN HARE, JOHN MARKEL, ALLEN WOOD, 1981. LEFT START: R. ROSSITER.

Begin at the bottom of a right-leaning rotten crack, about ten feet right of a large juniper tree. Stem off a rock wall that rims the ledge along the base of the wall, and place a stopper in a black crack. Make a difficult traverse left to a small ledge, then climb up and left to a higher ledge at the bottom of a shallow, right-facing dihedral. Climb the dihedral to the top of the buttress. This route may also be started just right of the juniper tree.

6. SACRIFICIAL VIRGIN 11B ★
FA: DAN HARE AND MIKE DOWNING, 1995.

Climb to the second bolt on *Inca Stone*, then work up and left to the arête past four more bolts. Step right and lower off from the anchor on *Inca Stone*.

7. INCA STONE 11D ★

Climb to the initial ledge on *Elegant Peasant*, then follow four bolts up and right to a hand crack. Lower off from a two-bolt anchor. Bring stoppers and small Friends.

8. SPEAK SOFTLY 10D
FA: DAN HARE AND GEORGE RUSSELL, 1981.

Stem off the rock wall just left of the "window" and jam a right-leaning crack through an orange lichen streak.

9. PRAYER WHEEL 8
FA: DAN HARE, 1981. SR PLUS A #3.5 FRIEND.

Climb the next significant crack right of *Speak Softly*, which has a three-foot spike at its base.

10. TRUTH SERUM 7
FA: DAN HARE, 1981.

Climb a right-leaning crack to the right of *Prayer Wheel*. Look for a sharp jug about four feet from the top.

11. VENOM 10
FA: DAN HARE, KURT GRAY, CHARLY OLIVER, 1981.

Locate a black streak dotted with orange and gray lichen on the right side of the wall. Climb a short crack and flared grooves up the middle of the lichen streak.

12. MASQUERADE 9
FA: DAN HARE AND ALAN BRADLEY, 1981.

Climb an overhanging thin crack at the far right end of the wall.

LOCAL ANESTHETIC 9
FA: JOEL SCHIAVONE AND DAN HARE, 1981.

This route ascends a short, right-facing dihedral on the south side of the creek, about 200 yards before Boulder Falls. The dihedral may be seen from the east end of the parking area at Boulder Falls.

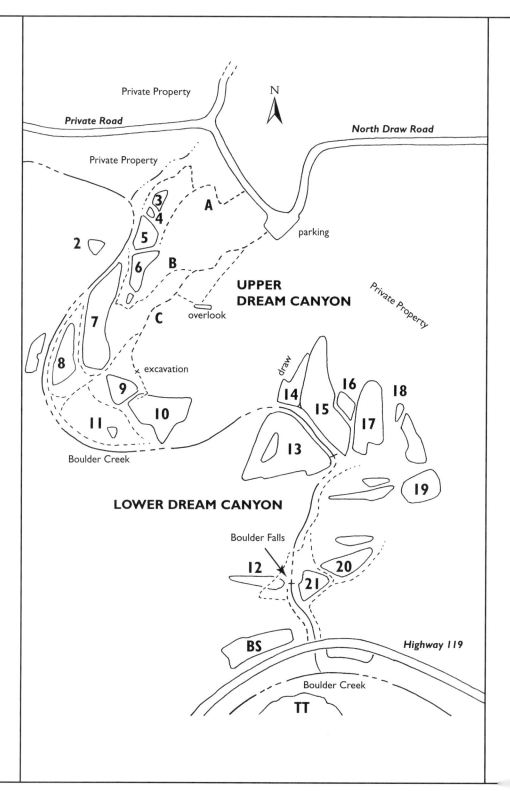

Lower Dream Canyon

North Boulder Creek cascades southward from a deep S-shaped gorge called Dream Canyon and joins Middle Boulder Creek (Boulder Creek) about 7.6 miles up Boulder Canyon. At this confluence and on the south side of the highway is a paved parking area rimmed by a castellated stone wall. The prominent tower to the west of the parking area and on the south side of the creek is Tonnere Tower, which has several seldom-climbed and unnamed routes. Just north of Tonnere Tower on the north side of the road is Boulder Slips, another crag that sees little action, though it has a couple of good routes. Boulder Falls, a tourist attraction, is reached by a short trail that begins on the north side of the highway. The clandestine gorge above the falls is best thought of as two different areas, Lower Dream Canyon and Upper Dream Canyon, as their approaches are separate and unrelated.

Lower Dream Canyon can be said to begin above Boulder Falls or at the actual opening of the gorge at Highway 119. Park as for Boulder Falls at 7.6 miles. Hike up the paved trail to the falls, then scramble about 150 feet up the slope on the left (west). Traverse right on a ledge and pass through a hole beneath a big boulder, then scoot down a gully to North Boulder Creek, just above the falls. It is necessary to ford the creek to reach crags on the east side of Dream Canyon. If the water is too high, one may scramble over the top of Boulder Falls Wall (Class 3) and enter the canyon on grassy ledges just below Chrome Dome. Note that the slope west of the trail is signed "No Tresspassing." Hikers and climbers have, however, been using this approach to pass the falls for at least fifty years. Proceed at your discretion.

Crags are described from left to right along the west bank of North Boulder Creek, then downstream (left to right) along the east bank.

MAP LEGEND			
Upper Dream Canyon		**Lower Dream Canyon**	
A.	West Trail	12.	Boulder Falls West
B.	Dream Dome Trail	13.	Bhakti Point
C.	South Trail	14.	Serenity Spire
1.	Universal Crag	15.	Krishna
2.	The Terrace	16.	Berlin Wall
3.	Thunder Point	17.	Wall of Winter Warmth
4.	The Icon	18.	Melons
5.	Oceanic Wall	19.	Pin Dome
6.	Dream Dome	20.	Chrome Dome
7.	Lost Angel	21.	Boulder Falls East
8.	Water Slabs	BS.	Boulder Slips
9.	Midnight Rock	TT.	Tonnere Tower
10.	Vanishing Point		
11.	Bat Cove		

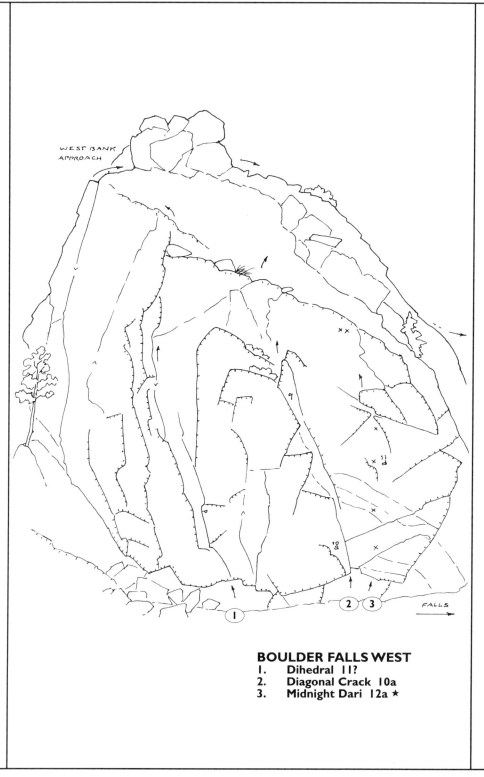

WEST BANK
APPROACH

FALLS

BOULDER FALLS WEST
1. Dihedral 11?
2. Diagonal Crack 10a
3. Midnight Dari 12a ★

BOULDER FALLS WEST

This is the small buttress on the west (left) side of Boulder Falls. The paved tourist path leads almost directly to its base.

1.   DIHEDRAL 11?
Climb a right-facing dihedral with a fixed pin, then step left and climb another right-facing dihedral to the top of the buttress.

2.   DIAGONAL CRACK 10A
Climb a left-leaning crack about 25 feet right of the preceding route.

3.   MIDNIGHT DARI 12A ★
FA: PAUL GLOVER AND DARI DEAVERS.
Climb the steep wall just right of *Kodak Crack*. Four bolts to a two-bolt anchor (no rappel rings).

EARLY WARNING 10D
FA: DAN HARE AND JIM SOUDER, 1978.
On a small rock above the falls, climb a short overhanging crack and a left-facing corner to a tree.

BHAKTI POINT

Also known as Plotinus, Bhakti Point is located on the west side of the gorge just across from Krishna, about 100 yards above Boulder Falls. It has a long steep south face and a distinctive summit block that overlooks the lower half of Dream Canyon.

1.   SLEEPLESS CHILD 9
FA: DAN HARE AND ALLEN WOOD, 1980.
At the west end of the wall is a square-cut buttress reminiscent of *Wind Ridge* in Eldorado Canyon. Follow cracks up the center of the buttress and finish with a short headwall.

2.   SOMETHING OBSCURE 10A
FA: JIM ERICKSON AND ART HIGBEE, 1975.
Climb a finger crack about 80 feet up and left from a big dihedral at the east end of the south face and just left of a 15-foot flake.

3.   NERVE DAMAGE 11A s
FA: DAN HARE AND CHRIS PEISKER, 1986.
Begin about 15 feet up and left from *Plotinus*. Climb the slab past a bolt, then work up and left into a small corner with very poor pro.

4.   PLOTINUS 10
FA: MICHAEL TOBIAS AND BILL PIERCE, 1969. FFA: ART HIGBEE AND JIM ERICKSON, 1974.
Plotinus – A neoplatonic philosopher of the third century AD. At the east end of the south face is a big dihedral with a smooth right wall. Climb the right edge of the wall past a bolt, then go up and left along a finger crack and on to the top of the wall.

Summit Knob

The following routes ascend the summit block of Bhakti Point. To reach the summit block, hike up the grassy slope beneath the south face and pass through a spectacular notch at the southwest end of the buttress, or scramble up the steep slope on the northwest side of the buttress.

BHAKTI POINT
Summit Knob

5. **Northeast Gully Class 4**
6. **The Talon 10**
7. **Sport Crystal 11b ★**
8. **West Ridge 6**

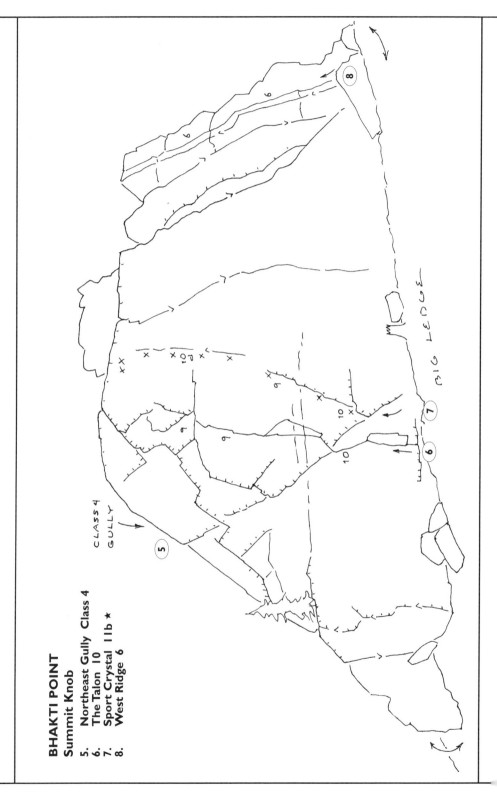

5.   NORTHEAST GULLY CLASS 4
This is the easiest way to reach the summit of Bhakti Point (and the easiest way to climb off).

6.   THE TALON 10
FA: DAN HARE AND JOEL SCHIAVONE, 1981.

This route ascends a zigzag crack system on the northwest side of the summit knob. Climb a short, overhanging fist crack to a ledge. Work up and left, then back right and follow a thin crack to the top.

7.   SPORT CRYSTAL 11B ★
FA: BOB HORAN AND MARK KALIN. RACK: 10 QDS.

Begin a few feet right of *The Talon*. Work up and right along flakes, then follow bolts along a beautiful black streak with many crystals.

8.   WEST RIDGE 6
FA: RICHARD ROSSITER.

Climb a hand and fist crack up good rock on the southwest side of the summit block.

WALL OF WINTER WARMTH MASSIF
The Wall Of Winter Warmth and its appendages Krishna and the Berlin Wall present a wide array of "traditional routes" and not much in the way of "sport climbs." These features are located on the east side of North Boulder Creek, across from Bhakti Point. Approach: Once above Boulder Falls, hike along the east stream bank to the bottom of the buttresses. This area may also be reached from the parking area used for Upper Dream Canyon, but beware of private property boundaries.

Serenity Spire
This small crag is located on the right side of a narrow gully about 200 feet above the stream, at the far north (left) end of Krishna.

1.   ADAM'S ARÊTE 10C/D
FA: BOB HORAN AND WERNER BRAUN.

Climb the arête at the left side of the north face. Five bolts to a two-bolt anchor.

2.   BOBBY'S WALL 10C
FA: BOB HORAN AND WERNER BRAUN.

Climb flake system up center of north face. Nine bolts to a two-bolt anchor.

3.   NORTH FACE 12B
FA: BOB HORAN, TR.

Climb thin edges and incipient cracks between *Bobby's Wall* and *Afro Sheen*.

4.   AFRO SHEEN 10 s
FA: JOHN SHERMAN AND MIKE BENGE, 1981.

This route ascends the overhanging, north-facing wall of an unnamed buttress just upstream from Wall Of Winter Warmth. Scramble over the upper waterfall (below Krishna) and continue upstream to a gully on the right side of the stream. Work up and right to a left-facing dihedral and climb to a ledge at its top. Steep cracks lead to the top. Walk off.

Krishna
Krishna rises directly out of North Boulder Creek, and with Bhakti Point on the west side, forms a narrow gap with a waterfall that makes passage into the upper canyon difficult. The upper right

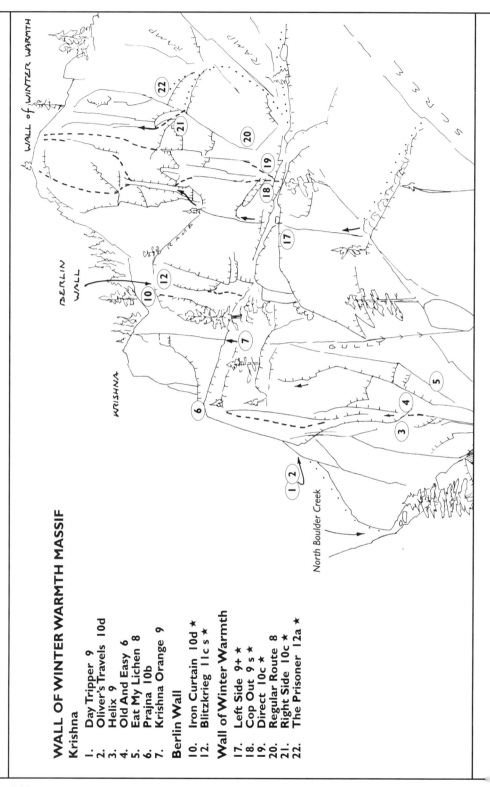

WALL OF WINTER WARMTH MASSIF

Krishna

1. Day Tripper 9
2. Oliver's Travels 10d
3. Helix 9
4. Old And Easy 6
5. Eat My Lichen 8
6. Prajna 10b
7. Krishna Orange 9

Berlin Wall

10. Iron Curtain 10d ★
12. Blitzkrieg 11c s ★

Wall of Winter Warmth

17. Left Side 9+ ★
18. Cop Out 9 s ★
19. Direct 10c ★
20. Regular Route 8
21. Right Side 10c ★
22. The Prisoner 12a ★

aspect of Krishna lies immediately northwest of the Berlin Wall. Approach by hiking along the east (right) bank of the stream to the foot of the buttress. To descend from the top, rappel from trees and down-climb the gully below the Berlin Wall.

The following routes are located on the long main wall and south buttress of Krishna.

1.   DAY TRIPPER 9
FA: PAT HEALY AND JOEL SCHIAVONE, 1981.

Climb discontinuous thin cracks left of the long roof mentioned in the following route.

2.   OLIVER'S TRAVELS 10D
FA: DAN HARE, PAT HEALY, JOEL SCHIAVONE, 1981.

This route begins about 100 feet north (upstream) from *Helix* (the right edge of the face). Work your way through the narrows in the stream and continue north until it is possible to scramble back right onto a ledge beneath the upper part of the face. Climb a large flake and continue up cracks to the center of a long roof. Move right to a big block, turn the roof at a flake, and continue in a vertical crack.

3.   HELIX 9
FA: KATY CASSIDY AND DAN HARE, 1982.

Step off a boulder just below the upper falls and climb a crack into the left of two dihedrals. Finish with an arête formed by the right edge of a west-facing wall.

4.   OLD AND EASY 6

Begin just right of *Helix* and follow a long, curving, left-facing dihedral up to the large terrace below the Berlin Wall.

5.   EAT MY LICHEN 8
FA: CARL MOYER, 1987.

This route lies between *Old And Easy* and the gully that leads up to the Berlin Wall. Begin on the boulder mentioned above, but take the next dihedral to the right up to a roof, and continue in a crack from the right end of the roof.

The following two routes begin from a big ledge up and left from the Berlin Wall.

6.   PRAJNA 10B
FA: MAC HESTER AND CHRIS BURGESS, 1989.

Climb the overhanging arête left of *Krishna Orange*. One bolt.

7.   KRISHNA ORANGE 9
FA: JOEL SCHIAVONE AND DAN HARE, 1981.

Climb a crack in the middle of the orange, southeast-facing wall.

Berlin Wall

This 90-foot vertical wall occupies an amphitheater between the Krishna buttress and Wall Of Winter Warmth. The routes have an intimidating appearance and are not well protected. Approach via a steep gully that climbs to a terrace at the base of the wall. To escape from the top of the wall, rappel 85 feet from a tree above *Checkpoint Charlie*.

8.   WALPURGISNACHT 11A
FA: DAN HARE AND MIKE GILBERT, 1986.

Night of the spirits. This is the farthest left route on the wall. Look for a bolt about 40 feet off the deck.

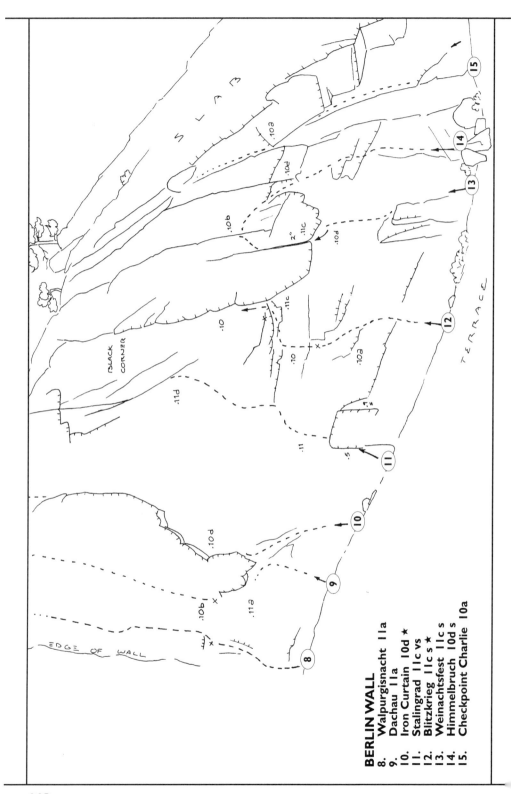

BERLIN WALL
8.   Walpurgisnacht 11a
9.   Dachau 11a
10. Iron Curtain 10d ★
11. Stalingrad 11c vs
12. Blitzkrieg 11c s ★
13. Weinachtsfest 11c s
14. Himmelbruch 10d s
15. Checkpoint Charlie 10a

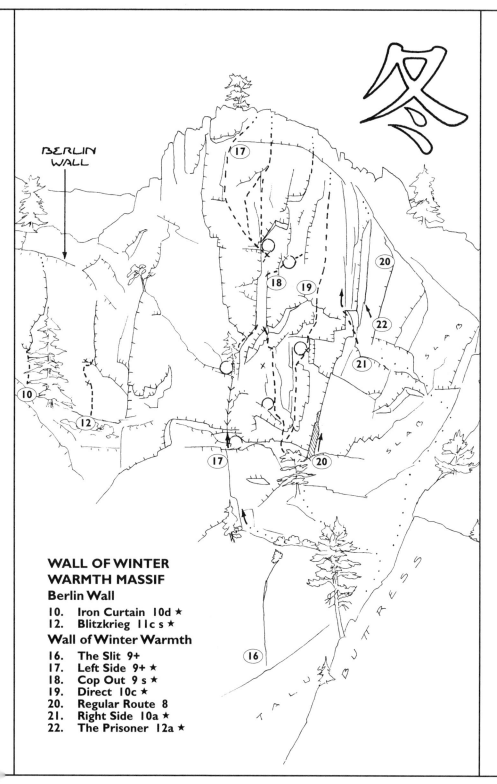

冬

BERLIN
WALL

WALL OF WINTER
WARMTH MASSIF
Berlin Wall

10. Iron Curtain 10d ★
12. Blitzkrieg 11c s ★

Wall of Winter Warmth

16. The Slit 9+
17. Left Side 9+ ★
18. Cop Out 9 s ★
19. Direct 10c ★
20. Regular Route 8
21. Right Side 10a ★
22. The Prisoner 12a ★

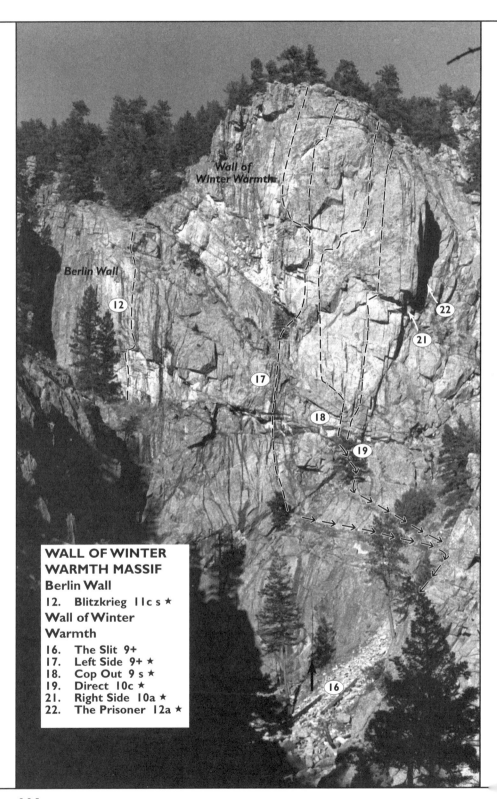

**WALL OF WINTER
WARMTH MASSIF**
Berlin Wall
12.   Blitzkrieg 11c s ★
**Wall of Winter
Warmth**
16.   The Slit 9+
17.   Left Side 9+ ★
18.   Cop Out 9 s ★
19.   Direct 10c ★
21.   Right Side 10a ★
22.   The Prisoner 12a ★

9. DACHAU 11A
FA: DAN HARE AND SCOTT WOODRUFF, 1984.

Climb up to a downward-pointing flake, then angle up and left past a bolt.

10. IRON CURTAIN 10D ★
FA: DAN HARE AND ?, 1981.

Climb up to a downward-pointing flake as for the preceding route, then follow its right margin to the top of the wall.

11. STALINGRAD 11C VS
FA: DALE GODDARD AND DAN HARE, 1985.

Climb onto a pedestal behind a large fir tree and place a #2 Friend, then work up and right to double cracks and continue to the top of the wall.

12. BLITZKRIEG 11C S ★
FA: BOB HORAN AND DAN HARE, 1984.

Move boldly up to a bolt (10b), traverse right under a roof, then crank into a black, left-facing corner (11c) that leads to the top of the wall.

13. WEINACHTSFEST 11C S
FA: DAN HARE AND ALAN BRADLEY, ON CHRISTMAS DAY, 1984.

Begin near the low-point of the wall and gain the top of a pillar. Climb up and left and jam a two-inch crack through a roof. Crank right into another crack and follow it to the top of the wall.

14. HIMMELBRUCH 10D S
FA: DAN HARE AND DAVE BATTEN, 1985.

Begin a few feet right of *Weinachtsfest*. Climb straight up to a roof, then go up and left to finish in the crack of *Weinachtsfest*.

15. CHECKPOINT CHARLIE 10A
FA: DAN HARE AND ALLEN WOOD, C. 1981.

At the right edge of the wall is a large, left-facing dihedral formed by a buttress. Climb the buttress up to a roof, then angle into the corner and continue to the top.

Wall of Winter Warmth

16. THE SLIT 9+
FA: RICHARD AND JOYCE ROSSITER, 1981.

Climb a seductive fissure in a wall directly beneath the main face.

17. LEFT SIDE 9+ ★
FA: UNKNOWN. FFA: KEVIN DONALD, JIM WALSH, AND JIM ERICKSON, 1970.

Begin from the left end of a grassy ledge above *The Slit*. Climb an easy crack up and left to a ledge at the base of a black groove and belay. Climb a difficult bulge and the groove above to a tree (9+) and belay. Angle up to the right and climb a flared right-facing dihedral to a small ledge beneath a roof. Work out left near the edge of the face and continue to the top. It is also possible to climb straight up from the belay.

18. COP OUT 9 S ★
FA: JIM ERICKSON AND JIM WALSH, 1971.

Approach as for the preceding route, but on the ledge beneath the black groove, move about 20 feet. Pass an overhang at a knob (8) and belay after another 30 feet. Move left into a dihedral, turn a roof, then step right and belay on a small ledge. Work up and right for ten feet, then follow cracks to the top of the wall.

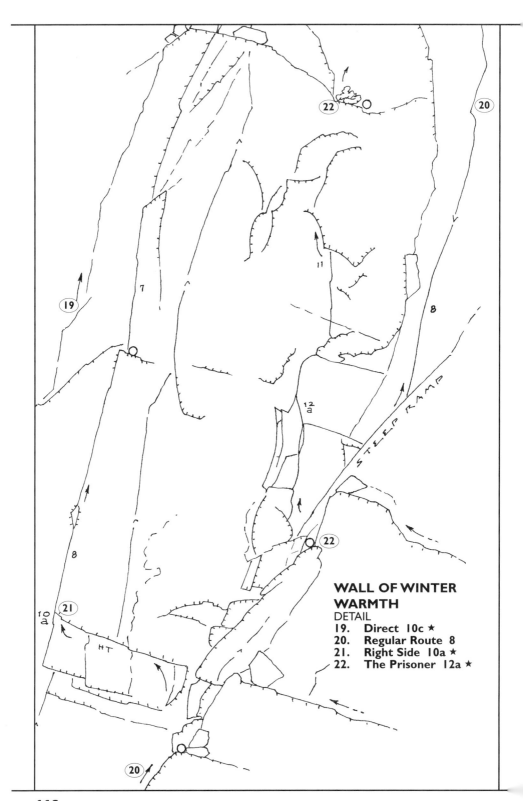

WALL OF WINTER WARMTH

DETAIL

19. Direct 10c ★
20. Regular Route 8
21. Right Side 10a ★
22. The Prisoner 12a ★

19. DIRECT 10c ★
FA: JOHN AND JIM MCMILLAN, 1971. FFA: SCOTT WOODRUFF AND DAN HARE, 1977.

Begin just right of *Cop Out*. Follow cracks up the right side of the face to a sling belay at a bolt beneath a series of roofs. Climb up through the roofs and belay on a sloping ledge or continue up discontinuous cracks to the top of the wall in one long pitch.

20. REGULAR ROUTE 8
FA: PAT AMENT AND PAUL MAYROSE, EARLY 1960S.

Begin in a deep slot and follow a right-facing dihedral system along the right side of the buttress.

21. RIGHT SIDE 10a ★
FA: JOHN BEHRENS AND ROB CULBERTSON, 1969. FFA: JIM ERICKSON AND CINDY STANLEY, 1975.

Begin with *Regular Route* or scramble up and left across slabs to a huge roof halfway up the right side of the buttress. Traverse out left beneath the roof (crux), then follow cracks up the right margin of the west face.

22. THE PRISONER 12a ★
FA: ALEC SHARP AND CHUCK FITCH, 1980.

The upper right side of the crag forms a very steep, south-facing wall. Move up and left into a pod, then make very hard moves up into a left-facing, left-leaning corner.

23. MELONS 9
FA: PAT HEALY AND DAN HARE, 1981.

This route is located on a small buttress at the top of the gully above the south side of Wall Of Winter Warmth. Climb a dihedral followed by a right-facing flake in the middle of the buttress.

24. PIN JOB 11?

This route is located on The Pin Dome, a rounded buttress high on the rim of the canyon, about 200 feet south of Melons. Locate a fixed pin in an open-book dihedral on the north side of the rock.

CHROME DOME

Chrome Dome is located several hundred feet up the east slope behind Boulder Falls East. It may be reached by fording the stream above Boulder Falls or by scrambling over the top of Boulder Falls East. The dome is divided into lower and upper halves by a prominent horizontal fault. Also note a vertical dike along the left side of the dome. Most routes have poor protection, but the rock is great and the lift lines are short. Walk off from the top.

1. SPLENDOR IN THE GRASS 9 s
FA: DAN HARE AND MARK HESSE, 1982.

Begin at the upper left side of the dome. Climb a small right-facing dihedral, then veer right to a dike and follow it to the top.

2. HEADSTRONG 10a s
FA: DAN HARE AND PAT HEALY, 1981.

Climb a vague, left-facing corner and gain the dike that climbs along the left side of the dome. Break right and follow shallow cracks to the top. One may also climb straight up the dike from a fault that runs across the middle of the northwest face, which is also the start to the following two routes.

3. PLATINUM BLOND 10d s
FA: GREG DAVIS AND DAN HARE, 1984.

Begin from the left end of the fault that spans the face. Climb up and right to a small roof above a tree. Turn a roof on the right, then step left and follow a seam to the top of the wall.

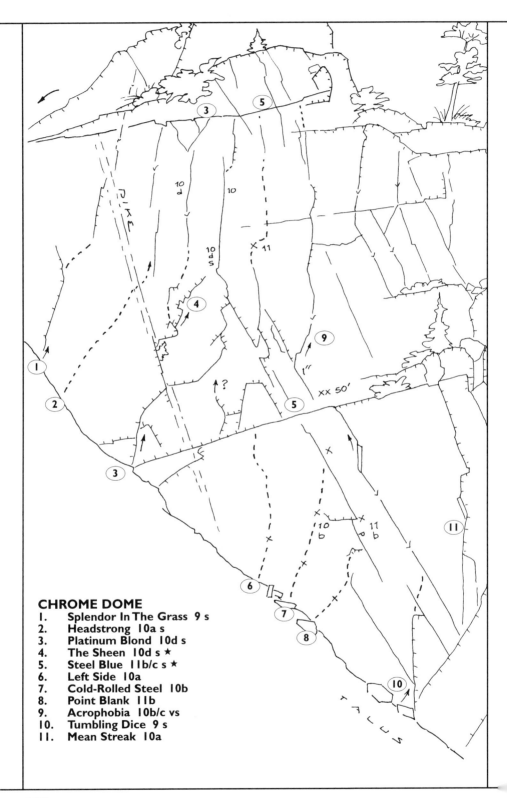

CHROME DOME
1. Splendor In The Grass 9 s
2. Headstrong 10a s
3. Platinum Blond 10d s
4. The Sheen 10d s ★
5. Steel Blue 11b/c s ★
6. Left Side 10a
7. Cold-Rolled Steel 10b
8. Point Blank 11b
9. Acrophobia 10b/c vs
10. Tumbling Dice 9 s
11. Mean Streak 10a

4.   THE SHEEN 10D S ★
FA: DAN HARE AND PAT HEALY, 1981.

Climb up to the tree and roof as for the preceding route, and turn the roof on the right. Work up and right along a flake, then step right and climb a difficult crack.

5.   STEEL BLUE 11B/C S ★
FA: DAN HARE AND ALFREDO LEN, 1981.

Traverse right along the fault and belay at a one-inch crack right of an arch. This point may also be reached climbing a route on the lower wall. Climb through a shallow left-facing dihedral, then veer right to a bolt. Move a few feet right, then work straight up to the top of the dome.

5A.   BLUE SHEEN 10D S ★
Climb Steel Blue to the bolt, then go up and left and join *The Sheen*.

The following routes begin below the horizontal fault.

6.   LEFT SIDE 10A
Climb the left side of the lower wall past a single bolt.

7.   COLD-ROLLED STEEL 10B
FA: DAN HARE AND SCOTT WOODRUFF, 1985.

Begin down and right from the left end of the horizontal fault. Climb the steep slab past 2 bolts and gain the fault.

8.   POINT BLANK 11B
FA: DAN HARE AND NOEL CHILDS, 1987.

Begin down and right from a small, right-facing dihedral. Climb up to a bolt and traverse a few feet right, then climb straight up past another bolt and continue to the fault.

9.   ACROPHOBIA 10B/C VS
FA: ALFREDO LEN AND DAN HARE, 1982.

Begin just below the preceding route. P1. Climb out right past a bolt to some knobs below a small roof. Climb past the right side of the roof and follow a shallow crack to the fault. P2. Start up the one-inch crack of *Steel Blue*, then break right and follow a mossy groove to the top of the dome.

10.   TUMBLING DICE 9 S
FA: DAN HARE AND GEORGE RUSSELL, 1983.

Begin down and right from some protruding steel cable. Climb along a flake, then follow a groove up and left to the horizontal fault.

11.   MEAN STREAK 10A
FA: DAN HARE AND MIKE DOWNING, 1983.

Climb the flake as for the preceding route, but continue straight up a black streak with a fixed pin.

BOULDER FALLS EAST

This is the steep buttress just right of Boulder Falls. Approach via the short tourist path and ford the stream or scramble along the east bank of the stream. To descend from the top, rappel from trees or scramble off to the south and down a gully.

1.   DARI DESIGN 11C
Begin with *Hubris*, then break left and climb up through the right side of an arched roof. Three bolts to a two-bolt anchor. Bring a stick clipper.

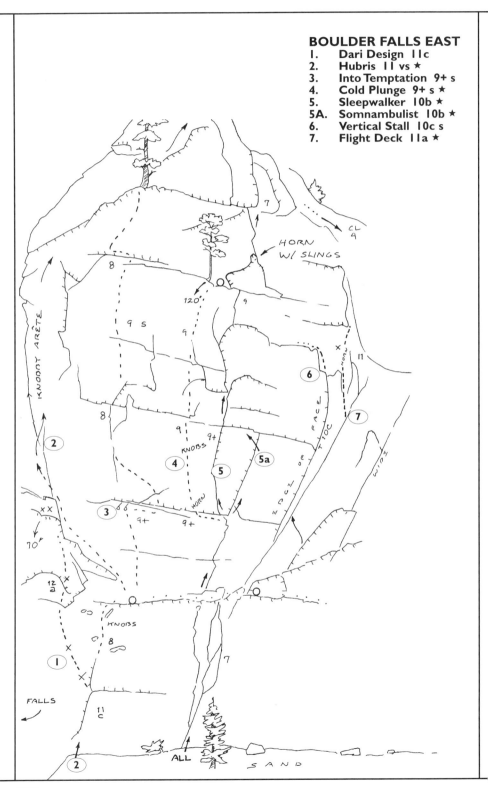

BOULDER FALLS EAST
1. Dari Design 11c
2. Hubris 11 vs ★
3. Into Temptation 9+ s
4. Cold Plunge 9+ s ★
5. Sleepwalker 10b ★
5A. Somnambulist 10b ★
6. Vertical Stall 10c s
7. Flight Deck 11a ★

2. HUBRIS 11 vs ★
FA: Roger Briggs, solo, 1976.

Boulder up a shallow, right-facing dihedral about 20 feet right of the falls (crux) and continue via knobs to a ledge (8). Angle up and left along a ramp, then up along a knobby arête to the top of the wall. The initial crux moves can be protected by stick clipping the first bolt on *Dari Design*.

3. INTO TEMPTATION 9+ s
FA: Dan Hare and Scott Woodruff, 1983.

Begin in parallel cracks about 20 feet right of *Hubris* and traverse left to belay. Climb up to a pair of fixed pins and proceed as shown in the topo. Belay at a tree.

3A. DIRECT
FA: Steve Dieckhoff and Kristin Peterson.

Above the ledge with a tree, climb a left-facing flake, etc.

4. COLD PLUNGE 9+ s ★
FA: Dan Hare and Scott Woodruff, 1982.

Begin as for the preceding route, but from the initial crack system, continue straight up to a small roof, move left, then work up the steep face to a tree. Belay from a horn. Rappel (120 feet) or climb an easier pitch to the top of the wall.

5. SLEEPWALKER 10b ★
FA: Scott Woodruff, Brad Gilbert, Dan Hare, 1978.

Climb up to the small roof mentioned in the preceding route, then follow a crack up to the belay at the tree.

5A. SOMNAMBULIST 10b ★
FA: Dan Hare and Scott Woodruff, 1982.

At the first shallow roof mentioned above, climb a right-facing, right-leaning corner to another roof, then hand traverse back left to *Sleepwalker*.

6. VERTICAL STALL 10c s
FA: Dan Hare and Jeff Koenig, 1983.

Climb the braided crack as for the preceding routes, then move right and belay. Climb up onto a pedestal and move left into a thin, flared crack—the left of two cracks.

7. FLIGHT DECK 11a ★
FA: Dan Hare and Dale Goddard, 1983.

Begin as for *Vertical Stall*, but climb the crack on the right. Where the crack fades, climb an arête past a bolt (crux) and continue to a belay. Traverse left to a horn with slings, or continue to the top of the wall and scramble off to the south.

Richard Rossiter on *The Vanishing*. Photo by Dan Hare.

Upper Dream Canyon

The rugged gorge above Boulder Falls continues upstream for about 0.7 mile, above which the cliff walls drop back to wooded slopes and the drainage traverses private property. This gorge remains in a primitive state, completely free of the usual contemporary riff raff such as signs, fences, roads, cars, paved walkways or the ever-expanding wildlife closures. Dream Canyon is said to have been named during the 1920s by the Trussel family who lived above the gorge. It is among the most beautiful places in Boulder County, and likely appears now much as it did when Christopher Columbus first set foot upon the "new world" and claimed it for the queen of Spain.

Upper Dream Canyon is characterized by a large point of land that protrudes to the southwest and features a host of outstanding crags. The relatively flat top of the point, the Lost Angel Plateau, is traversed by a network of trails that originally led to various mining excavations (see map). A large commune of disenfranchised citizens lived in this area during the 1960s and may have begun a tradition of nude sunbathing that happily continues to this day.

Please carry out all trash, even that left by others. The small dirt parking area above the gorge opens directly off a road leading to people's homes. DO NOT BLOCK THE ROAD. Dream Canyon is a very special place with a wealth of great climbing, but it is surrounded by private property. Our only hope of keeping this area open, is to be considerate of local residents and not draw attention to ourselves by parking on private property or blocking roadways. Remember, the gorge has long been a popular haunt among nudists and gay people. If you have a problem with nudity or homosexuality, climb somewhere else.

Upper Dream Canyon is most easily approached from the north: Drive up Boulder Canyon for 3.9 miles, turn right on Sugarloaf Road and continue for about 3.1 miles. Turn left on Lost Angel Road and continue to an intersection after one mile. Go straight on North Draw Road (Lost Angel Road goes right), veer right at 1.1 miles, and reach a dirt parking area at 1.5 miles. Three trails lead down into the gorge.

South Trail– A well-developed path (an old mining road) leads southwest from the parking area across a flat rocky section and descends to a mining excavation at the lip of the gorge, about 200 yards from the trailhead. After the first 50 yards, a left branch in the trail follows an old barbed wire fence straight south to sandy terraces with a good view of the lower gorge. About 50 yards before the excavation, a right branch in the main trail leads to a notch just east of a large buttress called Lost Angel. From this notch, a rugged path continues steeply down into the bottom of Dream Canyon.

Dream Dome Trail–This trail veers right from the South Trail after the first 100 yards and leads to the notch between Dream Dome and Lost Angel. It passes between the halves of a log cut in two pieces, then descends west to the top of Zen Garden Wall where one may rappel to the bottom of the gorge. The trail, however, continues down a large forested ramp (to the north) beneath Dream Dome to the bottom.

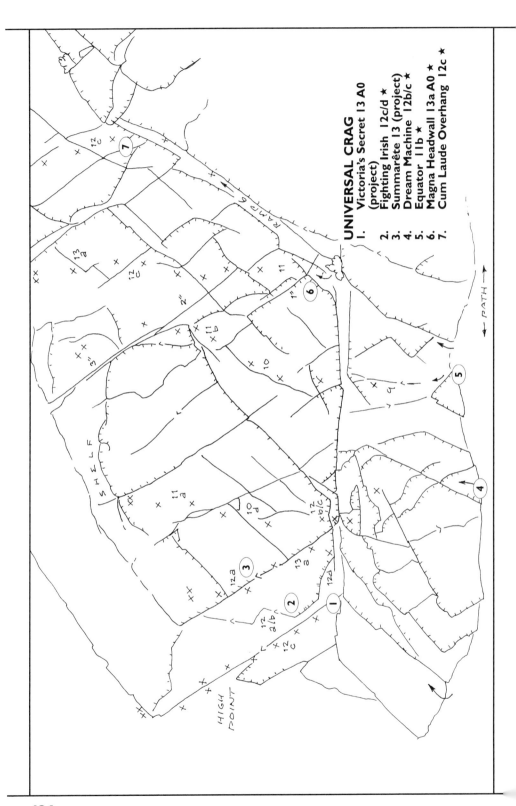

UNIVERSAL CRAG
1. Victoria's Secret 13 A0 ★ (project)
2. Fighting Irish 12c/d ★
3. Summarête 13 (project)
4. Dream Machine 12b/c ★
5. Equator 11b ★
6. Magna Headwall 13a A0 ★
7. Cum Laude Overhang 12c ★

West Trail–From the parking area, head north down a dirt road, and after about 150 feet, break left onto a well-worn path that leads without difficulty into the bottom of the gorge, just upstream from the main crags. Note that an obvious left branch in the trail leads to the top of Oceanic Wall and Dream Dome. At high water the shoreline cannot be followed to the main west face of Lost Angel: Use the South Trail.

Note: Crags are listed left to right (upstream) along the west bank of the creek and left to right (downstream) along the east bank.

UNIVERSAL CRAG

Universal Crag is a small, square-cut buttress across the gorge from the south end of the Lost Angel. It features extremely difficult face climbs and overhanging arêtes. It is most easily reached by descending the South Trail to the bottom of the gorge, where a ford of North Boulder Creek brings one directly to the foot of the buttress.

1.   VICTORIA'S SECRET 13 A0 (PROJECT)
TR: JOHN BALDWIN AND MARK ROLOFSON.

Climb a severely overhanging arête on the south side of the buttress. Seven bolts to a two bolt anchor.

2.   FIGHTING IRISH 12C/D ★
FA: BOB HORAN AND MARK KALIN.

Traverse out right on a shelf to start and climb the overhanging dihedral just left of *Suma Arête*.

3.   SUMMARÊTE 13 (PROJECT)
Begin at the right end of a shelf at the southeast corner of the buttress. Move right past two bolts, then climb a radically overhanging arête. Five bolts to a two-bolt anchor.

4.   DREAM MACHINE 12B/C ★
FA: BOB HORAN AND JOHN BALDWIN.

Start below the southeast corner of the buttress. Follow bolts up through a stepped roof and continue up the beautiful face above. Nine bolts to a two-bolt anchor.

5.   EQUATOR 11B ★
FA: BOB HORAN AND JOHN BALDWIN.

Begin from a pointed block in a recess near the middle of the crag. Follow bolts along a right leaning roof/dihedral, turn the right end of the roof and continue up the face to a two-bolt anchor. Seven bolts.

6.   MAGNA HEADWALL 13A A0 ★
FA: BOB HORAN.

Begin in a recess near the middle of the crag. Climb up and right along a ramp, then follow bolts up a steep face using zigzag cracks for holds. The last ten feet have not been climbed free. Seven bolts to a two-bolt anchor.

7.   CUM LAUDE OVERHANG 12C ★
FA: BOB HORAN AND SHANE RYMER.

Begin in a recess near the middle of the crag. Climb up and right along a ramp, then follow bolts up a bulging wall. Five bolts to a two-bolt anchor.

8.   TEMPTRESS 9
FA: DAN HARE, ALAN BRADLEY, DAVE WEBER, 1981.

Climb a steep diagonal finger crack in the right side of the buttress.

THUNDER POINT
1. Sunset Arête 11d ★

THE ICON
3. Mantra 11b ★

OCEANIC WALL
2. The Deep 11c ★ or 12a ★
3. Sargasso Sea 12a ★
5. Leviathon 11c ★
6. Mud Shark 11d ★
7. Creature From The Black Lagoon 11d ★
10. Shiny Toys 9 ★

DREAM DOME
11. A Brief History Of Time 9 ★

Dream Dome

Oceanic Wall

The Icon

Thunder Point

THE TERRACE

The Terrace is the small but apparent buttress across the river from Dream Dome and about 100 yards upstream from Universal Crag. Ford the stream and hike directly up the hillside to the bottom of the buttress or cross at a tyrolean below Lost Angel.

1.   ARÊTE 8 ★
FA: BOB HORAN AND STEVE MESTDAGH.

Climb the arête at the southeast corner of the crag.

2.   DREAM SCENE 11B ★
FA: HORAN AND MESTDAGH.

Begin at the southeast corner of the crag. Climb a steep wall just right of an arête, then join the arête and continue to the top. Nine bolts to a two-bolt and ring anchor.

THUNDER POINT

This small buttress is located along the east stream bank, immediately south from the bottom of the West Trail.

1.   SUNSET ARÊTE 11D ★
FA: BOB HORAN AND STEVE MESTDAGH.

Follow bolts up the arête at the left side of a conspicuous dihedral. Eight bolts to a two-bolt anchor.

2.   CENTER TAP CORNER 7
FA: ALISON SHEETS AND KYLE COPELAND, 1986. SR PLUS A #4 FRIEND.

Climb a right-facing dihedral just right of a prominent arête.

THE ICON

The following routes are located on a narrow slab between Thunder Point and Oceanic Wall. All routes by Richard Rossiter and Gail Effron, 1996.

1.   BUDDHIST PEST 9

I said, "I'm from Budapest," you fool. Climb a right-facing dihedral and wide crack along the left side of the slab.

2.   CRUCIFICTION 11B (INCOMPLETE)

Climb to the second bolt on *Mantra*, then follow a shallow groove up and left to a roof. Turn the roof on the right, and follow a wide crack to the top. Move right and lower off from the anchor on *Mantra*. Bolts have not been placed at time of writing; TR only.

3.   MANTRA 11B ★
Follow eight bolts along the right margin of the slab. Lower off, 85 feet.

OCEANIC WALL

Oceanic Wall is located about 200 feet downstream from the bottom of the West Trail. The dead-vertical wall rises directly above a narrow stretch of beach along the east side of North Boulder Creek and features several excellent sport climbs.

1.   IN YOUR DREAMS 10C ★
FA: MARCELLA AND JOHN BALDWIN. (TR).

This is the farthest left route on the wall. Climb through an apex, go up and left over a bulge, then up and right to join *The Deep* after 50 feet. To be bolted.

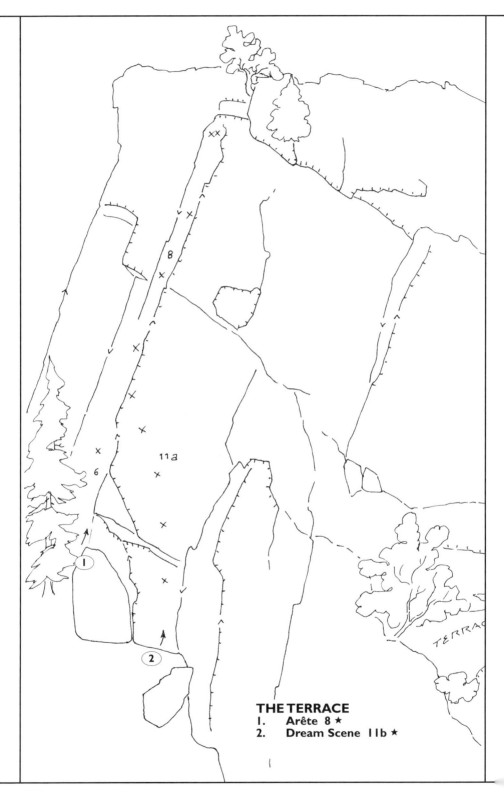

THE TERRACE
1. Arête 8 ★
2. Dream Scene 11b ★

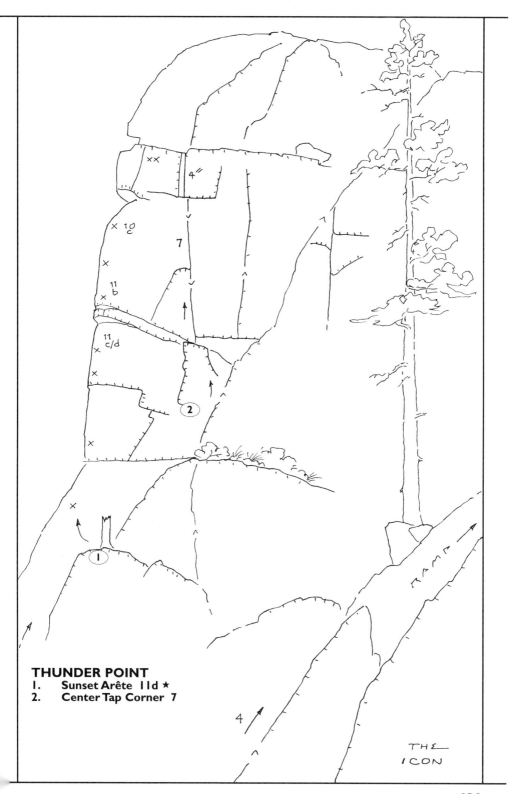

THUNDER POINT
1. Sunset Arête 11d ★
2. Center Tap Corner 7

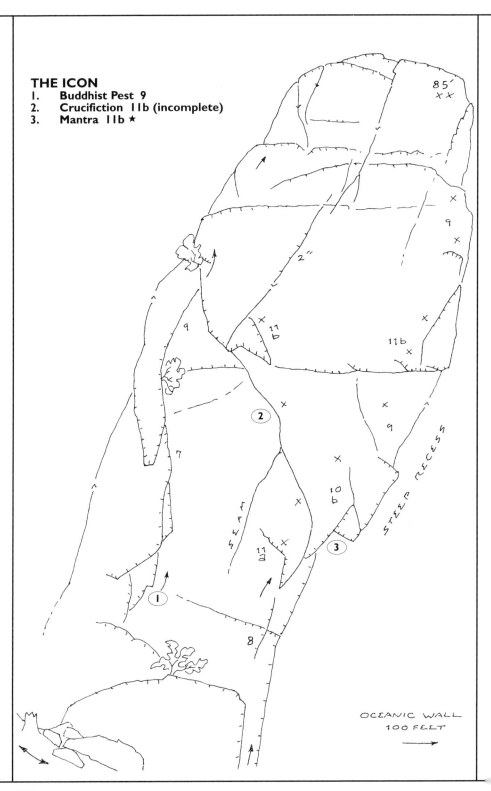

THE ICON
1.   **Buddhist Pest** 9
2.   **Crucifiction** 11b (incomplete)
3.   **Mantra** 11b ★

85'
××

9

2"

11b

11b

9

9

10b

SEAM

11a

STEEP RECESS

7

8

OCEANIC WALL
100 FEET

2.   THE DEEP 11C ★ OR 12A ★
FA: RICHARD ROSSITER AND LEAH MACALUSO, 1996.

This is a varied route on excellent steep rock along the left side of the wall. Begin with a mantle and work up to a roof. Traverse left and crank the roof, then balance up to a stance (11c). Angle up and left and climb the left side of a slab (9). Ten bolts to a two-bolt anchor.

3.   SARGASSO SEA 12A ★
FA: RICHARD ROSSITER, MOE HERSHOFF, DAN HARE, BOB HORAN. REDPOINT: CHIP RUCKGABER. ORIGINALLY TOP-ROPED BY ROSSITER AND MACALUSO (1996); RUCKGABER AND MIKE BROOKS (1997).

Begin about 20 feet right of *The Deep*. A difficult opening move leads to athletic climbing along a seam. Lieback and stem through a bulge (crux), then continue more easily to a two-bolt anchor. Nine bolts.

4.   WAKE OF THE FLOOD 13 (PROJECT)
FA: BOB HORAN.

Follow bolts up the bulging wall about 35 feet right of *The Deep*.

5.   LEVIATHON 11C ★
FA: TOP-ROPED BY RICHARD ROSSITER AND GAIL EFFRON, 1996; SET UP AS A SPORT CLIMB BY ROSSITER, JOHN BALDWIN, KEVIN KLEE, BOB HORAN, 1997. FIRST LEAD: STEVE SANGDAHL AND JOHN BALDWIN.

Begin at a line of holds near the middle of the wall. Climb straight up past three bolts to a two-bolt anchor at 50 feet (10a), then work up and left over increasingly difficult terrain and negotiate the final bulge. Nine bolts.

5A.   DREAM ON 11C ★
FA: SANGDAHL AND BALDWIN.

Climb to the fifth bolt on *Leviathon*, then break right in a shallow crack. Step up and left to anchor atop *Leviathon*. Eight bolts.

6.   MUD SHARK 11D ★
FA: SANGDAHL AND BALDWIN.

From the ring bolts on *Leviathon*, follow a flared groove up and right, then continue straight up to a bolt anchor. Nine bolts.

7.   CREATURE FROM THE BLACK LAGOON 11D ★
FA: STEVE SANGDAHL, JANET ROBINSON, JOHN BALDWIN.

Begin as for *Twistin' By The Pool*, then follow a line of bolts more or less straight up the wall past a black flake to a two-bolt anchor. Eleven bolts.

8.   TWISTIN' BY THE POOL 10D S ★
FA: KYLE COPELAND AND ALISON SHEETS, 1986. SR.

Begin near the right side of the buttress, just left of an A-shaped roof. Climb up and right along the left of two parallel cracks, then traverse right past fixed pins and move up to a bolt. Crank up and right (crux), then back left to easier ground. Work straight up the headwall, then veer left and finish in a flared crack (10a) with a two-bolt anchor at its top. 85 feet.

9.   SHEIK YER BOUTI 11D ★
FA: SANGDAHL, ROBINSON, BALDWIN.

Begin 20 feet right of the parallel cracks at a shallow A-shaped roof with a bolt. Turn the roof and climb straight up to the crux on *Twistin'*. Break left out of the right-leaning dihedral, then continue straight up the wall to a two-bolt anchor.

OCEANIC WALL
1. In Your Dreams 10c ★
2. The Deep 11c ★ or 12a ★
3. Sargasso Sea 12a ★
4. Wake Of The Flood 13
5. Leviathon 11c ★
5A. Dream On 11c ★

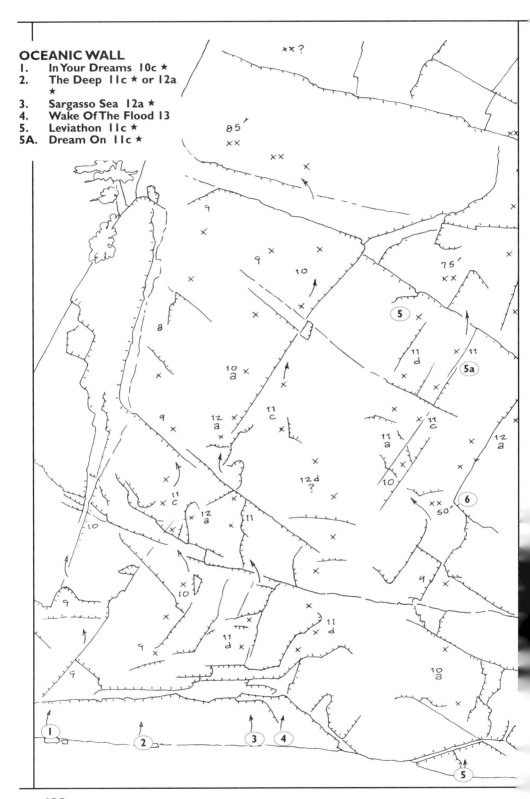

132

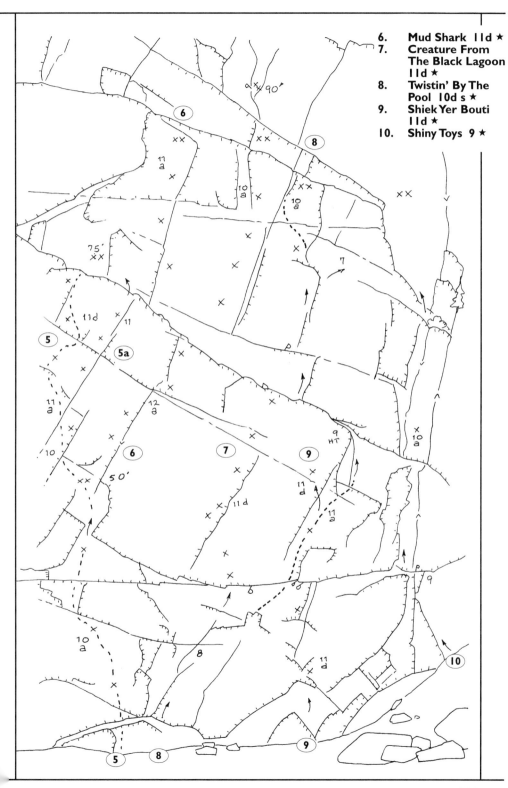

6. Mud Shark 11d ★
7. Creature From
   The Black Lagoon
   11d ★
8. Twistin' By The
   Pool 10d s ★
9. Shiek Yer Bouti
   11d ★
10. Shiny Toys 9 ★

133

Oceanic
Wall

DREAM DOME
1. Dreamscape 8 ★
2. Sea Of Dreams 11b ★
3. Flying Vee 10a s ★
4. Soul On Ice 11a ★
5. Dry Ice 11a ★
6. Wrinkles In Time 9 ★
9. Tales Of Power 11b ★
10. Journey To Ixtlan 11a ★
11. A Brief History Of Time 9
12. Gully Washer 9 ★

10. SHINY TOYS 9 ★
FA: COPELAND AND SHEETS, 1986. SR.

Climb a black-streaked, right-facing dihedral along the right edge of the wall, then go up and left to a two-bolt anchor. One fixed pin and one bolt.

11. TRANS-OCEANIC TRAVERSE 11D s
FA: CHIP RUCKGABER AND STEVE SANGDAHL (RIGHT TO LEFT); LED LEFT TO RIGHT BY SANGDAHL.

Begin with *Shiek Yer Bouti*, and follow the lowest horizontal break all the way left across the wall, then downclimb *The Deep* to finish. One may also climb the other direction, which may be harder. Ten bolts, three pins, plus gear.

12. DREAM COME TRUE 12A ★
FA: JOHN BALDWIN AND STEVE SANGDAHL.

Follow bolts up the overhanging headwall above *Creature From The Black Lagoon*. Five bolts to a two-bolt anchor.

DREAM DOME

Dream Dome is the large buttress (or dome) to the right of Oceanic Wall. The dome is divided by a blunt arête (see Wrinkles In Time) with a series of clean dihedrals on the left and a big roof and slab on the right. Routes on the left side of Dream Dome are most easily reached by hiking a branch in the West Trail and then rappelling from trees. These routes may also be reached by scrambling up a steep gully from the bottom of the wall. Routes on the right side are reached via the Dream Dome Trail and the long ramp that descends between Dream Dome and Lost Angel.

1. DREAMSCAPE 8 ★
FA: RICHARD ROSSITER AND BONNIE VON GREBE.

Begin from a broken pedestal below the upper left side of the wall. Follow cracks up into a V-shaped dihedral and climb to its top where it merges with the following route. 100 feet, six bolts. Belay from a tree on a big ledge.

2. SEA OF DREAMS 11B ★
FA: ROSSITER AND VON GREBE.

Begin about 30 feet down and right from the preceding route, below a long right-facing dihedral. Start up the dihedral, then crank left and follow the arête to the top. 140 feet, eight bolts.

3. FLYING VEE 10A s ★
FA: KYLE COPELAND, TIM HUDGEL, CARL RASSMUSEN, 1984.

This route ascends the big V-shaped dihedral in the middle of the left wall, about twelve feet right of the preceding route. Fixed gear (at time of writing) consists of an old button-head bolt, a fixed nut, and a couple of rusty pitons. 150 feet to top of wall.

4. SOUL ON ICE 11A ★
FA: DAN HARE.

Begin as for *Dry Ice*, then break left and follow bolts up the super-clean arête just right of *Flying Vee*. Reach the anchor at the top of *Dry Ice*. 100 feet, eight or nine bolts.

5. DRY ICE 11A ★
FA: DAN HARE AND JOHNNA TIPTON, C. 1991. RACK: RPS TO A #2 FRIEND WITH 12 OR SO QDS.

Rappel 150 feet from a tree at the top of the wall or scramble about 50 feet up a steep (and usually wet) corner to reach the beginning of the route. Follow eight or nine bolts up a tricky, left-facing dihedral and belay from two bolts in a shallow, right-facing dihedral near the top of the wall. Continue up the short headwall or rappel 160 feet to talus at the bottom of the wall.

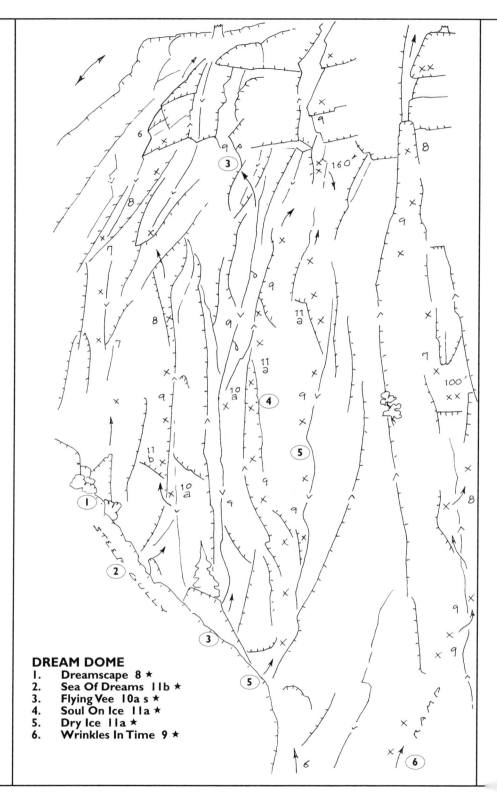

DREAM DOME
1. Dreamscape 8 ★
2. Sea Of Dreams 11b ★
3. Flying Vee 10a s ★
4. Soul On Ice 11a ★
5. Dry Ice 11a ★
6. Wrinkles In Time 9 ★

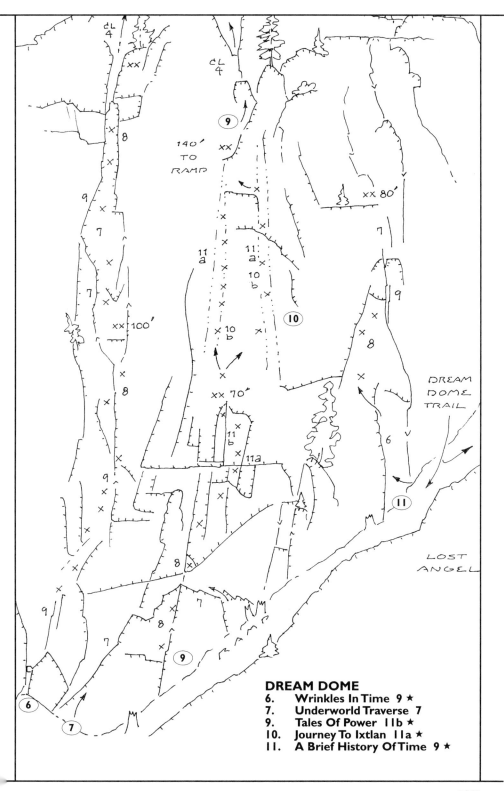

DREAM DOME
6. Wrinkles In Time 9 ★
7. Underworld Traverse 7
9. Tales Of Power 11b ★
10. Journey To Ixtlan 11a ★
11. A Brief History Of Time 9 ★

6.   WRINKLES IN TIME 9 ★
FA: ROSSITER AND VON GREBE. LIGHT SR WITH 10 OR 11QDS.

This route ascends the long "wrinkled" arête in the middle of the buttress. Begin at the bottom of the steep gully between Oceanic Wall and Dream Dome. P1. Climb a thin crack, then work up and right to the arête and continue to a good stance with a two-bolt anchor (9, 100 feet, eight bolts). P2. Climb the left side of the arête to the top of the wall and lower off from a two-bolt anchor. (8, 80 feet, six bolts).

7.   UNDERWORLD TRAVERSE 7
FA: RICHARD ROSSITER, SOLO.

Begin fifteen feet right of *Wrinkles In Time*. Follow a perfect flake/hand crack up and right beneath an overhanging wall. Cross *Tales Of Power* and continue right until it is easy to climb back down to the approach ramp.

8.   DRY HUMP 10 S ★
FA: KYLE COPELAND AND TIM HUDGEL, 1984.

The only known description of this route has it 50 feet left of *Flying Vee*, which does not match any actual terrain. Climb through two roofs to a sling belay on a slab. Climb a short finger crack, then move right (left?) to a black streak and continue to the top of the wall.

9.   TALES OF POWER 11B ★
FA: RICHARD ROSSITER AND BONNIE VON GREBE. FIRST REDPOINTED AS ONE LONG PITCH.

Begin about 70 feet right from *Wrinkles In Time*, below the left side of an arête. One may also begin farther up to the right and hand traverse left to the initial roof. P1. Work up and right through an easy roof (8), then continue up and right to a hanging block. Turn the main roof along the left side of the block, then crank up and left past a smaller roof to a stance with a two-bolt anchor (11b, 80 feet, nine bolts). P2. Friction up a black-washed dike in a hanging slab and gain a two-bolt anchor after about 70 feet (11a, seven bolts).

10.   JOURNEY TO IXTLAN 11A ★
FA: RICHARD ROSSITER AND BOB HORAN.

Climb the first pitch of *Tales Of Power*. Friction up and right, then follow a dike through a roof. Veer left after the sixth bolt and gain the anchor on *Tales Of Power*.

11.   A BRIEF HISTORY OF TIME 9 ★
FA: RICHARD ROSSITER. SR WITH SIX OR SEVEN QDS.

Begin about 60 feet up and right from *Tales Of Power*. Climb to the end of an obvious crack, then move up and left past a bolt to a flared crack and continue to where it fades. Move up and right past two bolts and climb a finger crack with perfect stopper placements, then go up and left to a ring bolt anchor and lower off (80 feet).

12.   GULLY WASHER 9 ★
FA: JANET ROBINSON AND STEVE SANGDAHL.

Climb a mottled wall about 75 feet right of *A Brief History Of Time*. Six bolts to a two-bolt anchor.

13.   WET DREAMS 10A
FA: ROBINSON AND SANGDAHL. (TR).

Climb through a black streak right of *Gully Washer*. Look for a directional bolt.

LOST ANGEL

Lost Angel is likely the largest granite formation in Boulder County. Reminiscent of Yosemite, the broad central slab is clean and continuous and features several superb routes more than 300 feet high. The south end of Lost Angel culminates in a separate summit called the South Tower. Most

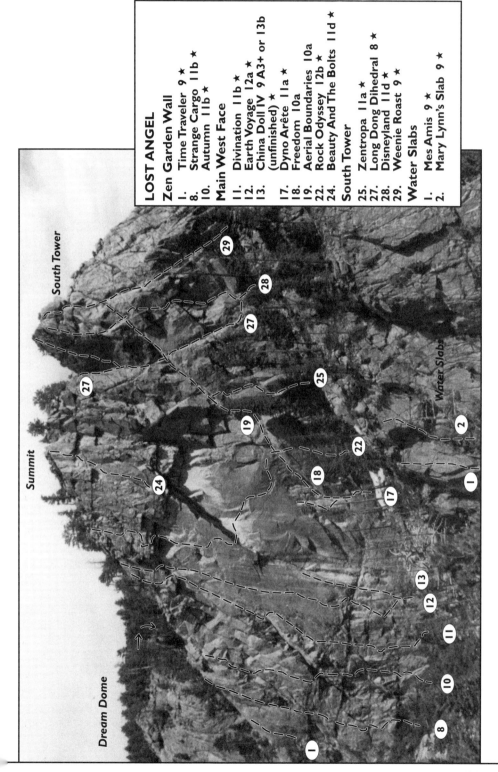

LOST ANGEL

Zen Garden Wall
1. Time Traveler 9 ★
8. Strange Cargo 11b ★
10. Autumn 11b ★

Main West Face
11. Divination 11b ★
12. Earth Voyage 12a ★
13. China Doll IV 9 A3+ or 13b (unfinished) ★
17. Dyno Arête 11a ★
18. Freedom 10a
19. Aerial Boundaries 10a
22. Rock Odyssey 12b ★
24. Beauty And The Bolts 11d ★

South Tower
25. Zentropa 11a ★
27. Long Dong Dihedral 8 ★
28. Disneyland 11d ★
29. Weenie Roast 9 ★

Water Slabs
1. Mes Amis 9 ★
2. Mary Lynn's Slab 9 ★

routes on Lost Angel are reached by hiking the South Trail to where it drops into the gorge just southeast of Lost Angel. Break right at a large pine and follow a faint path down and up around the south side of the South Tower, cross over a high point, and behold the main west face to the north. A long, forested ramp leads down along the base of the wall. It is also possible to reach the bottom of the wall from the West Trail or from the Dream Dome Trail when the stream is low. A third option is to rappel from the belay anchors on several of the west face routes. Routes along the far left side of the west face are most easily reached via the Dream Dome Trail.

Zen Garden Wall

The following routes are located on the far left side of the west face. The upper left part of the wall forms a rounded slab with several moderate crack climbs. A bolt anchor at the bottom of the first two routes can be reached by scrambling down along the north margin of the slab or by rappelling 80 feet from a bolt anchor near the top. The next four routes (all crack climbs) begin from a lower ledge and require a 120-foot rappel from the same anchor. The last four routes begin from the edge of the stream and are most easily reached by scrambling west along the streambank or by rappel. Routes 1 through 9 were established by Richard Rossiter with the help of Bonnie Von Grebe, Gail Effron, and other friends. First ascents of these routes involving other people are noted.

1.   TIME TRAVELER 9 ★

Begin from a bolt anchor below a large pine tree at the lower left corner of the slab. Climb a fabulous hand and finger crack up the left side of the slab. SR.

2.   SHAPE SHIFTERS 9 ★

Start up *Time Traveler*, then break right at a bolt and climb a thin crack until it fades. Continue up a blank slab (two bolts) to the top. Rack up to a #2 Friend with eight or nine QDs.

3.   BE HERE NOW 8 ★

From the bolt anchor beneath the pine, step down and cross a "catwalk" to gain the line, or begin as for the following routes and go up and left at the roof. Climb a left-facing dihedral with a good crack to a stance, then work up and left past three bolts and finish as for *Shape Shifters*.

4.   KNOWONENESS 9 ★

Rappel 120 feet to a good ledge with a bolt anchor. Climb past a small roof and follow a wide crack to a stance, then finish as for *Be Here Now*. Bring gear up to a #4 Friend.

5.   CRAZY WISDOM 11A ★

Start up and right along a ramp. Turn a bulge with two bolts (crux), then follow a hand crack to a stance on the left and finish with *Be Here Now*.

6.   SHUNYATA 8

Begin a few feet right of the preceding route. Climb through a small roof and follow a hand crack to easier terrain. One may also break left from the crack and join *Crazy Wisdom* as shown in the topo.

7.   RAISE THE TITANIC 11B ★

That'd be yer bum, mate. Begin from the edge of the stream beneath a right-facing dihedral, 30 feet left of *Strange Cargo*. Climb the dihedral, then hand-traverse left and pull through the roof. Five bolts. Lower off from a two-bolt anchor or continue up and right to join the second pitch of *Strange Cargo* (10a).

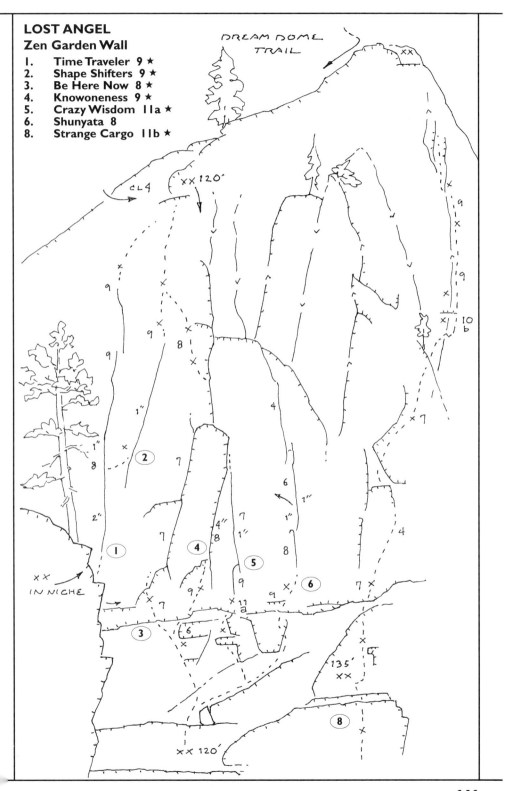

LOST ANGEL

Zen Garden Wall

1. Time Traveler 9 ★
2. Shape Shifters 9 ★
3. Be Here Now 8 ★
4. Knowoneness 9 ★
5. Crazy Wisdom 11a ★
6. Shunyata 8
8. Strange Cargo 11b ★

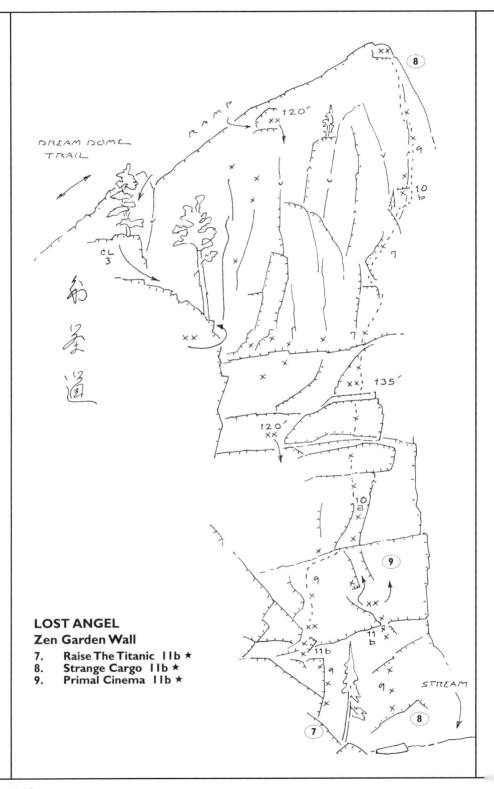

DREAM DOME
TRAIL

RAMP

120'

120'

135'

120'

10
b

9

10
a

9

11
b

9

9

11
b

9

STREAM

LOST ANGEL
Zen Garden Wall

7.   Raise The Titanic 11b ★
8.   Strange Cargo 11b ★
9.   Primal Cinema 11b ★

8.   STRANGE CARGO 11B ★
FA: RICHARD ROSSITER, COLLEEN GREENE, MOE HERSHOFF, DAN HARE. EIGHT QDS.

This route ascends the lower wall and final arête just right of the upper slab. When the water is low, hike to the bottom of the Dream Dome Trail, then scramble downstream to the start of the climb. During high water, make two 120-foot rappels starting from the ring bolts above Time Traveler. P1. Climb straight up black rock, turn the crux roof, and belay in a big scoop with a two-bolt anchor (11b, 60 feet, six bolts). P2. Step left and climb a steep wall to a good ledge with a two-bolt anchor (10a, 70 feet, six bolts). P3. Climb through a small roof, then work up and right to a prominent arête and continue to the top (10b, 130 feet, seven bolts).

9.   PRIMAL CINEMA 11B ★
FA: RICHARD ROSSITER AND BOB HORAN. 12 QDS.

This steep route links *Strange Cargo* with the crux of *Autumn*. P1. Climb the first pitch of *Strange Cargo* (11b, 60 feet, six bolts). P2. Step right and climb a right-facing dihedral, then move right again and belay on a narrow ledge with a two bolt anchor (10a, 60 feet, five bolts). P3. Climb up and right across the vertical headwall, up a shallow open book, then up the final pillar on *Autumn* (11b, 130 feet, 12 bolts). To reduce rope weight, one may pendulum right to the second belay on *Autumn*, which breaks the route into four pitches. It is also possible to exit left before the last two bolts (9) and avoid the final crux.

10.   AUTUMN 11B ★
FA: BOB HORAN AND RICHARD ROSSITER. 8 QDS.

This route begins from a boulder in the stream between *Strange Cargo* and *Divination* and can be reached only by rappel except during low water at the end of summer. P1. Climb the face of a large pillar just left of the first pitch of *Divination* (10c, 75 feet, eight bolts). P2. Continue up steep rock, then turn a roof on the left and climb more easily to a bolt belay in a broad groove or channel (10a, 70 feet, six bolts). P3. Climb up and left along a rounded arête, then crank the final overhanging wall (11b, 85 feet, seven bolts). It is possible to climb left before the last two bolts (9) and avoid the final crux.

Main West Face

The following routes are located on the broad central face of Lost Angel and begin from a forested ramp that climbs to the south along the bottom of the wall.

11.   DIVINATION 11B ★
FA: RICHARD ROSSITER, DAN HARE, AMY REYNOLDS. 11 QDS.

A big, forested ramp begins from the stream and climbs southward beneath the main west face of Lost Angel. Divination begins about 30 feet up and right from the bottom of this ramp. P1. Follow eleven bolts up the steep black wall and belay on a narrow ledge with a two-bolt anchor (11b, 130 feet). P2. Follow a dihedral system up and right to where it fades, then crank up and left to the arête. Work up and right along a steep ramp, then step left and belay from two bolts (11a, 100 feet, eight bolts). P3. Climb up and right along a black ramp, work up and left beneath a roof, then climb straight up to a nice ledge with a two-bolt anchor (10a, 100 feet, seven bolts). From the top of the black ramp, one may also continue up and right and finish with the final roof on *Earth Voyage* (10b).

12.   EARTH VOYAGE 12A ★
FA: BOB HORAN, JOHN BALDWIN, 1996. 14 QDS.

Earth Voyage ascends the very steep wall just left of *China Doll*. Begin about 35 feet up and right from *Divination*. One may avoid the initial crux by climbing the first pitch of *China Doll* and traversing up and left past two bolts to the first belay station. P1. Climb to the first bolt on *China Doll* (Horan's start) and break left beneath bulges (crux) to a hand crack, then climb up and right to a sling belay at a roof band (12a, 60 feet). P2. Climb up and left through the roof band, then work up and right on a slab to a bolt belay (12a, 70 feet). P3. Work straight up the steep slab to another bolt belay at a narrow ledge (11d, 65 feet). P4. Continue up the wall and turn the left side of a large roof (10b), then continue more easily to the top of the wall (80 feet).

13. CHINA DOLL IV 9 A3+ OR 13B (UNFINISHED) ★
FA: KYLE COPELAND AND MARC HIRT, 1981. FFA OF FIRST AND SECOND PITCHES: BOB HORAN, 1996.

This route follows the long right-leaning, right-facing dihedral system in the middle of the wall. No details of the original aid ascent are known; the free climb shown in the topo covers only the second pitch of the route and adds a direct start. Begin along the left side of the huge block as for *Earth Voyage*, climb to the first bolt, then continue straight up, and belay from bolts beneath the awesome white granite dihedral. Climb the continuously difficult dihedral, then lower off or rappel from a three-bolt anchor. The original route includes three more pitches up the dihedral system. The fourth pitch has been free climbed (Horan) and leads out through a roof to connect with a two-pitch headwall route called *Beauty And The Bolts*.

14. RASPBERRY MANHANDLER IV 6 A3+
FA: MATT BUCKNER AND JIM FUNSTEN, C. 1990.

This aid climb begins from a flat boulder right of *China Doll*. Traverse left along a horizontal fault, up a right-facing corner, and climb what is now the second pitch of *Divination*. Start up a steep ramp, then traverse left and finish at a break in the roofs. Four pitches.

15. ARCHANGEL 12C ★
FA: THOM BYRNE, 1988. FIRST PITCH AND ANCHORS ADDED BY RICHARD ROSSITER AND THOM BYRNE, 1997. ENHANCED SR.

This route ascends the beautiful arching dihedral to the right of *China Doll*. Climb an easy pitch with three bolts and belay on a ledge with a two-bolt anchor (9). Climb the awesome dihedral to where it fades into a blank wall and lower off from a two-bolt anchor (not in place at time of writing).

16. FALLEN FROM GRACE 12D (PROJECT)
TR: BOB HORAN.

This route ascends the roofs and dead vertical wall just right of *Archangel*. Incomplete at press time.

17. DYNO ARÊTE 11A ★
FA: BOB HORAN AND RICHARD ROSSITER.

Begin from the approach ramp about 150 feet up and right from *China Doll*. Face climb up to the bottom of a large right-facing dihedral, then break left and climb a steep arête past several bolts. Lower off, 75 feet.

18. FREEDOM 10A
FA: BOB HORAN AND MARK KALIN.

Begin as for *Dyno Arête*, but climb up and right past several bolts to a two-bolt anchor on *Rock Odyssey*. Lower off (85 feet) or continue with the following route.

19. ESCAPE FROM FREEDOM 10A
FA: RICHARD ROSSITER AND RAOUL DE ROSSITER. SR.

This route follows a long diagonal ramp system up and right across the west face of Lost Angel. **P1**: Climb *Freedom* and belay at the two-bolt anchor (10a). **P2**: Move right and climb a short steep section (6), then friction up and right along a big ramp (7) and belay as for *Zentropa*. One may join *Zentropa* from this belay. **P3**: Follow the fading ramp up and right past a gap (8) and join the last pitch of *Weenie Roast* (9). One may also climb a steep corner and roof system before reaching the last pitch of *Weenie Roast* (gear up to a #4 Friend, 11a). Or, as a final option, continue up and right along the easy ramp and gain the south shoulder of the South Tower.

20. WIDE CRACK 9

Begin about 25 feet right of *Freedom*. Climb mossy rock into a left-facing dihedral with a wide crack. Continue to the bolt belay on *Freedom*.

21. LITTLE WING 11A

FA: THOM BYRNE AND DAVID SCHIPPER, 1988.

This route ascends the steep slab just left of the first pitch of *Rock Odyssey*. Two bolts plus gear.

22. ROCK ODYSSEY 12B ★

FA: BOB HORAN, JOHN BALDWIN, SHANE RYMER.

P1. Climb the steep wall and slab right of *Wide Crack* to a two-bolt anchor (11d, 85 feet, 11 bolts). P2. Traverse up and left, then up along a curved flake past a fixed anchor (rappel point) and a slab to an anchor in the dihedral of *China Doll* (11d, 75 feet, 11 bolts). P3. Crank left out of the dihedral, then climb up the steep slab to a three-bolt anchor (11d, 50 feet, five bolts). P4. Work up and left and climb through the big stepped roofs, then continue to the top of the wall (12b, 100 feet, 10 bolts).

23. TRIPENDICULAR WILDMAN 12B ★

FA: BOB HORAN AND MARK KALIN.

This upper wall route can be reached from the third pitch of *Earth Voyage*, the third pitch of *Rock Odyssey*, or by rappel from the top. Climb through the big roof and up the headwall just left of the upper *China Doll* dihedral. Two pitches.

24. BEAUTY AND THE BOLTS 11D ★

FA: BOB HORAN AND JOHN BALDWIN.

This spectacular route may be reached by rappelling from a bolt anchor near the summit or by climbing *Rock Odyssey* and the fourth pitch of *China Doll*. From a bolt anchor just above the main roof, climb the narrow face right of the final pitches of *China Doll* and belay from a bolt anchor (10b, six bolts). Continue up the steep face, pass a bulge, and belay at the top of the wall (11d, nine bolts).

AWAKENINGS 12A ★

FA: DAN HARE, LOTUS STEELE, MOE HERSHOFF, 1998. SR

P1: Climb past the first two bolts on *Rock Odyssey*, then break right and continue past six more bolts to a big ledge (10b, 60 feet). **P2**: Climb past a bolt and up a thin crack to a right-facing dihedral. Climb the dihedral and turn a roof at its top (11b/c), then follow a thin crack up the vertical wall to another good ledge (12a, 110 feet). Can rappel from here. **P3**: From the left side of the ledge, climb a left-facing corner and discontinuous cracks to a flat ledge at the top of the wall (9+, 70 feet).

South Tower

The following routes are located on the South Tower of Lost Angel, which is continuous with the main rock, but has a separate summit.

25. ZENTROPA 11A ★

FA: RICHARD ROSSITER AND GAIL EFFRON. SR WITH 10 OR 11 QDS.

This is a three-pitch route up the west side of the South Tower. Begin about 200 feet down and left from the high point of the approach ramp. P1. Start at a bolt or climb a hand crack ten feet to the right. In either case, gain a finger crack that leads to a short headwall with three bolts (crux). Above the headwall, climb up and right along a ramp and gain a two-bolt anchor. P2. Climb the second pitch of *Long Dong Dihedral*, and belay at a two-bolt anchor after 50 feet (8). P3. Follow seven bolts and a finger crack (stoppers) up the middle of the northwest face of the South Tower (10c, 80 feet). Locate a belay bolt next to the summit.

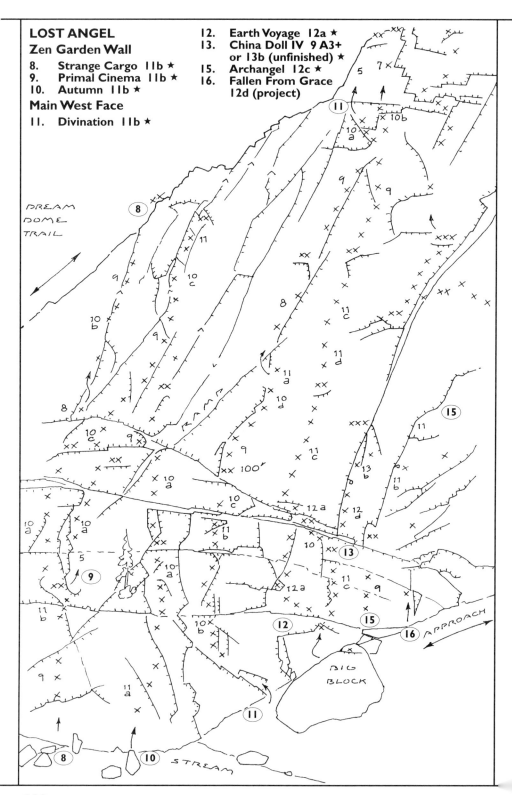

LOST ANGEL

Zen Garden Wall

8. Strange Cargo 11b ★
9. Primal Cinema 11b ★
10. Autumn 11b ★

Main West Face

11. Divination 11b ★

12. Earth Voyage 12a ★
13. China Doll IV 9 A3+
    or 13b (unfinished) ★
15. Archangel 12c ★
16. Fallen From Grace
    12d (project)

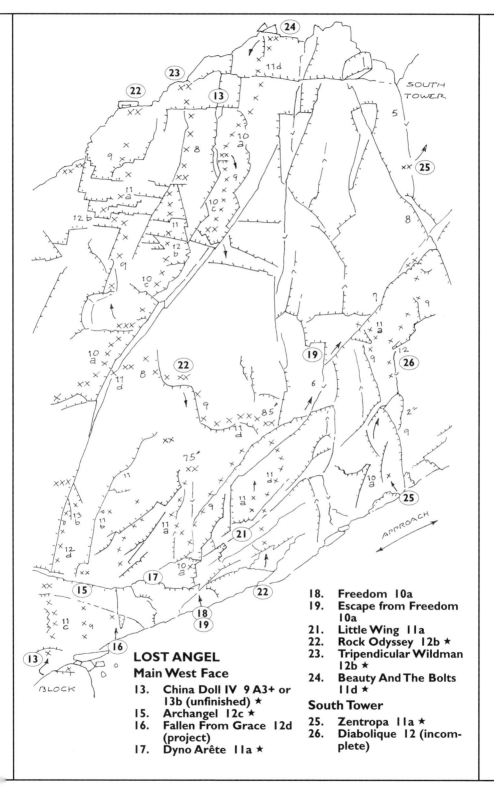

LOST ANGEL

Main West Face

13. China Doll IV 9 A3+ or 13b (unfinished) ★
15. Archangel 12c ★
16. Fallen From Grace 12d (project)
17. Dyno Arête 11a ★

18. Freedom 10a
19. Escape from Freedom 10a
21. Little Wing 11a
22. Rock Odyssey 12b ★
23. Tripendicular Wildman 12b ★
24. Beauty And The Bolts 11d ★

South Tower

25. Zentropa 11a ★
26. Diabolique 12 (incomplete)

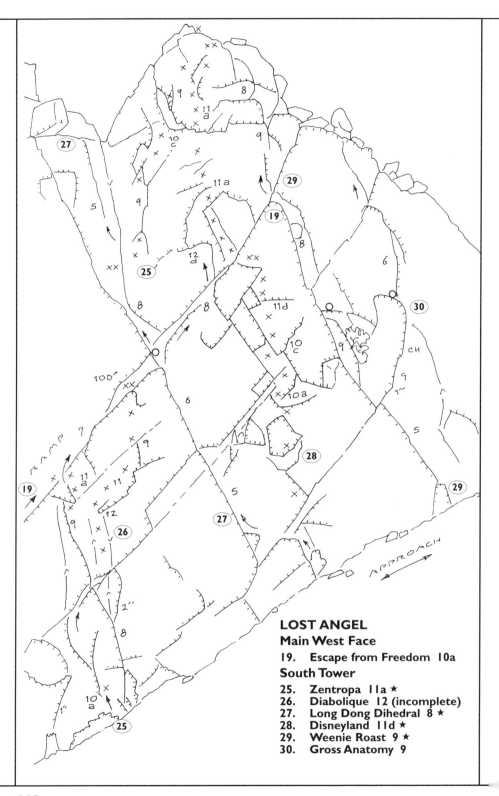

LOST ANGEL

Main West Face

19. Escape from Freedom 10a

South Tower

25. **Zentropa 11a ★**
26. **Diabolique 12 (incomplete)**
27. **Long Dong Dihedral 8 ★**
28. **Disneyland 11d ★**
29. **Weenie Roast 9 ★**
30. **Gross Anatomy 9**

26. DIABOLIQUE 12 (INCOMPLETE)
FA: RICHARD ROSSITER.

Take either start to *Zentropa* and gain a diagonal fault about 60 feet up. Climb a difficult shallow corner just right of the finger crack on *Zentropa*, turn a small roof (crux), and follow bolts up the headwall as shown in the topo. A 60-meter rope is required to lower off.

27. LONG DONG DIHEDRAL 8 ★
FA: RICHARD ROSSITER, SOLO, 1997. SR.

Begin as for the following route, but break left into a long dihedral system that angles up and left to the notch between the main summit and the South Tower. Three pitches.

28. DISNEYLAND 11D ★
FA: BOB HORAN AND KEVIN KLEE.

Begin about 50 feet down and left from where the approach trail rounds the southwest corner of Lost Angel. P1. Climb a steep face with a right-leaning roof and dihedrals near the top and belay from bolts just below a long ramp that cuts across the upper west face of Lost Angel (11d, ten bolts). P2. Climb up and left around the corner, then up the steep west arête of the South Tower (11a, ten bolts).

29. WEENIE ROAST 9 ★
FA: RICHARD ROSSITER AND COLLEEN GREENE, 1997. SR.

Begin a short way up and right from the preceding route at the top of the long approach ramp. Climb a large V-shaped dihedral, pass a steep section on the left, and belay after about 90 feet. Continue up the clean dihedral to a ramp where one could escape up and right, then climb straight up a series of short, steep cracks (crux) and finish with a flared hand crack.

30. GROSS ANATOMY 9
FA: ROSSITER.

Start up *Weenie Roast*, then break right at a dihedral/chimney and belay at its top. A moderate crack leads to the south shoulder of the South Tower.

Wake Up Wall

Dedicated to the spirit of freedom in an unfree world. Recommended listening: Rage Against The Machine (Epic ZK52959). The following routes are located on the sunny south side of the South Tower, just above the approach path after it breaks west from the main South Trail. Routes by Richard Rossiter with Bonnie Von Grebe unless otherwise noted.

31. KILLING IN THE NAME 9 ★
Begin from the left side of a shelf, just right of a small tree. Climb past a bolt, then follow a crack system through a bulge and reach a two-bolt anchor after about 75 feet. SR.

32. TAKE THE POWER BACK 9 ★
Begin about seven feet right of the preceding route. Follow a good crack through a bulge and continue to the same anchor as *Killing In The Name*. SR.

32A. CRACK IN THE WALL 10A ★
Climb a hand crack through the bulge about three feet left of the main line. SR.

33. RUSH 11B ★
Begin as for *Take The Power Back*, but break right at a bolt, pass a strenuous bulge, and lieback through a roof. Go right or left at the last bolt depending on which anchor you want to use. Five bolts.

LOST ANGEL
Wake Up Wall

31. Killing In The Name 9 ★
32. Take The Power Back 9 ★
33. Rush 11b ★
34. Rage Against The Machine 11b ★
35. Jungle Blues From Jupiter 10c ★
36. Spiders From Mars 11b ★
37. Drop Zone 10b ★
38. Boys' World 8 ★

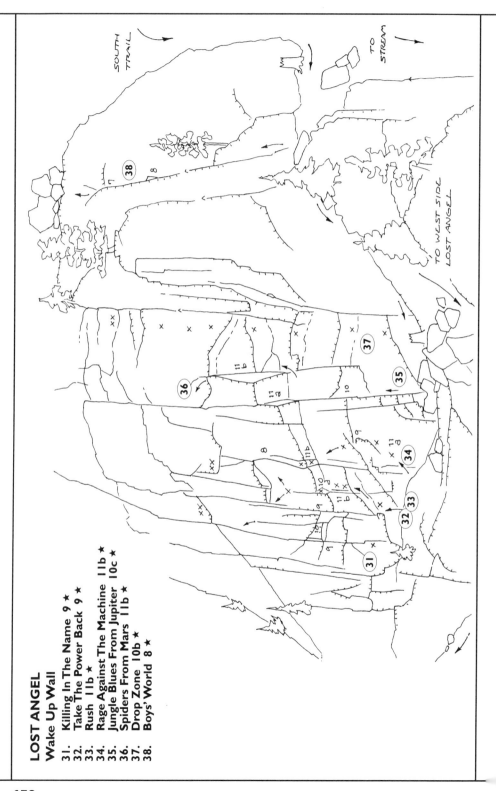

LOST ANGEL
APPROACH RAMP

WATER SLABS
1.   Mes Amis 9 ★
2.   Mary Lynn's Slab 9 ★

34. RAGE AGAINST THE MACHINE 11B ★

Begin toward the right side of the ramp and left of the big dihedral of Jungle Blues. Follow bolts up and right through a bulge, then jam parallel cracks through the main roof and continue more easily to a two-bolt anchor. Five bolts. A couple of mid-range Friends can be used above the roof.

35. JUNGLE BLUES FROM JUPITER 10C ★
FA: Bob Horan, Skip Guerin, Harrison Dekker, 1981. SR.

Climb two consecutive, overhanging, right-facing dihedrals. This is the left of two right-facing dihedral systems.

36. SPIDERS FROM MARS 11B ★
FA: Dekker, Guerin, Horan, 1981.

Begin with the preceding route, then move up and right into a steep, thin crack in a right-facing dihedral. Step left at the top.

37. DROP ZONE 10B ★
FA: Rob Stanley and Stef Streich, 1997.

Climb the steep arête just right of the preceding routes. Six bolts to a two-bolt anchor at 95 feet. Lower off or scramble to walking terrain.

38. BOYS' WORLD 8 ★
FA: Richard Rossiter, solo.

Begin about 50 feet up and right from the preceding routes. Climb a clean, V-shaped dihedral with a pine tree near its bottom.

WATER SLABS

Just above the creek and directly below the South Tower of Lost Angel are some low-angle arêtes and slabs. The easiest approach is to follow the South Trail all the way to the bottom of the gorge, then hike upstream until beneath the north end of the formation. Routes by Bob Horan and Werner Braun.

1. MES AMIS 9 ★

Climb over a prow, then follow bolts up a smooth slab and gain a bolt anchor at upper left. Nine bolts.

2. MARY LYNN'S SLAB 9 ★

Start up a narrow slab a short way right of *Mes Amis*, climb an arête and finish with a hanging slab. Nine bolts to a two-bolt anchor.

MIDNIGHT ROCK

Midnight Rock is located east of Lost Angel just across the South Trail, where it first drops steeply into Dream Canyon. The main wall faces west and is characterized by steep, shallow cracks and big roofs. To reach the west and south sides of the buttress, follow the South Trail down into the gorge until is apparent to break left and contour to the base of the rock. To reach the upper southeast face, approach as for Vanishing Point and descend to a ledge that leads west to the wall.

1. THE CAGE 9+ S
FA: Dan Hare and Kurt Gray, 1982. SR.

Begin from blocks beneath the upper left side of the west face. Pull up and right to a flake, then follow thin cracks to a shelf. Scramble off to the left.

Steve Bartlett on *Strange Cargo*. Photo by Richard Rossiter.

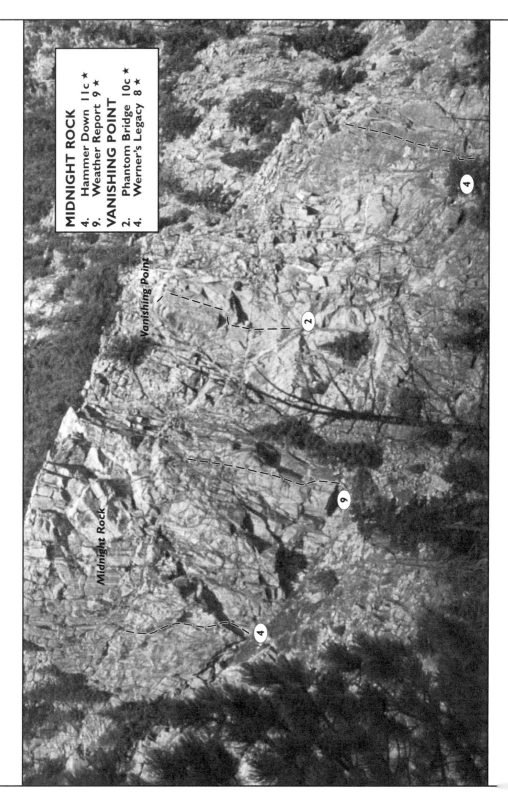

MIDNIGHT ROCK
4. Hammer Down 11c ★
9. Weather Report 9 ★
VANISHING POINT
2. Phantom Bridge 10c ★
4. Werner's Legacy 8 ★

Vanishing Point

Midnight Rock

2. BIRDS OF PREY 10
FA: DAN HARE AND DAVE BREWSTER, 1981. SR.

Climb a thin crack through a bulge with a wedged flake. Climb the right of two parallel thin cracks, then work up and right and belay on a ledge. A short crack leads to a bigger ledge.

3. CIRQUE DU SOLEIL 12c ★
FA: BOB HORAN, CHULE LEE.

Begin just right of the preceding route. Follow bolts up and right, then lieback off an arête. Gain a two-bolt anchor and lower off.

4. HAMMER DOWN 11c ★
FA: BOB HORAN, CHULE LEE, JORGE.

Follow bolts up a right-facing dihedral just right of *Cirque*, turn the roof as for *Union With Earth*, then work up and right to a final bulge (crux).

5. UNION WITH EARTH 10a
FA: BOB HORAN, SKIP GUERIN, DICK CILEY, 1981. SR.

Begin ten feet right of the preceding route. Climb a V-slot and follow a crack through a four-foot roof with a bolt. Continue up a right-facing dihedral, followed by a left-facing dihedral and gain a ledge with a two-bolt anchor.

6. AROUND MIDNIGHT 12d A0
FA: BOB HORAN AND CHULE LEE.

Begin ten feet right of the preceding route. Follow bolts up the face to a huge roof with a fixed pin. Turn the roof and join *Hammer Down*. Bolts plus gear.

7. PIRATE RADAR 11d ★
FA: BOB HORAN AND CHULE LEE.

Begin beneath a large roof at the lower right side of the west face. Climb straight up via jugs, then traverse left along flakes to a crack that pierces the roof. Crank up and left through the roof and gain a two-bolt anchor. Three bolts and three pins.

7A. VARIATION 12a ?

Begin about 15 feet up and left from regular start. Climb up and right past two bolts to gain the roof/crack.

8. JET STREAM 12a ★
FA: BOB HORAN AND JOHN BALDWIN.

Begin about 25 feet down and right from *Pirate Radar*. Climb a clean right-facing dihedral, then work up and left and finish with a perfect hand crack. Four bolts plus gear to a two-bolt anchor. Bring Friends #0.5 to #2.5 or equivalent.

9. WEATHER REPORT 9 ★
FA: RICHARD ROSSITER AND BONNIE VON GREBE, 1997.

From the low-point of the buttress, follow bolts up a steep arête, a slab, and a narrow gully. Nine bolts to a two-bolt anchor. From the seventh bolt it is possible to traverse up and right 20 feet to the anchor on *Grande Finale* (7).

10. GRANDE FINALE 13 A0 ★
FA: BOB HORAN AND CHULE LEE.

Begin about 50 feet up and right from *We And They*. Go left on a ledge, then climb an overhanging wall, round the arête at left and gain a two-bolt anchor. Seven bolts.

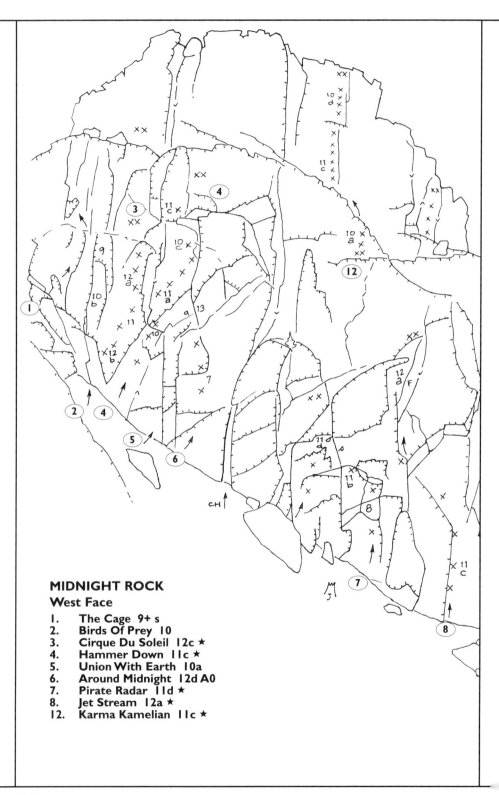

MIDNIGHT ROCK

West Face

1. The Cage 9+ s
2. Birds Of Prey 10
3. Cirque Du Soleil 12c ★
4. Hammer Down 11c ★
5. Union With Earth 10a
6. Around Midnight 12d A0
7. Pirate Radar 11d ★
8. Jet Stream 12a ★
12. Karma Kamelian 11c ★

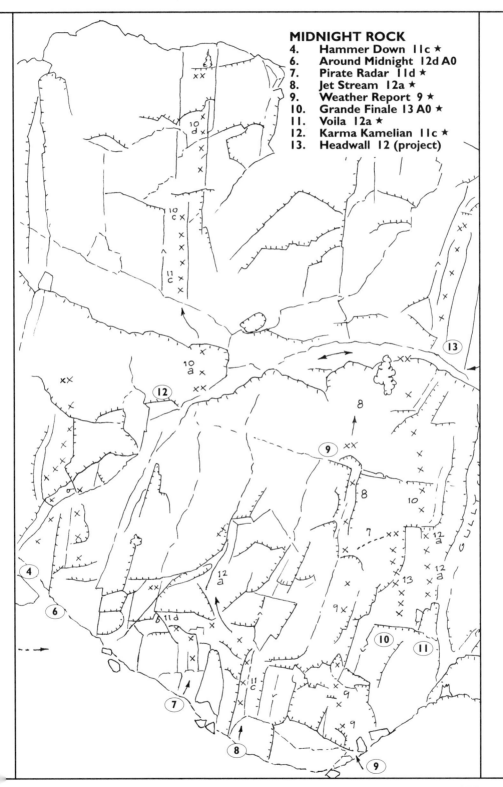

MIDNIGHT ROCK
4.   Hammer Down 11c ★
6.   Around Midnight 12d A0
7.   Pirate Radar 11d ★
8.   Jet Stream 12a ★
9.   Weather Report 9 ★
10. Grande Finale 13 A0 ★
11. Voila 12a ★
12. Karma Kamelian 11c ★
13. Headwall 12 (project)

11. VOILA 12A ★
FA: BOB HORAN AND CHULE LEE.

Begin just right of the preceding route. Follow eleven bolts up the bulging wall and gain a two-bolt anchor on a big ledge where one may lower off or scramble off to the right.

12. KARMA KAMELIAN 11C ★
FA: BOB HORAN, "CLEAN DAN" GRANDUSKY, JERRY GREENLEAF.

This route is located on the south side of Midnight Rock, just above a big ledge system that runs across the upper buttress. Approach as for *Vanishing Point*, then traverse west along the ledge to a two-bolt anchor at its end. Climb up to a ledge and up along a thin crack to another ledge, then up the head-wall crack to a two-bolt anchor. Twelve bolts, 75 feet.

13. HEADWALL 12 (PROJECT)
TR: DAN HARE.

This route ascends an overhanging wall at the far east end of the big upper ledge. Approach as for the preceding route. Follow four bolts up the steep wall between two shallow grooves. Lower off from a tow-bolt anchor.

VANISHING POINT

Vanishing point is the next buttress east of Midnight Rock. It is characterized by a super-clean monolithic pillar at its upper west side, some dihedrals around to the east, and a long rib that descends to the bottom of the gorge. Vanishing Point is easily reached by following the main South Trail to its end at a mining excavation. The top of Vanishing Point is located 150 feet down to the southeast from the excavation. The bottom of the rock may be reached as for Midnight Rock.

1. THE VANISHING 11C ★
FA: RICHARD ROSSITER, DAN HARE, AMY REYNOLDS.

This route climbs the stunning southwest arête of the monolith. Rappel 85 feet from a two-bolt anchor atop the prow to a two-bolt anchor in an open book dihedral. Follow bolts up the left side of the open book and gain a stance at the left end of a large roof, then work up and right to the exposed arête and continue straight to the top. 12 bolts.

2. PHANTOM BRIDGE 10C ★
FA: RICHARD ROSSITER, GAIL EFFRON, DAN HARE.

Begin as for the preceding route. Climb past the first four bolts, then hand-traverse right along a crack between two big roofs. Step right around the arête, then follow bolts up a steep dihedral and veer left at the top. 12 bolts.

3. VANISHING INK 12A A0 ★
FA: DAN HARE AND RICHARD ROSSITER. REDPOINT: DAN HARE AND BRUCE ADAMS.

Rappel 85 feet to a bolt anchor in an open book as for the preceding routes. Follow an easy crack up and right through a slab, then turn double roofs (crux) and climb the steep wall between the arête at left and the dihedral of *Phantom Bridge* (12a). The steep wall has been redpointed from *Phantom Bridge*, which avoids the crux roofs and provides an excellent route.

4. WERNER'S LEGACY 8 ★
FA: BOB HORAN AND WERNER BRAUN.

The lower south rib of Vanishing Point climbs directly out of North Boulder Creek. This route ascends the west arête of the rib. Approach as for Midnight Rock, but continue all the way to the bottom of the gorge, then hike downstream until below the arête. Follow eight bolts up the arête and lower off.

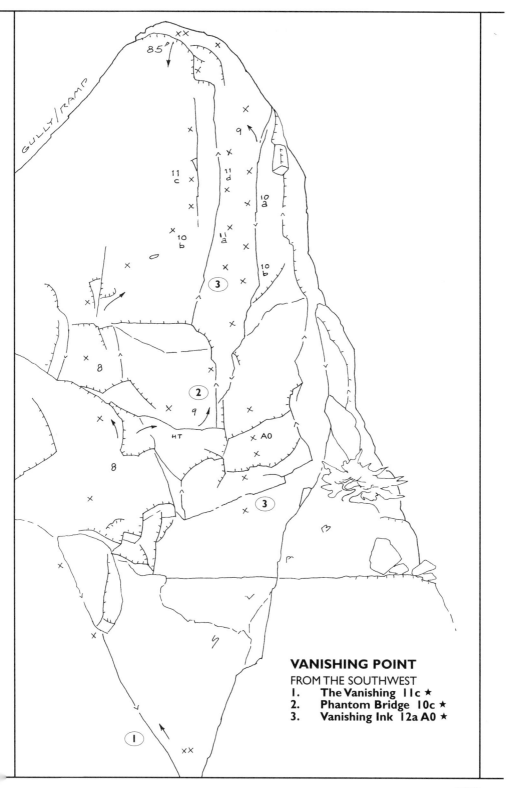

GULLY/RAMP

85°

11
c

11
d

11
a

10
b

9

10
a

10
b

3

8

2

9

8

HT

A0

3

1

VANISHING POINT

FROM THE SOUTHWEST
1.　The Vanishing 11c ★
2.　Phantom Bridge 10c ★
3.　Vanishing Ink 12a A0 ★

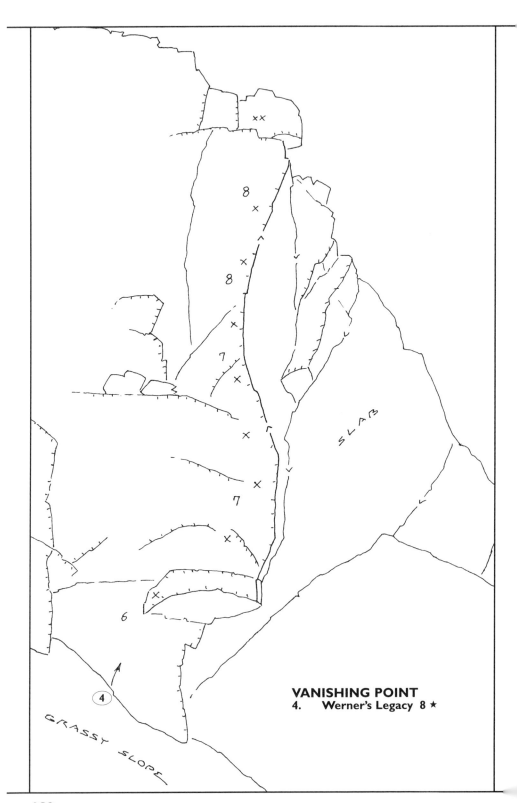

SLAB

GRASSY SLOPE

VANISHING POINT
4.   Werner's Legacy 8 ★

BAT COVE

The Bat Cove is a small buttress located along the stream directly below Midnight Rock. The following short routes are located on the west side of the buttress. All routes by Bob Horan and Chule Lee.

1.   HOW BIZARRE 11A
Climb a corner near the left side of the wall and hand traverse right at the top. Five bolts to a two-bolt anchor.

2.   BATARANG 12B
Climb an overhanging scoop in the middle of the wall. Four bolts to a two-bolt anchor.

3.   BAT BOY 11C/D
Climb the arête at right via a large flake and pockets. Three bolts to anchor on *Batarang*.

BOULDER SLIPS
1. Minutia 8
2. La Lune 12d/13a ★
6. The Threshold 11b

Road Routes II

BOULDER SLIPS

Boulder Slips is located on the north side of the highway, just west of the path to Boulder Falls. Park in the large pull-out as for Boulder Falls or on the gravel shoulder just below the crag. The first three routes are located on the east side of a gulch at the west end of Boulder Slips, about 100 yards west of the Boulder Falls Trail. The remainder are located along the main wall farther to the right.

1.   MINUTIA 8
FA: DAN HARE, KURT GRAY, CHARLY OLIVER, 1980.
Begin about 100 feet up the gulch. Climb a hand crack and slab and finish in a corner.

2.   LA LUNE 12D/13A ★
FA: BOB HORAN, 1988 (ALL GEAR). BOLTS ADDED LATER BY A SECOND PARTY.
This route is located on an overhanging black-streaked wall above *Minutia*. Follow bolts up and left along a thin crack, pull over the lip, and finish with a hand crack in the head wall. Lower off from a two-bolt anchor.

3.   USELESS ONE 10
FA: RANDY LEAVITT AND DAN HARE, 1981.
Begin at a vertical wall about 60 feet right of *La Lune*. Follow thin cracks from lower left to upper right.

4.   QUAGMIRE 9+ S
FA: DAN HARE AND GREG DAVIS, 1982.
Climb a thin crack to a ramp and move left to another thin crack.

5.   THE THROTTLE 10B/C S
FA: ALEX LOWE, GREG DAVIS, DAN HARE, 1983.
Near the center of the rock, locate a small bowl at the base of some water streaks. Climb up 30 feet or so into this bowl, then go up to the right.

6.   THE THRESHOLD 11B ★
FA: RANDY LEAVITT AND DAN HARE, 1981.
Climb onto a pillar at the southeast corner of the buttress, then jam discontinuous handcracks just left of the arête.

7.   BOULDER SLIPS 9 S
FA: LARRY DALKE AND PAT AMENT, 1964. FFA: JIM ERICKSON, SOLO, 1972.
Take the right-facing dihedral just right of the *Threshold* arête, go left at a roof, and jam to the top.

TOWER OF BABEL

The Tower of Babel is a narrow spire on the south side of the stream, about 500 feet west of the Boulder Falls parking area. Park on the north side of the highway and ford the stream or cross via tyrolean 100 yards upstream. The tower is 90 feet high and has two known routes. Rappel 90 feet to the stream from two bolts on the summit.

1.   PINNACLE 9
FA: LARRY DALKE, C. 1965.
This route ascends the "north side" of the tower, though its exact line is not known.

2.   BABYLON IS BURNING 11D/12A ★
FA: ROB STANLEY AND STEF STREICH, 1997. SR TO A #3.5 FRIEND.
Follow seven bolts and short cracks up the north face of the tower.

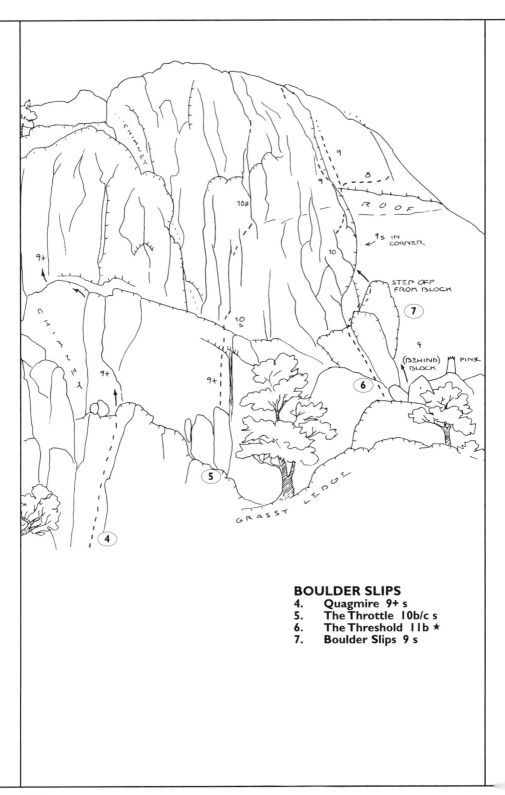

CHIMNEY

9

8

10a

9

ROOF

9s IN CORNER

9+

10

STEP OFF FROM BLOCK

⑦

C
H
I
M
N
E
Y

9+

10
5

9+

9
(BEHIND) BLOCK

PINE

⑥

⑤

GRASSY LEDGE

④

BOULDER SLIPS

4.   **Quagmire 9+ s**
5.   **The Throttle 10b/c s**
6.   **The Threshold 11b ★**
7.   **Boulder Slips 9 s**

TOWER OF BABEL
2.   Babylon Is Burning 11d/12a ★
3.   Ziggurat 11a

11a

12
a

RAMP

②

③

HIGH WATER

3.   ZIGGURAT 11A
FA: STANLEY AND STREICH, 1997.
Follow eleven bolts up the northwest corner of the tower. Bring a #2.5 Friend.

MIND SHAFT AREA
The following crags are located above and to either side of an old mine at 7.9 miles on the north side of the highway.

Mind Warp Cliff
Just left of the mine entrance on the north side of the highway at 7.9 miles is a short cliff with four routes that can be led or top-roped: a right-facing dihedral, parallel finger cracks, a right-leaning hand crack, and a flake/crack on the right.

Mindless Cliff
Below and slightly west of Mind Shift Cliff is a small but beautiful south-facing wall with a pillar on the right that forms a left-facing dihedral. One may scramble directly up to the wall about 150 feet west of the mine.

1.   GROUND SWELL 10B ★
FA: DAN HARE AND FRED KNAPP, 1996. BRING A #2 FRIEND.
Begin from a pedestal and climb the left side of the face past four bolts.

2.   QUICK CHILL 9 ★
FA: SCOTT WOODRUFF AND DAN HARE, 1979.
Climb the excellent finger crack in the middle of the wall.

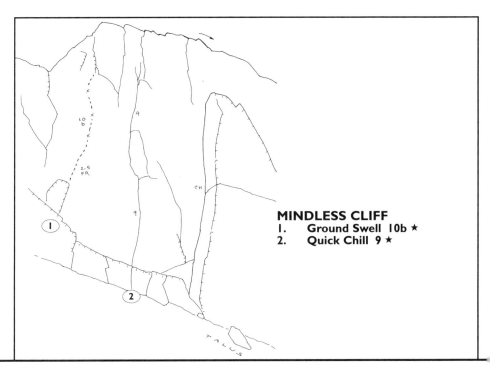

MINDLESS CLIFF
1.   **Ground Swell 10b ★**
2.   **Quick Chill 9 ★**

MINDLESS CLIFF
2. Quick Chill 9 ★
MIND SHIFT CLIFF
3. Stickshift 11a/b
3. Spellbound 11b ★
4. Downshift 12a/b ★
8. Mental Imbalance 11b ★

Mindless
Cliff

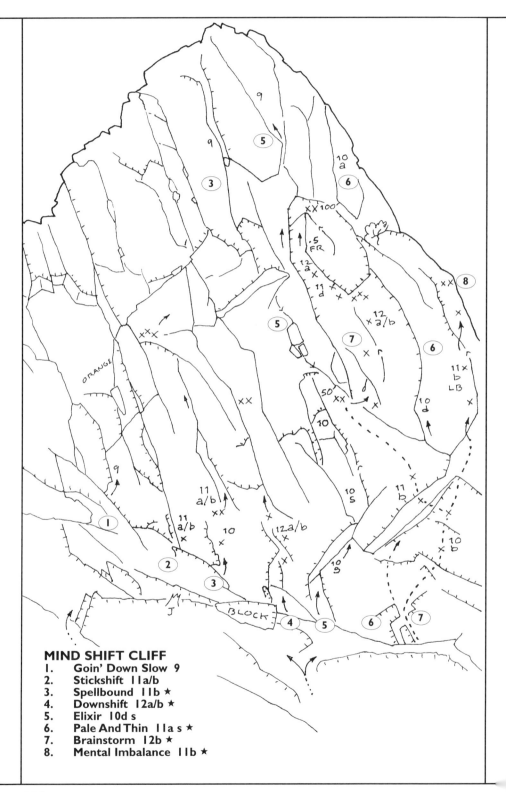

MIND SHIFT CLIFF
1. Goin' Down Slow 9
2. Stickshift 11a/b
3. Spellbound 11b ★
4. Downshift 12a/b ★
5. Elixir 10d s
6. Pale And Thin 11a s ★
7. Brainstorm 12b ★
8. Mental Imbalance 11b ★

Mind Shift Cliff

Mind Shift is located up and left from the mine and to the west of Lion's Den. From the right side of the mine entrance, follow a steep footpath up to a platform with a second mine opening. Continue up and left to the bottom of the steep face.

1.   GOIN' DOWN SLOW 9
FA: DAN HARE AND SCOTT WOODRUFF, 1979.

Near the left side of the rock, climb an arch, exit left, and take the roof.

2.   STICKSHIFT 11A/B
FA: MIKE DOWNING, JOHN WARREN, DAN HARE, 1983.

Locate a thin crack that is 20 feet off the ground and leads to an apex. The first ascent party placed protection with a stick on this pitch. Climb past a bolt and gain a wide crack that leads to a dihedral. Lower off 50 feet from a two-bolt anchor.

3.   SPELLBOUND 11B ★
FA: LEONARD COYNE AND DAN HARE, 1982.

Locate left-leaning, parallel thin cracks 30 feet up and right of *Stickshift*. Start at an overhanging flake with a bolt and continue up to a second bolt. Move right and climb parallel cracks to a belay. Work straight up past some loose blocks or lower off from the anchor on the preceding route.

4.   DOWNSHIFT 12A/B ★
FA: DAN HARE, ROB STANLEY, DAN LEVISON, 1994. RACK: #7 AND 8 ROCKS, #0.5, 1.5, 2.5 AND #3 FRIENDS.

Begin below the left side of the initial roof on *Elixir*. Climb through a bulge with three bolts and gain a finger and hand crack. Lower off from a bolt anchor.

5.   ELIXIR 10D S
FA: JEFF ACHEY AND DAN HARE, 1984.

Begin at the lower left corner of a big diagonal roof. Climb up and right and turn the roof, then continue up a dihedral and jam an overhanging fist crack. Climb off to the east.

6.   PALE AND THIN 11A S ★
FA: DAN HARE AND SCOTT WOODRUFF, 1979.

Begin 10 feet right of *Elixir*. Angle up and right beneath a roof and belay (10). Move left into a difficult, right-facing dihedral and belay at its top (11a). Jam a finger crack on the right (10a).

7.   BRAINSTORM 12B ★
FA: DAN HARE AND FRED KNAPP, 1996. RACK: #3 AND 4 RPS, #4 - 6 ROCKS, TWO #0.5 FRIENDS, PLUS ENOUGH QDS FOR EIGHT BOLTS.

Begin just right of *Pale And Thin*. Climb to a jug and continue up the wall past two bolts. Go straight left over a roof (two bolts), then up and slightly left to a ledge with a bolt anchor. Follow bolts along the left side of an overhanging buttress, then step right and back left into a left-leaning crack and follow it to the top of the buttress.

8.   MENTAL IMBALANCE 11B ★
FA: DAN HARE AND DENNIS SANDERS, 1995. RACK: #5 - 9 ROCKS, #1.5, #2.5 AND #3 FRIENDS.

Climb to the right end of the roof as for the preceding route, then go up and slightly right and follow three bolts up the arête along the right edge of the face. Five bolts.

Valor

Straight above Mind Shift Cliff is a small south-facing wall with the following routes.

1. VALOR 9
FA: Dan Hare, solo, 1981.
Face climb up the center of the wall.

2. LIMITED PARTNERSHIP 9
FA: Dan Hare, solo, 1982.
To the right of *Valor*, foxy face climbing leads to a crack.

3. DISCRETION 8
FA: Dan Hare, solo, 1980.
Climb a crack that diagonals up to the left along a fin at the right side of the formation.

4. SCHIZOPHRENIA 11c
FA: Dan Hare and Dan Levison, 1995.
Begin just right of the preceding route. Climb a small, right-leaning arch, then go up and left along an arête. Four bolts to a two-bolt anchor.

PINNACLE OF SUCCESS 11b
FA: Dan Hare and Dennis Sanders, 1995. Gear: two #2 and #5 Rocks, one each #6 and #7 Rocks plus #1 and 1.5 Friends and 11 QDs.
Locate a 40-foot pinnacle 100 yards uphill and right of Mind Shift Cliff. Climb past two bolts, then follow a finger crack to a bolt anchor.

Lion's Den
Up and right from the mine, east of Mind Shift, is a steep cliff above a sloping ledge system.

1. GRAY PANTHER 10
FA: Dan Hare and Alan Bradley, 1980.
Begin to the right of a big roof. Climb overhanging hand and finger cracks with a wedged flake near the top.

LION'S DEN
1. Gray Panther 10
2. Simba 10
3. Skin And Bones 9
4. Lion's Den 9

2. SIMBA 10
FA: DAN HARE AND RANDY LEAVITT, 1981.

Climb a dirty, left-facing dihedral near the center of the formation.

3. SKIN AND BONES 9
FA: DAN HARE AND CHARLY OLIVER, 1980.

Climb a left-facing dihedral with a wide crack.

4. LION'S DEN 9
FA: DAN HARE, SOLO, 1979.

Climb an overhanging fist crack in the right side of the wall.

Laws of Physics

This is a compact, west-facing buttress above and east of Lion's Den. It may be reached from the top of Lion's Den or from below.

1. IF SIX WERE NINE 9+
FA: GREG DAVIS AND DAN HARE, 1982.

Begin at a black streak (with a bolt) near the center of the rock, below a large roof that angles up to the right. Climb double thin cracks and turn the left side of the roof. SR.

2. THE LAW COMES DOWN 12A
FA: DAN HARE, 1994.

Begin as for *If Six Were Nine*, then angle right under the roof. From the highest bolt under the roof, traverse straight right to a jug and join *Trouble With The Law*. Nine bolts. Lower off. SR.

3. TROUBLE WITH THE LAW 11C ★
FA: DAN HARE AND TOM PAINTER, 1994.

Begin beneath the right side of the west face. Climb the slab past two bolts, step right and climb a short crack, then left along a diagonal crack and straight up a small arête. Eight bolts to a three bolt anchor.

Sentinel Slab

Sentinel Slab is a west-facing wall above a gulch on the south side of the canyon and east of Bell Buttress. Several routes have apparently been climbed, but only one has been documented. To approach, ford the stream and hike up the brushy gulch to the bottom of the wall.

INVEIGLE 8+
FA: PAT AMENT, MID 1960s.

Climb a bulging slab left of a tree and left of a dihedral in the middle of the wall.

PRACTICE ROCK AREA

About 8 miles up the canyon and on the north is a confusing area of small crags and discontinuous cliffs. The landmark feature of this group is the very popular Practice Rock, easily seen from the road 25 yards upslope on the right. The routes are described first along the road, including the Practice Rock, up the hillside to the northeast, then back along the road to the west of the Practice Rock.

FIN 10

At 8.0 miles and near the north side of the road is a 35-foot fin or arête with a couple of bolts.

LAWS OF PHYSICS
1. **If Six Were Nine** 9+
2. **The Law Comes Down** 12a
3. **Trouble With The Law** 11c ★

ZEE ELIMINATOR 10C
FA: Dan Hare and Charly Oliver, 1980.

Begin about 50 feet east of a large tree along the north side of the road. Hike up to a bench beneath a left-curving dihedral. Start with a lieback and climb a difficult slot.

TRICK OR TREAT 9
FA: Dan Hare and Kurt Gray, 1980.

Begin just right of the big tree along the north side of the road. Climb a small inside corner to a roof and go left to a ledge.

The following routes lie uphill to the northeast from the Practice Rock.

1.   BLOODSTONE 11
FA: Dan Hare and Kurt Keiner, 1979.

Scramble up to the second level of cliffs (above some orange streaks) and traverse left into a left-leaning dihedral. Above this, move left and ascend vertical rock.

2.   THE HARDER THEY COME 11
FA: Casey Newman and Kent Lugbill, 1980.

Scramble to the highest band of cliffs and jam a finger crack for 20 feet, then follow it up and left. One may also climb a flake up and left from the start of this route (8).

3.   GRAY HARES 11
FA: Dan Hare and Kurt Gray, 1980.

This route is on a separate cliff to the right of the previous route. Climb a similar crack that tops out at a large tree.

The Practice Rock

At 8.1 miles and on the north side of the highway is a sheer little buttress that faces across the canyon toward Bell Buttress. Numerous piton scars attest to its early popularity. Its three main lines may be top-roped or led.

1.   THIN CRACK 9+
FA: Mark Wilford and Ken Duncan, 1977.
Follow a thin crack through a roof at the left side of the south face.

2.   REGULAR ROUTE 11B ★
FA: Bill Putnam, 1971.
Climb the zig-zag crack in the center of the face.

3.   LIEBACK 10A
FA: Jim Erickson, 1973.
Undercling and lieback along a left-leaning flake on the right side of the face.

STINGER 9
FA: Dan Hare, 1980.
Climb the right of two dihedrals above and left of The Practice Rock.

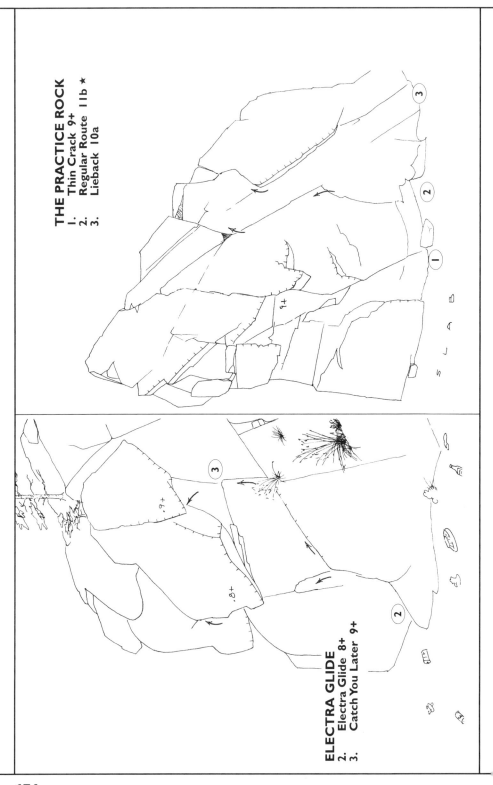

THE PRACTICE ROCK
1. Thin Crack 9+
2. Regular Route 11b ★
3. Lieback 10a

ELECTRA GLIDE
2. Electra Glide 8+
3. Catch You Later 9+

ELECTRA GLIDE

About 25 yards beyond The Practice Rock and on the same side of the highway is a small buttress with zig-zag cracks that lead to a tree.

1. BLOODY MONDAY 10D
FA: BILL MORCK, KATHE MORCK, ED WEBSTER, 1990.

Begin 25 feet up around the corner to the left of *Electra Glide*. Climb shallow cracks to a ledge, under-cling right at an overlap, then clip a bolt and face climb up to *Electra Glide* (10d). Climb thin cracks to the top (9).

2. ELECTRA GLIDE 8+
FA: SCOTT WOODRUFF AND DAN HARE, 1976.

Climb the crack on the left past the left side of a roof, then up and right to the tree.

3. CATCH YOU LATER 9+
FA: PAT AMENT, C. 1982.

Begin as for *Electra Glide*, but after a few moves, break right and follow a steep crack straight up to the tree.

SUPERDEATH 9
FA: KENT LUGBILL AND BILL FEIGES, 1980.

Locate a small crag about 100 feet beyond *Electra Glide* and some 50 feet above the road. Climb a thin crack to an arête, and finish with the face on the right.

TAILSPIN 9
FA: DAN HARE AND ALLEN WOOD, 1980.

A wee bit further up the road, lieback a mossy corner on the right margin of a long, smooth wall.

25. NEW BEGINNINGS 11C ★
FA: PAUL GAGNER.

Begin atop a large block just up and right from the preceding line. Follow bolts along a right-facing dihedral and finish with a steep slab on the right. Eight bolts to a two-bolt anchor, 75 feet.

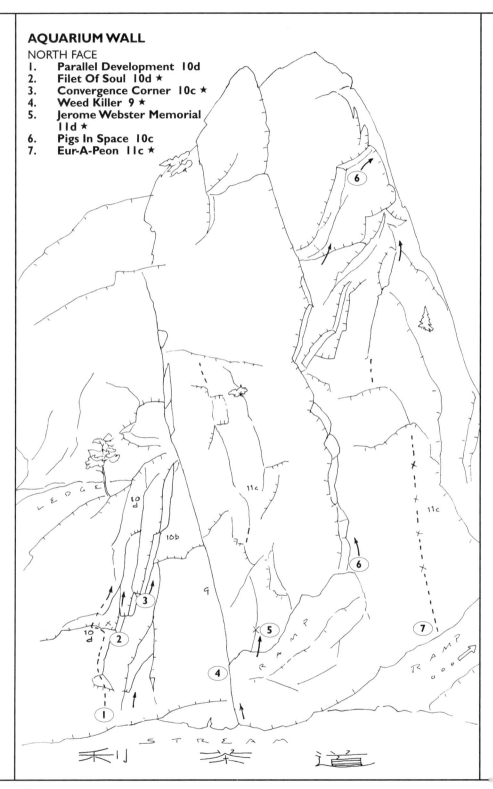

AQUARIUM WALL

NORTH FACE
1. **Parallel Development 10d**
2. **Filet Of Soul 10d ★**
3. **Convergence Corner 10c ★**
4. **Weed Killer 9 ★**
5. **Jerome Webster Memorial 11d ★**
6. **Pigs In Space 10c**
7. **Eur-A-Peon 11c ★**

The Narrows

The following crags are located along a steep and winding section of the canyon known as "The Narrows." All features are on the south side beginning with Bell Buttress and ending with Sleeping Beauty, and require a crossing of Boulder Creek.

AQUARIUM WALL

Across the stream from the Practice Rock and about 150 feet east of Bell Buttress is a steep wall or buttress characterized by a stepped right-facing dihedral and a left-leaning hand crack that converge at a ledge with a small pine tree. The climbing here is somewhat seasonal in that the wall faces north and to reach it one must ford the stream. Easiest access is from late summer to early winter. To escape from the top of the routes, rappel 75 feet from a couple of pitons.

1.   PARALLEL DEVELOPMENT 10D
FA: KYLE COPELAND AND BUSHY POTTASCH, 1987.

Start up the stepped dihedral, hand traverse left along the lip of a roof (crux), and climb braided cracks to a ledge with a pine tree.

2.   FILET OF SOUL 10D ★
FA: KYLE COPELAND, MARC HIRT, AND TIM HUDGEL, 1987.

Begin as for the preceding route, but turn the right side of the roof and follow a finger crack just left of the stepped dihedral.

3.   CONVERGENCE CORNER 10C ★
FA: KYLE COPELAND, 1987.

Climb the stepped dihedral to its top.

4.   WEED KILLER 9 ★
FA: BUSHY POTTASCH AND JOSH GEETER, 1987.

Or was it Killer Weed! Move in from the right and jam a left-leaning hand crack to the ledge with a small pine.

5.   JEROME WEBSTER MEMORIAL 11D ★
FA: BUSHY POTTASCH AND KYLE COPELAND, 1987.

Traverse in from the right as for the preceding route. Climb past a bolt, then follow discontinuous cracks to the east shoulder of the buttress. This route does not lead to the pine tree ledge. Escape as you will.

6.   PIGS IN SPACE 10C
FA: DAN HARE AND KURT GRAY, 1981.

This route begins from the edge of the creek and follows the right margin of the Aquarium Wall. Climb a thin crack up an open-book corner, then follow a right-facing dihedral to an alcove and belay on a narrow stance at left. Move right into a steep, right-facing dihedral that leads to a roof. Pass the roof on the right and continue more easily to the top of the buttress.

7.   EUR-A-PEON 11C ★
FA: KYLE COPELAND, MARC HIRT, TIM HUDGEL, 1987.

Begin from the bottom of the long ramp that leads to the upper tier of Bell Buttress. Climb past four bolts on the smooth wall to the right of *Pigs In Space*, then veer right and follow cracks and corners to the top of the buttress.

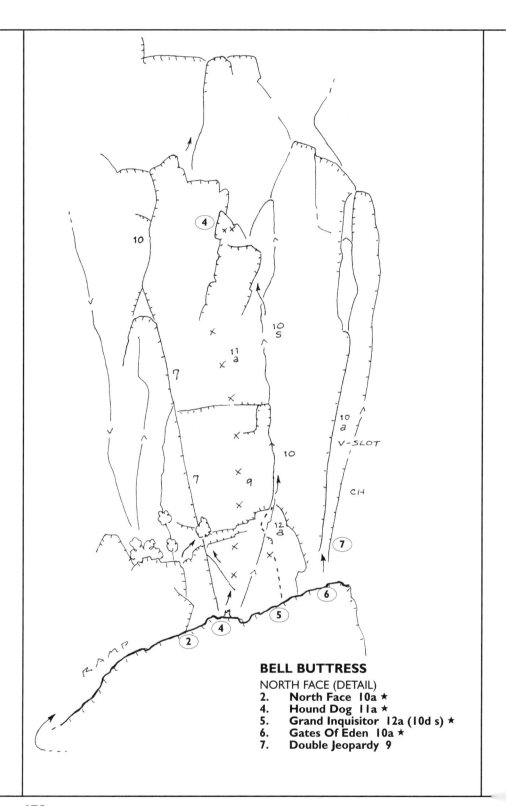

BELL BUTTRESS

NORTH FACE (DETAIL)
2.   **North Face 10a** ★
4.   **Hound Dog 11a** ★
5.   **Grand Inquisitor 12a (10d s)** ★
6.   **Gates Of Eden 10a** ★
7.   **Double Jeopardy 9**

BELL BUTTRESS

At about 8.1 miles and on the south side of the creek, Bell Buttress towers above the highway and draws the eye of the passing climber. Park on the wide shoulder along the right side of the road, near the Practice Rock. To reach the buttress, ford the stream and gain the east end of a long ramp/ledge that traverses the entire crag. One may also scramble directly up to this ledge from the stream, below the large, right-facing dihedral of *Cosmosis*. To reach routes on the upper west face, look for a cairn along the stream about 150 feet west of the buttress. From the cairn, follow a vague path up and left into the upper part of the gully along the west side of the crag. Descend from the summit by hiking south and reversing the approach for the upper west face.

1. THE PITTS 11A
FA: ROB CANDELARIA AND ROGER BRIGGS, 1975.

Just left of the north face is a funky gully about 200 feet high. Two-thirds of the way up and near a tree, branch off to the left and enter a crack system that leads to the top of the rock.

2. NORTH FACE 10A ★
FA: LARRY AND ROGER DALKE, 1964.

Begin at the far left side of the north face beneath a right-facing V-shaped dihedral. Start with a short chimney on the left or climb directly up the crack and follow the dihedral to a pedestal at its top. Climb a steep crack and belay on a ledge or continue up another crack in a short wall to a higher ledge. Finish as for *Cosmosis*.

3. THE BYPASS 8 A4
FA: LARRY AND ROGER DALKE, 1964.

Begin just right of *North Face* and climb straight up to the right of the groove.

4. HOUND DOG 11A ★
FA: CHIP RUCKGABER AND DAVE FIXX.

This may be a free version of the preceding route. Climb the beautiful wall right of the original *North Face* route and finish with a short crack that leads to a ledge with a two-bolt anchor. Nine bolts. Lower off, 85 feet. Include a selection of small to medium friends. A variation goes left somewhere along the route.

5. GRAND INQUISITOR 12A (10D S) ★
FA: ALEC SHARP AND CHUCK FITCH, C. 1980. RACK: RPS TO A #2.5 FRIEND.

This intimidating line takes the right side of the nose formed by the juncture of the north and north-west faces. Climb up to a bolt beneath a large overhang and proceed as shown in the topo.

6. GATES OF EDEN 10A ★
FA: PAT AMENT AND DANNY SMITH, 1967.

Begin with an overhanging hand crack just left of a large slot. Jam the crack to a sloping stance with a couple of fixed pins, or continue to a small ledge higher up and belay. Follow an obvious crack up and right and join the last pitch of *Cosmosis*.

7. DOUBLE JEOPARDY 9
FA: JACK LAUGHLIN AND KEN PARKER, 1960. FFA: JIM ERICKSON, SOLO, 1973.

A short distance right from the *Grand Inquisitor* is a steep slot or chimney that gives rise to a pair of cracks. Follow the cracks to a square-cut, left-facing corner and climb to its top. Move up and right and finish as for *Cosmosis*.

BELL BUTTRESS
5.   Grand Inquisitor 12a
     (10d s) ★
10. Cosmosis 9+ ★
10A. Swerve 12b
14. West Face 9+ ★
18. Arms Bazaar 12a s ★

Bean Liquor Wall

BELL BUTTRESS
18. Arms Bazaar 12a s ★
22. Daedalus 10c s ★

8.   THE SPOILS 12A S ★
FA: PAT AMENT AND TOM MENK, 1965. FFA: RON MATOUS, 1979.

A couple yards right from *Double Jeopardy*, climb a very steep, left-facing corner.

9.   VERVE 13B/C ★
FA: CHRISTIAN GRIFFITH, 1987.

Climb the overhanging arête just left of *Cosmosis*. Four bolts to a two-pin anchor. Lower off 75 feet.

10.   COSMOSIS 9+ ★
FA: PAT AMENT AND PAUL MAYROSE, 1965. FFA: DUNCAN FERGUSON AND BOB POLING, 1970.

This was, and still is, the most popular route on Bell Buttress. Just around the corner to the right from Verve is a large, clean, right-facing dihedral. Two or three pitches in all to the summit. There may be a rappel anchor at the top of the first pitch.

10A. SWERVE 12B
FA: GARY RYAN, STEVE DIECKHOFF, ANNIE WHITEHOUSE.

Climb about halfway up the first pitch of *Cosmosis*, then traverse up and left to the last clip on *Verve*.

11.   THE ROUTE THAT DAN MISSED 10A S ★
FA: MARC GAY AND MARK TARRANT, 1986.

Climb the arête to the right of the last 75 feet of *Cosmosis*. Two bolts.

12.   BEETHOVEN'S FIFTH 12D S ★
FA: OF ALL BUT THE CRUX BY ALEC SHARP, C. 1980 AND CALLED UNFINISHED SYMPHONY. DALE GODDARD COMPLETED THE FINAL DIFFICULT PASSAGE DURING 1986, BUT CHANGED COMPOSERS.

Climb the thin crack system just right of *Cosmosis*, pass a small roof, and eventually merge with the *West Face* route on the right.

13.   WEST CRACK 9+ ★
FA: ART HIGBEE AND LUKE STUDER, 1972.

About 20 feet right of *Cosmosis* are two parallel cracks, the right of which becomes a shallow right-facing corner that ends at a roof (*West Face*). Climb the crack on the left and eventually merge with *West Face*.

14.   WEST FACE 9+ ★
FA: TEX BOSSIER AND JOE OLIGER, 1962. FFA: JIM ERICKSON AND DAVE ERICKSON, 1972.

This is the last route along the approach ledge before the big chimney that splits the buttress from top to bottom. Climb the right of two cracks and belay on a ledge after a long pitch. Climb a right-facing dihedral to the top of the rock.

15.   HEADWALL 10
FA: DAN HARE, BRAD GILBERT, AND SCOTT WOODRUFF , 1975.

Climb the steep face to the left of the regular last pitch.

16.   LEFT WALL 12?
Follow bolts up the overhanging arête along the left side of the big chimney that splits the rock. Eight or ten bolts to a two-bolt anchor.

17.   EPIPHANY 11D S
FA: CHUCK FITCH, ALEC SHARP, RICHARD CAREY, 1980.

This route ascends the north-facing wall just right of the huge chimney that splits the rock from bottom to top. Climb the left side of the wall to a belay, then move right and follow thin cracks to a ledge.

BELL BUTTRESS

WEST FACE (LEFT)
5. **Grand Inquisitor** 12a (10d s) ★
6. **Gates Of Eden** 10a ★
7. **Double Jeopardy** 9
8. **The Spoils** 12a s ★
9. **Verve** 13b/c ★
10. **Cosmosis** 9+ ★
11. **The Route That Dan Missed** 10a s ★
12. **Beethoven's Fifth** 12d s ★
13. **West Crack** 9+ ★
14. **West Face** 9+ ★
15. **Headwall** 10
16. **Left Wall** 12?

17. **Epiphany** 11d s
18. **Arms Bazaar** 12a s ★
19. **Three Minute Hero** 11 b/c
20. **Joe Pontiac** 7
21. **Malaise** 10
22. **Daedalus** 10c s ★

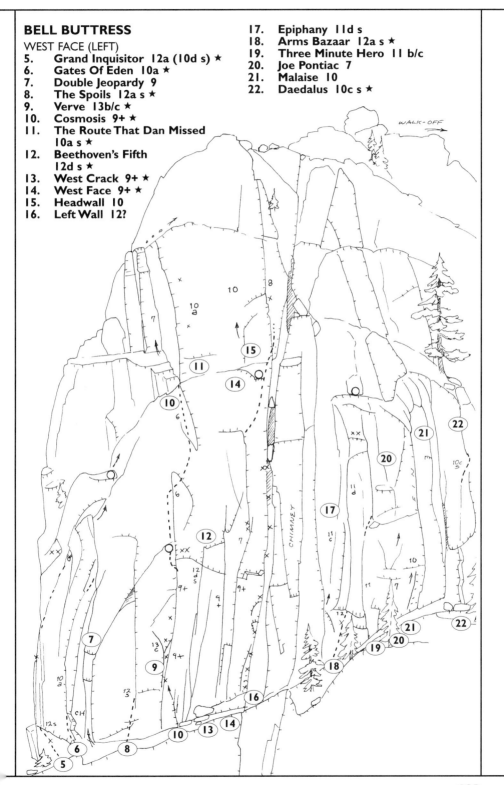

183

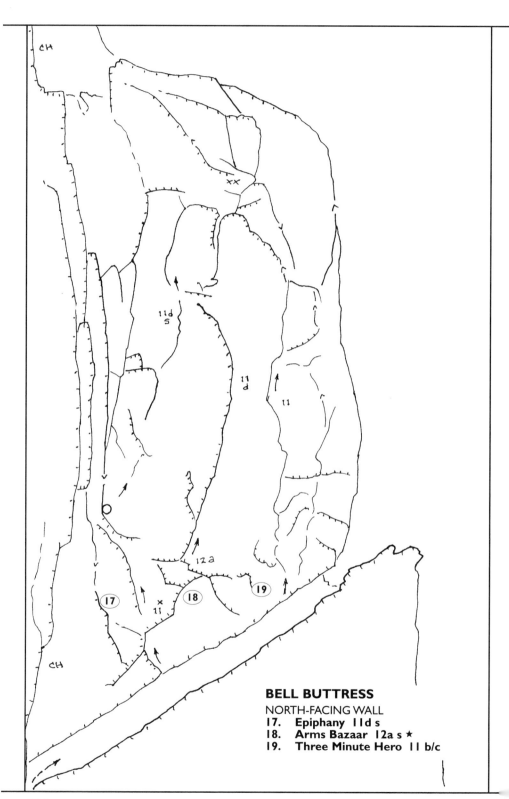

CH

XX

11d
s

11
d

11

O

12 a

17   ×   18   19
      11

CH

BELL BUTTRESS

NORTH-FACING WALL
17.   **Epiphany** 11d s
18.   **Arms Bazaar** 12a s ★
19.   **Three Minute Hero** 11 b/c

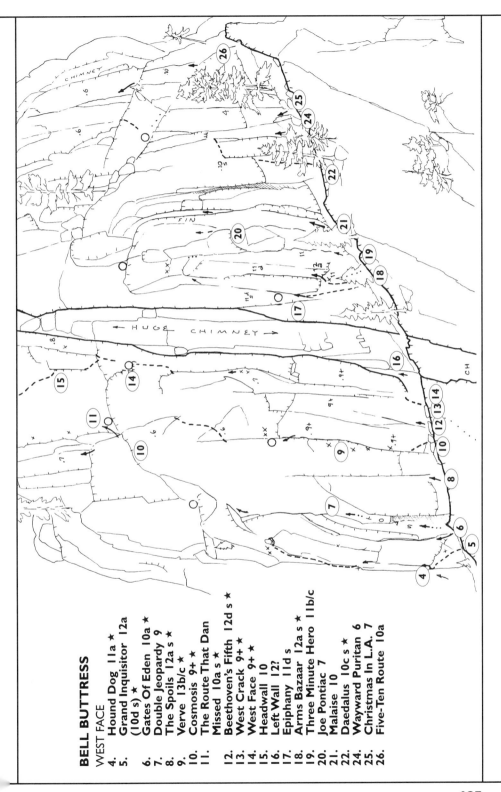

BELL BUTTRESS

WEST FACE

4. Hound Dog 11a ★
5. Grand Inquisitor 12a (10d s) ★
6. Gates Of Eden 10a ★
7. Double Jeopardy 9
8. The Spoils 12a s ★
9. Verve 13b/c ★
10. Cosmosis 9+ ★
11. The Route That Dan Missed 10a s ★
12. Beethoven's Fifth 12d s ★
13. West Crack 9+ ★
14. West Face 9+ ★
15. Headwall 10
16. Left Wall 12?
17. Epiphany 11d s
18. Arms Bazaar 12a s ★
19. Three Minute Hero 11b/c
20. Joe Pontiac 7
21. Malaise 10
22. Daedalus 10c s ★
24. Wayward Puritan 6
25. Christmas In L.A. 7
26. Five-Ten Route 10a

18. ARMS BAZAAR 12A S ★
FA: ALEC SHARP AND RICHARD CAREY, 1980.

Begin just right of *Epiphany*. Work up and left to a bolt, turn a roof, then follow cracks straight up the steep wall to a ledge.

19. THREE MINUTE HERO 11 B/C
FA: ALEC SHARP AND MARTIN TAYLOR, 1980.

Begin just right of *Arms Bazaar* and follow a flake and crack system to the same ledge.

20. JOE PONTIAC 7
FA: CHUCK FITCH, SOLO, 1980.

From the area of *Arms Bazaar*, pass beneath a large boulder and begin this route just right of a tree. Climb up over a bulge, then follow shallow corners to the same ledge as the preceding routes.

21. MALAISE 10
FA: JOHN KIRK, MURIEL AND ALEC SHARP, 1980.

This route begins with a small, left-facing corner at the bottom of a fin or narrow rib and finishes on the right side of the fin.

22. DAEDALUS 10C S ★
FA: ALEC SHARP AND DAN HARE, 1980.

A few yards right of the fin and right of a narrow chimney, climb a left-facing dihedral past a bulge, then make hairy moves out right to the crack of *Wrinkles*.

23. WRINKLES 9 S
FA: BRUCE SPOSI AND DAN HARE, 1979.

Begin from a ledge with a tree, not far above the stream. Climb a crack through a bulge, then move up and right to belay on the approach ramp. Climb the left of two cracks beginning with a right-facing dihedral and belay on a ledge with a big tree. Move the belay right, then follow another crack to the top of the buttress.

24. WAYWARD PURITAN 6
FA: ALEC SHARP, SOLO, 1980.

Beginning from the approach ramp, climb the crack system just right of *Wrinkles*. Two pitches.

25. CHRISTMAS IN L.A. 7
FA: CARL HARRISON AND AL TORRISI, 1982.

Begin about 50 feet right of the second pitch of *Wrinkles*, near two trees close to the wall. Undercling a flake, move up and right past a roof, then continue to a ledge. Climb a "fin" and the face above between two cracks.

26. FIVE-TEN ROUTE 10A

This route begins from a small ramp, up and left from the approach ledge where the wall bends around to face southwest. Climb a thin crack to a higher ramp and finish in the much easier crack just right of *Wayward Puritan*.

BELL BUTTRESS
22. Daedalus 10c s ★
27. Front Line 11b ★
28. Front Line Lefthand 11b ★
Bean Liquor Wall
34. Bean Bagger 11
35. Hambanger 10d ★

Bean Liquor Wall

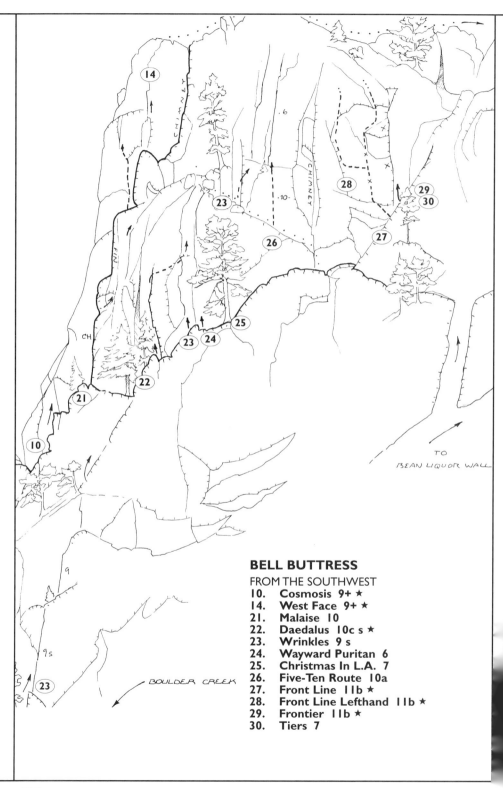

BELL BUTTRESS

FROM THE SOUTHWEST
10. **Cosmosis 9+ ★**
14. **West Face 9+ ★**
21. **Malaise 10**
22. **Daedalus 10c s ★**
23. **Wrinkles 9 s**
24. **Wayward Puritan 6**
25. **Christmas In L.A. 7**
26. **Five-Ten Route 10a**
27. **Front Line 11b ★**
28. **Front Line Lefthand 11b ★**
29. **Frontier 11b ★**
30. **Tiers 7**

BOULDER CREEK

TO
BEAN LIQUOR WALL

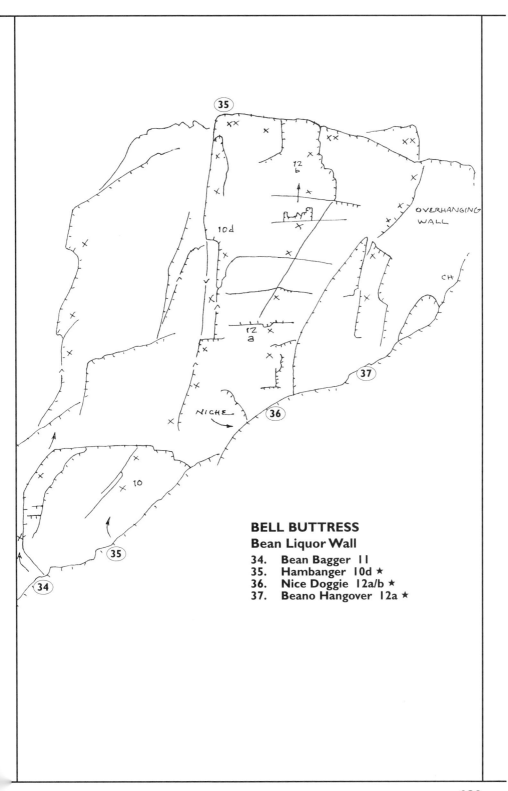

BELL BUTTRESS
Bean Liquor Wall

34. Bean Bagger 11
35. Hambanger 10d ★
36. Nice Doggie 12a/b ★
37. Beano Hangover 12a ★

189

The following routes are located high on the upper right side of Bell Buttress. Ford the creek about 150 feet west of the buttress (look for a cairn), then follow a trail up and left to the steep gully that runs along the wall. This area may also be reached from the south end of the approach ramp.

27. FRONT LINE 11B ★
FA: ALEC SHARP, 1980.
Above the south end of the approach ledge, a small but imposing buttress presses outward. A couple of bolts indicate this line up the center of the buttress.

28. FRONT LINE LEFTHAND 11B ★
FA: ALEC SHARP, CHRISTIAN GRIFFITH, JOHN ALLEN, 1981.
Climb past the first bolt on the preceding route, then traverse left to the arête and climb to the top.

29. FRONTIER 11B ★
FA: MARK TARRANT AND ANNE-MARIE BIERBAUM, 1986.
Climb the face along the right side of the buttress. Two bolts.

30. TIERS 7
FA: PAT AMENT AND TOM RUWITCH, 1970.
Climb the dihedral just right of the *Front Line* buttress.

31. DRY SOBS 10
FA: AL TORRISI AND ALAN BOWMAN, c. 1980.
A lieback somewhere to the right of *Tiers*.

32. THE WEB 10
FA: DAN HARE AND JOEL SCHIAVONE, 1982.
Climb the left of some short dihedrals to the right of *Tiers*. This route may be the same as the following.

33. EAT THE RICH 10
FA: CARL HARRISON AND AL TORRISI, 1982.
The Bolshevik Revolution of '82. Begin at a large tree about 100 feet up and right from *Tiers*. Face climb into a steep, shallow, right-leaning dihedral system and follow it to a roof. Traverse left and continue to the top.

Bean Liquor Wall

Bean Liquor? The following routes ascend a steep, south-facing wall at the top of the talus gully that climbs along the right side of Bell Buttress. Routes by Rick Leitner.

34. BEAN BAGGER 11
Begin from a small platform in the gully below where it narrows to a chasm. Turn a bulge at a bolt and climb more easily to the bottom right side of a left-facing dihedral. Follow bolts along the right side of its arête.

35. HAMBANGER 10D ★
Begin just right of the preceding route. Climb a short wall with two bolts, then step right on a ledge and climb the right side of a left-facing dihedral. Nine bolts to a two-bolt anchor.

36. NICE DOGGIE 12A/B ★
Begin up in the chasm about 40 feet right of the preceding route. Stem off a block and follow bolts up the middle of the wall. Seven bolts to a two-bolt anchor.

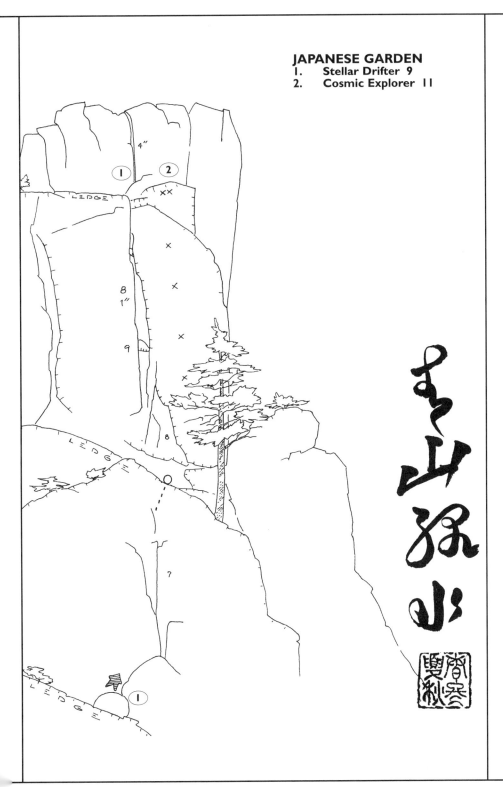

JAPANESE GARDEN
1. **Stellar Drifter** 9
2. **Cosmic Explorer** 11

37. BEANO HANGOVER 12A ★

Begin farther up in the chasm, just before it becomes a steep chimney. Climb a flake followed by a bulging wall. Five bolts to a two-bolt anchor.

JAPANESE GARDEN

This crag is located about 100 yards southwest of Bell Buttress. It is easily seen up on the right as one drives down the canyon. To reach the crag, ford the stream and scramble up brushy talus to the bottom of the west face. To descend from the summit, fashion a rappel on the southeast side or down-climb and rappel a gully on the northwest side.

1. STELLAR DRIFTER 9

FA: DAN HARF AND CHRIS WOOD, 1979.

This route climbs a crack/chimney in the upper west face. From the talus, scramble up to the left below a large Douglas fir tree that is visible from the road. Two pitches.

2. COSMIC EXPLORER 11

FA: DON DEBLIEUX AND PAUL LEMBECK, 1992.

Climb the wall 15 feet right of the second pitch of *Stellar Drifter*. Four bolts to a two-bolt anchor.

AVALON

Avalon is the large, complex crag between Japanese Garden and Vampire Rock, on the south side of the road. Avalon is about 500 feet high and is divided into three tiers by two big ledge systems that run across the north and west sides. Most of the known routes are located on the second tier. The upper tier culminates in an isolated summit with a spectacular view.

Approach: Park at a narrow pull-out just beyond the Practice Rock (8.2 miles), ford the stream, and hike up talus along the west side of the buttress. The gully along the east side is steep and brushy. Look for a Tyrolean traverse across the stream during high water.

1. SPARE RIB 10

FA: BRUCE SPOSI AND DAN HARE, 1977.

This is the only known route on the lower tier. Begin beneath a long roof at the bottom of a north-facing, hanging slab. Climb through the roof at an A-shaped break and continue up a crack to a ledge. Move left and climb a six-inch crack through a second overhang.

2. AH YA PUNTER 11

FA: DON DEBLIEUX AND PAUL LEMBECK, 1993.

Hike up the talus gully along the west side of the crag and gain the big ledge between the first and second tiers, then walk to its east end. Begin just left of a large roof. Climb up into a left-facing dihedral and through a difficult slot (crux), then move left and follow moderate cracks to a ledge with a tree.

3. EARTH ANGEL 12D ★

FA: BOB HORAN BELAYED BY PAT HORAN, 1996.

Begin a short way right of the preceding route. Climb a steep wall past three bolts, pull over a big roof, then climb just right of an arête past six more bolts to a two-bolt anchor. Lower off.

Three Walls

The following routes lie on three adjacent walls at the west side of the middle tier. The walls are set at right angles to each other and recall the foreboding battlements of some ancient castle. The left wall faces north and begins from a raised area behind a giant boulder. The middle wall faces

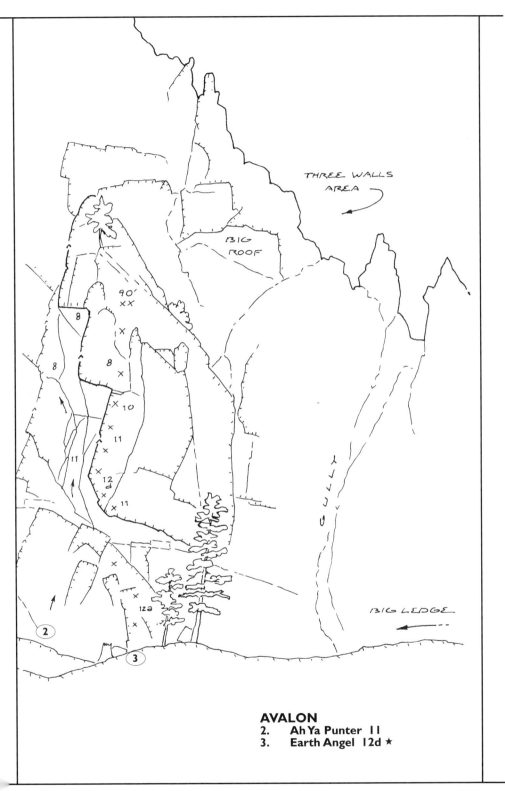

THREE WALLS AREA →

BIG ROOF

90'
XX

8

8   8 ×

× 10

11   ×
11

× 12
d

× 11

GULLY

×

2

×

12a

×

3

BIG LEDGE
←

AVALON
2.   **Ah Ya Punter 11**
3.   **Earth Angel 12d ★**

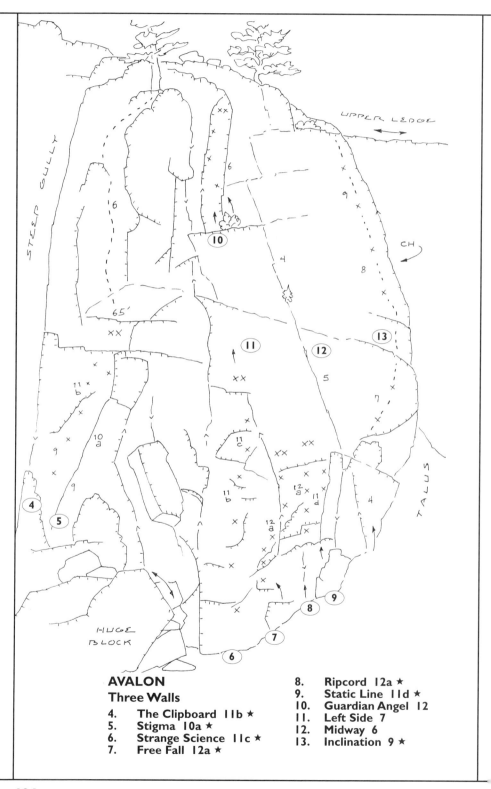

AVALON
Three Walls

4. **The Clipboard** 11b ★
5. **Stigma** 10a ★
6. **Strange Science** 11c ★
7. **Free Fall** 12a ★
8. **Ripcord** 12a ★
9. **Static Line** 11d ★
10. **Guardian Angel** 12
11. **Left Side** 7
12. **Midway** 6
13. **Inclination** 9 ★

west and has a significant overhang at lower left. The upper part of the wall is a steep slab. The right wall is just right of a chimney and faces north. This area is located about 500 feet up along the west side of the crag, just below the big upper ledge. All routes by Richard Rossiter and Bob Horan, 1996, unless otherwise noted.

4.   THE CLIPBOARD   11B ★
FA: RICHARD ROSSITER AND GAIL EFFRON.
Begin at the left corner of the left of the Three Walls. Follow five bolts up and right along a seam and gain a two-bolt anchor above a flat ledge.

5.   STIGMA   10A ★
FA: ROSSITER AND EFFRON.
Climb a finger crack that angles up and right across the wall. A bolt protects the final moves along a large detached flake. RPs to a #2.5 Friend.

6.   STRANGE SCIENCE   11C ★
Begin this beautiful route near the low point of the large scooped-out area just down and right from the Left Wall. Follow bolts up the steep concave wall left of *Free Fall*. Five bolts to a two-bolt anchor. Lower off or continue up the slab to *Guardian Angel*.

7.   FREE FALL   12A ★
Start beneath a big roof, just up and right from the low point. Climb a shallow finger crack along the left side of an overhanging arête, then crank right to a jug and continue more easily to the big slab. Six bolts to a two-bolt anchor.

8.   RIPCORD   12A ★
Battle up the west-facing overhang just right of *Free Fall*. Five bolts to a two-bolt anchor (incomplete at time of writing).

9.   STATIC LINE   11D ★
Follow a crack up the right side of the overhang. Gear plus two bolts at the crux (incomplete).

10.   GUARDIAN ANGEL   12
This route climbs the overhanging left arête of a monolithic pillar at the top of the big slab. It may be approached from any of the routes on the Middle Wall. Five bolts to a two-bolt anchor. Incomplete at time of writing.

11.   LEFT SIDE   7
FA: ROSSITER, SOLO.
Begin just right of the big overhang. Climb the right side of a short arête and gain the big slab, then traverse straight left to the bolt anchor at the top of Free Fall. Climb the left side of the slab to the bottom of *Guardian Angel*, and finish in the dihedral along the right side of the pillar.

12.   MIDWAY   6
FA: ROSSITER, SOLO.
Begin as for the preceding route, but continue up a crack system in the middle of the slab. Belay from a pine on the big upper ledge and walk off to the southwest.

13.   INCLINATION   9 ★
FA: ROSSITER, SOLO.
Gain the bottom of the slab as for the preceding routes, then angle up and right and follow a few bolts along the right side of the slab (bolts not placed at time of writing).

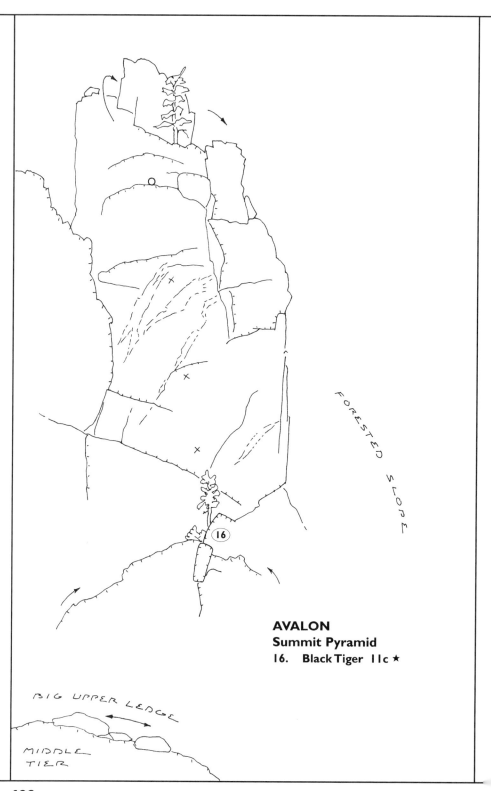

FORESTED SLOPE

16

AVALON
Summit Pyramid
16.   Black Tiger 11c ★

BIG UPPER LEDGE

MIDDLE
TIER

14. Tomb Of Sorrows 10c
FA: R. ROSSITER, TR, 1996.

Begin about 10 feet back in the chimney, at a black streak at right from the big slab. Follow bolts up the steep wall to the walk-off ledge and belay from a big Douglas fir. Fixed gear (incomplete at time of writing).

15. Isle Of The Dead 10a
FA: R. ROSSITER, TR, 1996.

This route ascends the blunt arête a short way right of the big chimney. Fixed gear (incomplete at time of writing).

Summit Pyramid

The upper tier of Avalon culminates in an isolated summit with a steep east face and a small clean buttress on the west. Scramble off to the south and west.

16. Black Tiger 11c ★
FA: CHRIS BRISLAWN AND JIM SWENSON, 1989.

This route ascends the middle of the smooth, clean buttress at the west side of the upper tier. Climb the steep slab past three bolts, then run it out to the top of the buttress. Small Friends or TCUs can be used above the third bolt. Belay from cracks near the top. Walk off to the west.

WATERMARK

Watermark is a smaller formation several hundred feet west of Avalon, just above the stream. The top of the buttress forms a quaint little pinnacle that is of limited interest to climbers, but the lower part forms a series of arêtes and slabs with a couple of interesting routes. To approach, ford the stream and walk directly up to the bottom of the formation. The routes top out on a big bench. To return to the bottom, hike down around the west side. It is also easy to traverse east to Avalon from the bench. Routes by Richard Rossiter, free soloed and retro-bolted.

1. Dark Tower 6
Climb the arête on the left-most buttress passing a small pine tree halfway up. Gear only.

2. The Memory Of Trees 9 ★
A song by Enya. Begin at the lower right side of the formation beneath a clean arête with two small roofs. Climb the arête turning the first roof on the left and second roof on the right. Belay from a large tree at the top and walk off. Bring QDs for five bolts plus stoppers and a few Friends up to #2.5. 120 feet.

3. Lothlorien 8 ★
Climb the narrow slab at the right side of the formation and belay from a tree at the top. Four bolts, no gear. 90 feet.

AVALON
3. Earth Angel 12d ★
SUMMIT PYRAMID
16. Black Tiger 11c ★
WATERMARK
1. Dark Tower 6
2. The Memory Of Trees 9 ★
3. Lothlorien 8 ★

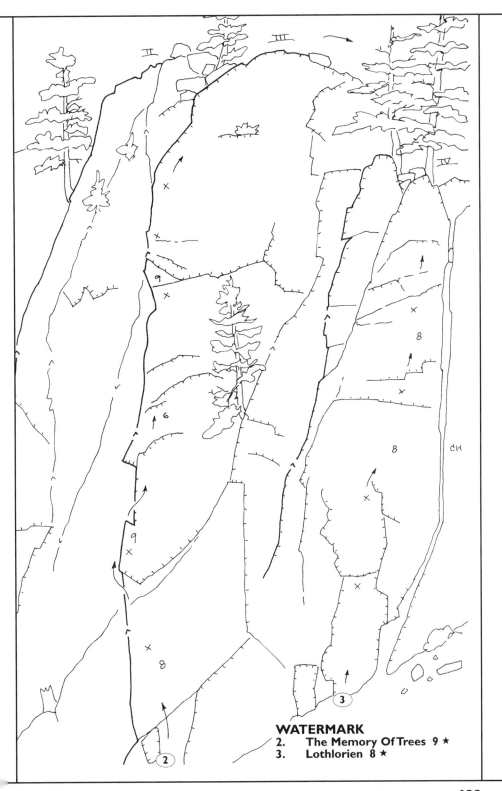

WATERMARK
2. The Memory Of Trees 9 ★
3. Lothlorien 8 ★

VAMPIRE ROCK

Vampire Rock is the large, sullen buttress at 8.4 miles and on the south side of the canyon. It is the left and larger of two similar buttresses and features a broad north face with many routes both old and new. A good path runs along the base of the wall and continues across to the north face of Black Widow Slab, on the right. Park at a pull-out about 200 yards west of Vampire Rock, then walk back along the stream and ford it below the west corner of the buttress. A Tyrolean traverse may be in place during high water. To descend from the summit, walk off to the south, then down along either side of the buttress. One may lower off and/or rappel from bolt anchors on the newer routes.

1.   CLIMB EYE KNIGHT 12c ★
FA: BOB HORAN, CHULE LEE, JOHN BALDWIN, 1996.

On the east face of Vampire rock, just left and up from the northeast corner, locate a large right-facing dihedral with bolts leading to a "blobular wall." P1. Climb the dihedral and belay from bolts. P2. Climb an obvious crack and continue up a face with bolts (crux and best pitch). P3. Climb the yellow headwall with a small overhang followed by good face climbing—a spectacular pitch, all bolts.

2.   VELVET OVERHANG 12 (PROJECT)
TR: BOB HORAN 1996.

This route ascends the steep white face and overhangs at the left side of the north face. Bolts lead to a bolt anchor with rings above the roofs. A second pitch goes up and slightly right to a prominent headwall just below the large shelf of the third pitch of *Climb Eye Knight*.

3.   RED SONJA 7
FA: DAVID ALLEN AND SUZ WAKEFIELD, 1978.

This route is located on the left side of the rock, supposedly left of *B.C.* Climb a left-leaning dihedral, then step left and follow a right-facing corner to a stance below an overhang. Climb up and right past the roof, then continue in a trough.

4.   B.C. 8
FA: BOB CULP AND MAC MAGARY, 1962.

This route is thought to ascend the face just right of the white overhangs, however, it may be farther right as indicated by an old bolt anchor on *Heart Of The Narrows*.

5.   TRANSYLVERLINA 12B ★
FA: BOB HORAN AND TOM MURPHY, 1996. RACK: 8 QDS.

Identify a line of bolts up the blunt arête just left of a prominent left-leaning, right-facing dihedral. P1. Start up face, then swing around to right side of arête and continue to anchor (10b/c, eight bolts). P2. Go up and right over roof, then up a thin face to a ledge with an anchor (12b, 11 bolts). P3. Go up and slightly right and past a bulge/roof to a wavy face, then up past ledges to arête that leads to a belay (12a, nine bolts). P4. Climb out a large roof and gain a bolt belay (12b/c, four bolts). Rappel or walk off.

6.   HEART OF THE NARROWS 12c ★
FA: BOB HORAN, RICHARD ROSSITER, CHULE LEE, 1996. RACK: 6 QDS.

This varied route ascends the middle of the north face in four pitches. Begin at the bottom of a prominent left-leaning, right-facing dihedral. P1. Start up the dihedral, then brake right and follow bolts up through a roof (10a). Belay at an anchor with two old bolts. P2. Move up and right, then climb a very steep wall with orange lichen (12b). Belay at two bolts. P3. Climb straight up to a long diagonal ramp and belay at two bolts (7). P4. Scramble up and right along the ramp and climb the overhanging arête (crux) just right of the last pitch of *The Vampire*.

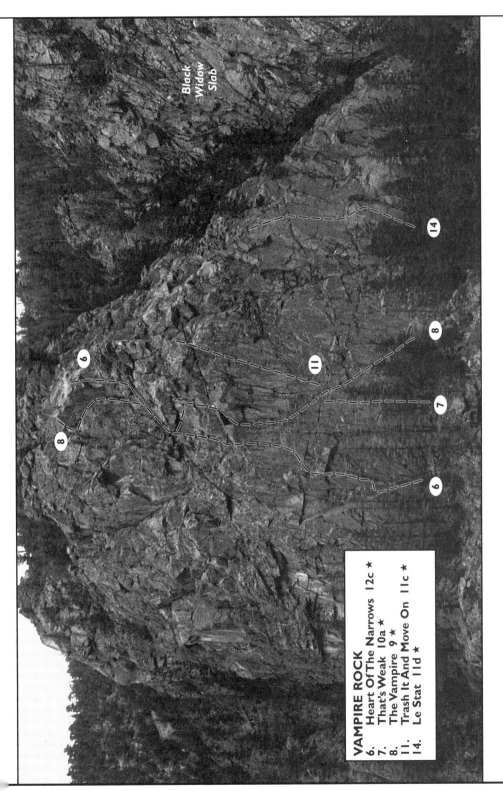

Black
Widow
Slab

VAMPIRE ROCK
6. Heart Of The Narrows 12c ★
7. That's Weak 10a ★
8. The Vampire 9 ★
11. Trash It And Move On 11c ★
14. Le Stat 11d ★

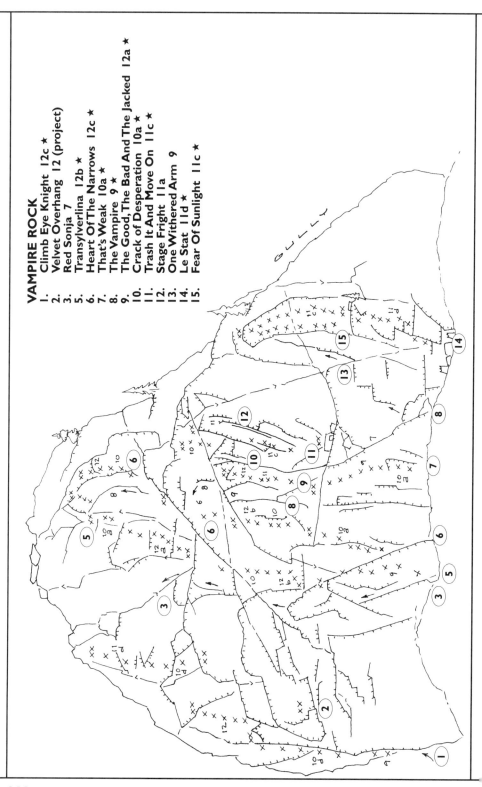

VAMPIRE ROCK
1. Climb Eye Knight 12c ★
2. Velvet Overhang 12 (project)
3. Red Sonja 7
5. Transylverlina 12b ★
6. Heart Of The Narrows 12c ★
7. That's Weak 10a ★
8. The Vampire 9 ★
9. The Good, The Bad And The Jacked 12a ★
10. Crack of Desperation 10a ★
11. Trash It And Move On 11c ★
12. Stage Fright 11a
13. One Withered Arm 9
14. Le Stat 11d ★
15. Fear Of Sunlight 11c ★

VAMPIRE ROCK
6. Heart Of The Narrows 12c ★
7. That's Weak 10a ★
8. The Vampire 9 ★
9. The Good, The Bad And The Jacked 12a ★
10. Crack of Desperation 10a ★
11. Trash It And Move On 11c ★
12. Stage Fright 11a
13. One Withered Arm 9

7. THAT'S WEAK 10A ★
FA: Steve Sangdahl and John Baldwin, 1996.

Begin near the center of the north face, about 25 feet right of a dirty groove. Follow eight bolts up the wall (10a) and belay from a two-bolt anchor below the second pitch of *The Vampire*.

8. THE VAMPIRE 9 ★
FA: Layton Kor and Warren Blesser, 1961. FFA: Bob Culp and Bob Beall, 1971.

1. Climb a left-leaning crack near the middle of the north face or begin with *That's Weak* a short way to the left. P2. Climb a flared, right-facing dihedral through a roof (crux) and belay on a slab. P3. Start up and right toward a roof, then traverse about 30 feet left to a grassy ramp with a two-bolt anchor. P4. Scramble about 75 feet up and right along the ramp, then climb a steep, left-arching dihedral to the top of the wall (8).

9. THE GOOD, THE BAD AND THE JACKED 12A ★
FA: Steve Sangdahl, Dave Salisbury, John Baldwin, 1996.

From the anchor atop *That's Weak*, climb straight up the steep face to a two-bolt anchor. Seven bolts.

10. CRACK OF DESPERATION 10A ★
FA: Layton Kor and Herb Swedlund, 1963.

Climb the original first pitch of *The Vampire* or *That's Weak*. Follow an obvious wide crack into a right-facing dihedral, through a roof, and gain a narrow ledge (optional belay). Step left and join *The Vampire* or traverse right to a two-bolt anchor above *Trash It* and rappel 85 feet to a ledge with a two-bolt anchor, then rappel 70 feet to the ground.

11. TRASH IT AND MOVE ON 11C ★
FA: Sangdahl and Baldwin, 1996.

Climb *That's Weak*, then traverse right along a ledge and belay from bolts beneath *Stage Fright*. Start up and left, then follow bolts and cracks up and right to a ledge. Climb up and around the right side of a bulge and gain a three-bolt anchor. Nine bolts. Bring a #1, #1.5, and #2 Friends. 90 feet.

12. STAGE FRIGHT 11A
FA: Mason Frischette, 1977.

Begin as for the preceding routes. Climb right-angling, parallel cracks to the right of *Trash It* and gain a ledge at 85 feet. Lower off from a two-bolt anchor or continue up to a big grassy ledge and exit right.

13. ONE WITHERED ARM 9
FA: Dudley Chelton and Bob Culp, 1972.

Climb the left-facing dihedral just left of the big slab of *Le Stat*.

14. LE STAT 11D ★
FA: Bob Horan and John Baldwin, 1996.

This fine route ascends the steep slab at the right side of the north face. Step off a block and follow nine bolts up and right to a bolt belay on a good ledge. Continue up the center of the slab past another nine bolts to a two-bolt anchor. Lower off and rappel or walk off to the right.

15. FEAR OF SUNLIGHT 11C ★
FA: Chris Archer, 1996.

Climb the left side of the upper slab past six bolts, then veer right and finish with *Le Stat*. Crux is near the top.

VAMPIRE ICE CLIMBS

During the winter of 1997, water was diverted down the very steep north face of Vampire Rock as well as the northeast face of Black Widow Slab. Three sensational routes have been climbed on Vampire.

1. LEFT RUNNEL WI6 M5
FA: HELGI CHRISTIANSON.

Begin at the bottom of a large left-leaning, right-facing ramp/dihedral as for *Heart Of The Narrows*. P1. Climb up and left to a bolt anchor on *Transylverlina* (WI3). P2. Climb to the very top of the ramp, then straight up a very thin and difficult runnel, passing the left end of a roof, and gain a ledge on what is likely the old route *B.C.*

2. NOSFERATU WI5-
FA: JAMES CASTRO, LESLIE COON, 1997.

Begin as for the preceding route and belay at the bolts on *Transylverlina*. Move right across the gully and climb a substantial runnel (by comparison) and belay on a ledge with a two-bolt anchor as for *Transylverlina* (WI4+). A long second pitch leads to the top of the rock (WI5-) and can be done as two pitches. Route originally done as four pitches.

3. LA BELLE MORTE WI5+
FA: JACK ROBERTS AND BRETT RUCKMAN, 1997.

Begin toward the right side of the north face, but up and left from a shallow cave (near the original start to *The Vampire*). Climb a left-angling crack/corner to a long ledge system where one could belay from the bolt anchor on *Trash It*. Continue up a prominent hanging icicle to a ledge on *Trash It And Move On* (WI5+). A second pitch goes right or left and up a series of steep steps, the last being the longest and most difficult (WI4+).

BLACK WIDOW SLAB

Black Widow Slab is located just west of Vampire Rock, on the south side of Boulder Creek. The broad northeast face has only one known route, which may not have been climbed since its first ascent. The rock is well-lichened and most cracks are filled with moss and bushes. The steep north face, however, is cleaner and the rock is good. Approach as for Vampire Rock. Ford the creek below either side of the buttress, then scramble up talus to a path that runs along the bottom of the north face.

1. LEFT SIDE 8
FA: LAYTON KOR AND WARREN BLESSER, 1961.

Begin about 50 feet up and left from *Dracula* at the northeast corner of the buttress, and scramble 15 feet up to a small ledge with a dead tree. Follow a shallow, mossy corner up and left to some roofs and go right at a bolt or fixed pin. Continue up steep rock to the crest of the buttress and belay. Two more pitches lead to the summit of Black Widow Slab.

2. DRACULA 12B ★
FA: BOB HORAN AND PAT HORAN, 1996.

This route climbs an overhanging arête at the northeast corner of the buttress. Climb a slab with four bolts, then work up and right across a yellow-streaked overhang and gain the arête at right (crux). Climb straight up to a two-bolt anchor and lower off. Ten bolts.

3. SPECTER 10D
FA: DAN HARE AND JOEL SCHIAVONE, 1982. SR.

Begin to the right of a chimney system, about 40 feet right of *Dracula*. Jam a hand crack through the middle of a six-foot roof and belay in an alcove. Climb an out-leaning, left-facing corner and finish up the arête on the right.

BLACK WIDOW SLAB
2.   Dracula 12b ★
5.   Bong Session 10a
6.   Pipe Dreams 12c ★
10. Right Side 8

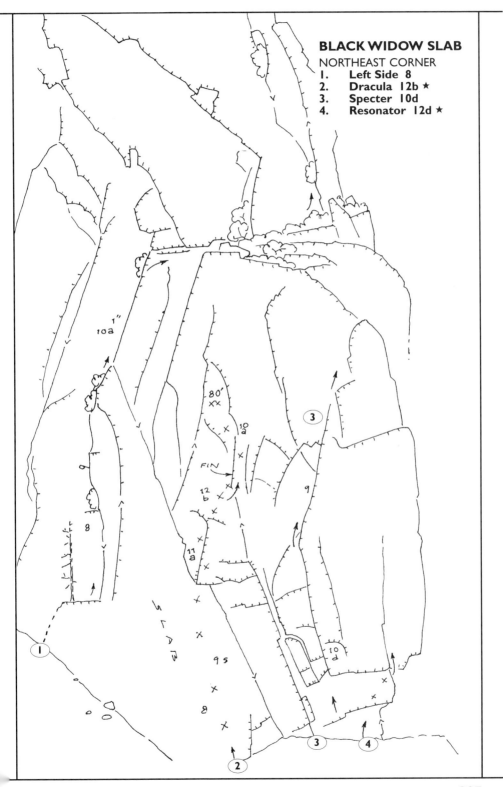

BLACK WIDOW SLAB
NORTHEAST CORNER
1. **Left Side** 8
2. **Dracula** 12b ★
3. **Specter** 10d
4. **Resonator** 12d ★

BLACK WIDOW SLAB
North Face

1. Left Side 8
2. Dracula 12b ★
3. Specter 10d
4. Resonator 12d ★
5. Bong Session 10a
6. Pipe Dreams 12c ★
7. Fuck You 11c
8. Bands Of Gold 11d ★
9. Center 8
10. Right Side 9
11. Smoke Down 10d

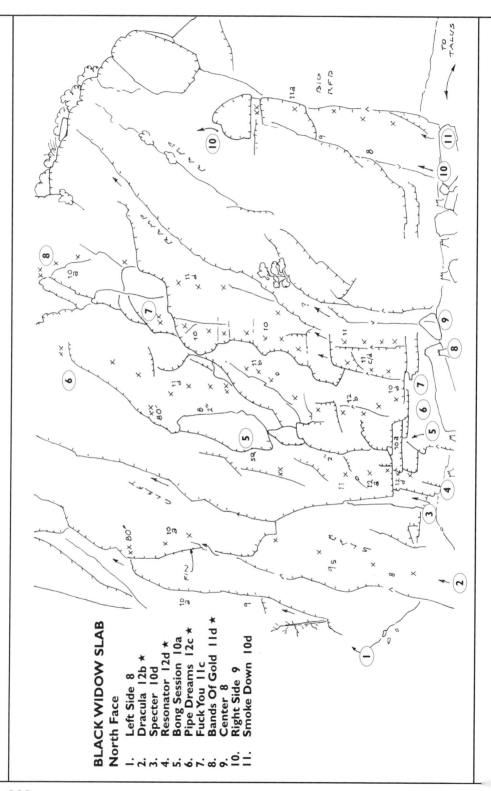

4.   RESONATOR 12D ★
FA: STEVE SANGDAHL, BOB HORAN, DAVE SALISBURY, CHIP RUCKGABER, JOHN BALDWIN (TR). FIRST LEAD: SANGDAHL, 1997.

Begin at the northeast corner of the buttress. Follow bolts up and right through a stepped roof, then crank up and left. Reach a two-bolt anchor at 50 feet. Six bolts.

5.   BONG SESSION 10A

Begin just around to the right from *Resonator*. Work up and left through a roof and follow a well-formed crack along the left edge of the north face. The crack varies from hands to offwidth to squeeze. About halfway up, one may branch right in a hand crack (8).

6.   PIPE DREAMS 12C ★
FA: BALDWIN, HORAN, SANGDAHL, 1996.

Begin about 20 feet right of *Resonator*. This is the left of two routes that begin from a large, flat boulder. Pull over a roof (10d) and follow bolts up a blunt arête on the left. Veer right past four bolts, pull onto a ramp, and belay at a two-bolt anchor (nine bolts in all). A second pitch goes up the headwall (12a, five bolts). Route can be done in one pitch.

7.   FUCK YOU 11C
FA: SANGDAHL, 1996.

Begin from the big boulder, a few feet right of the preceding route. Stick-clip the first bolt, then pull over the roof and gain a shelf about 40 feet up. Follow bolts up the arête above and reach a stance with a two-bolt anchor. Eleven bolts.

8.   BANDS OF GOLD 11D ★
FA: HORAN AND BALDWIN, 1996.

A few feet right of the preceding route a sharp arête forms the left margin of an open–book dihedral. Follow four bolts along the right side of the arête and gain the shelf mentioned in the previous route. Start up and right along a broken ramp, then follow bolts and cracks up the steep wall above to a bolt anchor. Twelve bolts.

9.   CENTER 8
FA: LAYTON KOR AND RAY NORTHCUTT, 1961.

This route is thought to begin with the open-book dihedral just right of *Bands Of Gold*. Climb the dihedral and gain a grassy ledge about 90 feet up. Two more long pitches up the spine of the buttress lead to the summit of Black Widow Slab. Scramble off to the southeast.

10.   RIGHT SIDE 9
FA: LAYTON KOR AND RAY NORTHCUTT, 1961.

Begin near a large tree at the base (bearing in mind that this description dates back 36 years). Climb the steep wall up and slightly right to a grassy ledge easily seen from the road. Follow the line of least resistance to the top of the buttress. The exact line of this route is not known, but it likely begins with the right-facing, right-leaning dihedral just left of *Smoke Down*.

11.   SMOKE DOWN 10D
FA: SANGDAHL AND BALDWIN, 1996.

Begin at a blocky arête toward the right side of the north face and near a small forked tree. Follow four bolts up the arête and gain a two-bolt anchor at about 60 feet.

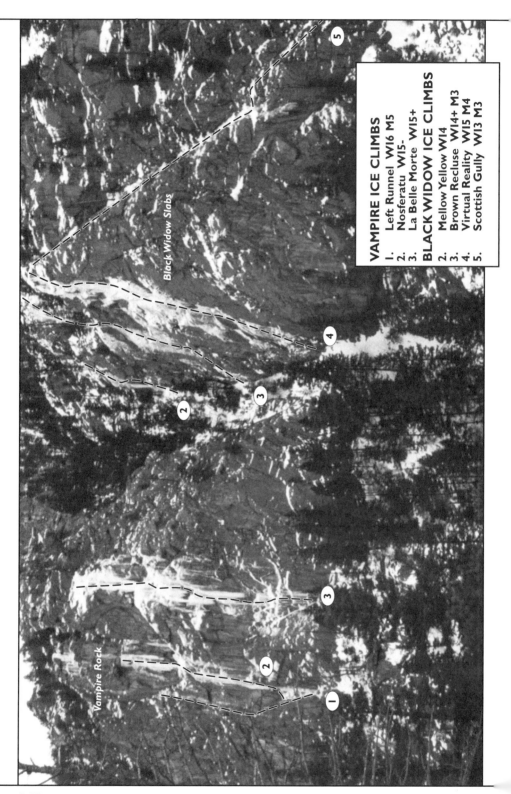

VAMPIRE ICE CLIMBS
1. Left Runnel WI6 M5
2. Nosferatu WI5-
3. La Belle Morte WI5+

BLACK WIDOW ICE CLIMBS
2. Mellow Yellow WI4
3. Brown Recluse WI4+ M3
4. Virtual Reality WI5 M4
5. Scottish Gully WI3 M3

Black Widow Slabs

Vampire Rock

BLACK WIDOW ICE CLIMBS

During the winter of 1997, water was diverted down the steep north face of Vampire Rock as well as the northeast face of Black Widow Slab. Five distinct routes have been climbed on Black Widow. All routes except *Scottish Gully* (aka *Hector Direct*) are located on the steep slab of the northeast face. To escape from the top, walk off to the east and down the gully beneath the northeast face or rappel from fixed anchors along *Scottish Gully* (two x 150 feet or four x 75 feet).

1.   MEOW MIX WI3
FA: BOB HORAN, ET AL.

Climb the farthest left formation at the top of the gully between Vampire Rock and Black Widow Slab.

2.   MELLOW YELLOW WI4
FA: JAMES CASTRO AND LESLIE COON, 1997.

Climb a yellowish column of ice from the upper part of the gully.

3.   BROWN RECLUSE WI4+ M3
FA: JAMES CASTRO AND LESLIE COON.

Begin about halfway up the gully beneath the northeast face. P1. Climb up and right along a groove and belay from a #3 Camalot (M3). P2. Climb a steep slab with no pro, pass through a narrow chute, and belay from a large dead tree (WI4+). These two pitches can be done as one (160 feet). P3. Climb a substantial flow to the top (WI4-).

3A. WINKELMAN WI5 M5

This is the farthest left of two variations to *Brown Recluse* originated by Eric Winkelman. Look for a dihedral with discontinuous ice.

3B. SECOND LEG WI4+

This variation ascends a left-facing dihedral/gully between *Winkelman* and the regular first pitch.

3C. VIRTUAL RECLUSE WI5 M3
FA: CARL PLUIM AND JERRY SCRITCHFIELD, 1997.

Climb the ramp on *Brown Recluse* and continue up and right into the upper part of *Virtual Reality*. Belay in a cave from mid-range cams. Finish as for *Virtual Reality*.

4.   VIRTUAL REALITY WI5 M4
FA: JAMES CASTRO AND LESLIE COON, 1997.

Begin a short way up the gully beneath the northeast face. P1. Climb thin verglas to a ledge with a small tree and a bolt (M5, bring two #3 Camalots). P2. Climb up and slightly right and finish with a vertical pillar (WI5-). One may also finish in a steep chimney on the left (WI4-).

5.   SCOTTISH GULLY WI3 M3
FA: UNKNOWN.

Also known as *Hector Direct*, this route ascends the long, narrow gully that runs up and left along the right side of the north face. Fixed anchors exist at 75-foot intervals along this route. Begin at the far right side of the north face. Climb a narrow ramp (M4) up and left to gain entrance to the hanging gully, which continues as good moderate ice for 250 feet.

5A. THE KERBASH WI5
FA: HELGI CHRISTIANSON, 1997.

Climb a vertical pillar into the bottom of the Scottish Gully.

SLEEPING BEAUTY

Sleeping Beauty is the large northeast-facing wall to the west of Black Widow Slab and on the same side of the canyon. Its gloomy appearance and vegetated cracks have kept exploration to a minimum. The rock, however, is excellent, and at least five routes have been established. Park at a pullout on the south, across from the Boulderado (8.6 miles). Ford the stream and hike up brushy talus to the bottom of the wall, or traverse up and right from the base of Black Widow Slab. The best approach is to park below Easter Rock (9.0 miles), ford the stream, then follow a faint trail through open forest to the top of the wall and rappel to the base. Look for cairns. To descend from the top of the wall, hike back down the west slope or rappel the northeast face.

1.   AERIAL BOUNDARIES 12B ★
FA: RICHARD ROSSITER, MORRIS (MOE) HERSHOFF, LEAH MACALUSO, 1998. REDPOINT: HERSHOFF.

Begin from a ledge at the far left side of the wall. Climb moderate rock to small roof that is passed with a very difficult move, then continue straight up the rounded arête to a sloping shelf (130 feet). The route is mostly 9 in difficulty and the crux can be aided (10a A0).

2.   SLEEPING BEAUTY 10 S
FA: DAN HARE AND SCOTT WOODRUFF, 1983.

Begin from the left end of a long ledge system at the upper left side of the rock. Pull over a roof at a black knob and follow thin cracks to a bulge, then go right to a crack and gain a ledge. Follow a vegetated crack for about 40 feet, go right at a flake and up to another flake (9+ s), then continue up the slab to the top of the wall.

3.   THE AWAKENING 11B ★
FA: ROSSITER, MACALUSO, HERSHOFF, 1998

Begin to the right of *Sleeping Beauty* and to the right of a tree. Turn a small roof and continue up steep rock to a sloping ledge. Climb through a blocky area straight up the wall to a sloping shelf (11b, 150 feet). Scramble 30 feet to the top of the wall or rappel.

4.   CRACK OF DAWN 10C ★
FA: RICHARD ROSSITER AND SERENA BENSON, DAN HARE. 1998.

Begin about 50 feet right of *The Awakening* and to the right of a large pine. **P1**: Climb a hand crack that soon goes wide and continues to the right end of a perfect ledge with a V-shaped pine tree. The crux is a roof about halfway up (10c, 90 feet). Double gear from one to four inches. **P2**: From the ledge, friction up a slab to the top of the wall and belay from a tree (9, 85 feet).

5.   THE HEX 9
FA: DAN HARE AND JOEL SCHIAVONE, 1984.

Begin at a tree about 40 feet right of *Crack of Dawn*. **P1**: Climb a mossy crack system and belay beneath a prominent left-facing dihedral. **P2**: Follow the dihedral up and left, turn a roof, and continue to the top of the wall.

THE BEER CAN

This is the square-cut buttress at the north end of Sleeping Beauty, across the stream from The Boulderado. Ford the stream and scramble up to the base. To descend from the routes, lower off or rappel 90 feet from a three-bolt anchor.

1.   BEER BELLY 9+
FA: UNKNOWN.

Climb a wide crack along the left edge of the east face. Gear needed.

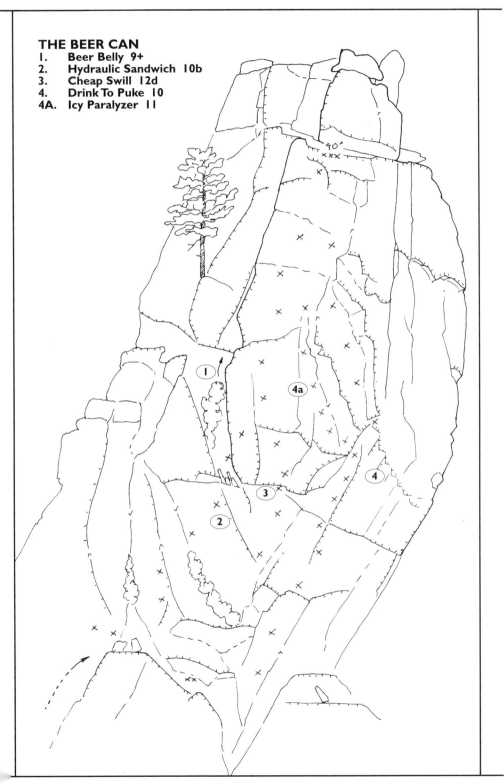

THE BEER CAN
1. Beer Belly 9+
2. Hydraulic Sandwich 10b
3. Cheap Swill 12d
4. Drink To Puke 10
4A. Icy Paralyzer 11

2. HYDRAULIC SANDWICH 10B
FA: Sangdahl and Baldwin, 1996.

Begin from the left of two belay stations with two-bolt anchors at the bottom of the buttress. Follow bolts up left side of east face. Beware of loose blocks at roof above fourth bolt. Twelve bolts.

3. CHEAP SWILL 12D (HANGERS REMOVED)
FA: Sangdahl and Baldwin, 1996.

This climb has a large, loose flake at the main roof. Hangers have been removed.

4. DRINK TO PUKE 10
FA: Sangdahl, Baldwin, Tom Englebach, Dave Salisbury, 1996.

Begin from the right of two belay stations with two-bolt anchors. Follow a line of bolts up and right around the right end of the big roof, then up and left to the top. 14 bolts.

4A. ICY PARALYZER 11
FA: Sangdahl and Baldwin, 1997.

Climb to the eighth bolt on *Drink To Puke*, then pull left through the roof and up the arête to rejoin the original line.

Bob Horan on *Heart of the Narrows*. Photo by Richard Rossiter.

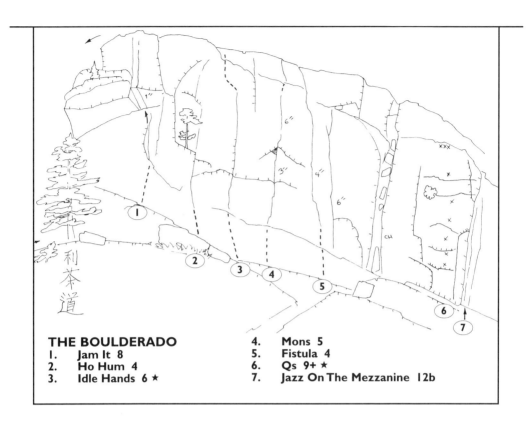

THE BOULDERADO

1. Jam It 8
2. Ho Hum 4
3. Idle Hands 6 ★
4. Mons 5
5. Fistula 4
6. Qs 9+ ★
7. Jazz On The Mezzanine 12b

ANIMAL WORLD & BEYOND

The following crags are located along the north side of the canyon beginning with Animal World (8.6 miles) at the top of The Narrows and ending with Nip and Tuck (10.5 miles). All formations are on the north side of the canyon with the exception of High Energy Crag (9.1 miles).

THE BOULDERADO

About 8.6 miles up the canyon and on the south side of the highway is an auto pull-out utilized to access Vampire Rock, Black Widow Slab, and Animal World. Directly across the road from this pull-out is a low, clean wall called The Boulderado. The main wall faces south and yields several excellent beginner routes. The steep block at the east end features harder fare.

1. JAM IT 8
Climb a hand crack through the right side of a roof at the left (west) side of the wall.

2. HO HUM 4
Climb a right-facing corner with a tree to the right of *Jam It*.

3. IDLE HANDS 6 ★
Climb over some bulges in the middle of the face, jam the crack, step left and master the headwall. The headwall is the crux and may be avoided by finishing to the right.

4. MONS 5
Climb the next crack right of *Idle Hands*.

5. FISTULA 4
Climb a wide crack near the right side of the main wall.

The following routes are on the steep block at the east end of the wall.

6. QS 9+ ★
FA: HEIDI BENTON AND FRED KNAPP, 1995.

Follow 6 bolts up the wall just left of the southeast corner. Lower off from a two-bolt anchor.

7. JAZZ ON THE MEZZANINE 12B
FA: FRED KNAPP AND DAN HARE, 1995.

Climb the first crack right of the northeast corner. Stick-clip the first bolt. Angle up and left toward the arête and finish on the left side. Lower off (50 feet) from a bolt anchor.

8. HELL IN A BUCKET 12D
FA: MIC FAIRCHILD (TR).

Climb the middle of three crack lines. This route may have been led with gear.

9. SUITE 11 11C
FA: STEVE MUEHLHAUSER AND MIC FAIRCHILD, 1985.

Climb the right of three crack lines with two bolts and the crux near the top.

THE BOULDERADO
6. Qs 9+ ★
7. Jazz On The Mezzanine 12b
8. Hell In A Bucket 12d
9. Suite II 11c

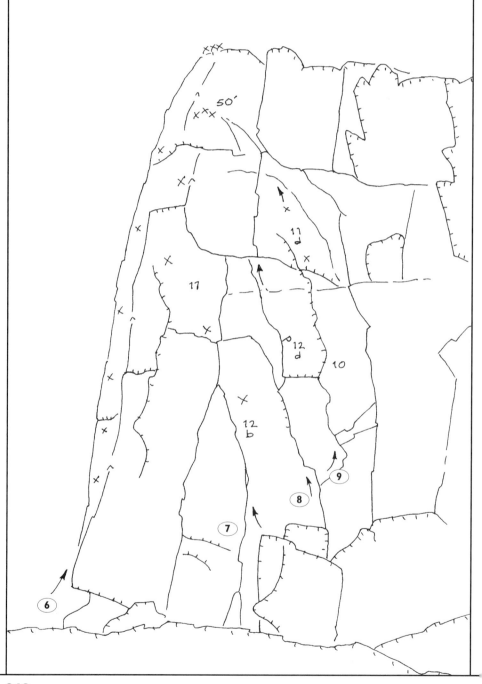

ANIMAL WORLD

Animal World is the large complex buttress above and to the northeast of The Boulderado. It is one of the best "sport crags" in Boulder County. The castle-like formation consists of prominent east and west buttresses separated by a large south-facing gully. A ledge system runs across the middle of the west buttress separating it into upper and lower tiers. The lower tier has several interesting routes that begin from a large shelf above The Boulderado. The upper tier is less visited and has two known routes. The multi-faceted, monolithic east buttress features a fine collection of difficult routes up to 55 meters in height.

Approach all routes by scrambling up through a little gap just west of The Boulderado. Veer right and continue up a scree gully to the large terrace above The Boulderado. This point may also be reached on a path that leads north from the west end of The Boulderado, then cuts back to the southeast. To reach the upper tier of the west buttress, continue up the gully, then scramble up and right onto a big ledge that runs along the base of the upper tier.

West Buttress

This cliff is located just above and east of The Boulderado. A faint trail runs along its base.

1.   ANIMAL RIOTS ACTIVIST   12A ★
FA: KEN TROUT AND RICK LEITNER.

This is the first bolt route at the left side of the buttress. Find it in a little alcove behind some trees. Follow seven bolts over a roof and up to a bolt anchor. Lower off.

2.   PILES OF TRAILS   12B ★
FA: BOB D'ANTONIO AND GREG HAND.

Begin a short way right of the preceding route and follow six bolts over a roof and up to a bolt anchor. Lower off.

3.   AUTOMATIC CHOKE   11B/C
FA: DAN HARE AND KENT LUGBILL, 1981.

To the right of the preceding routes, climb a thin, overhanging crack just left of the arête.

4.   CANNABIS SPORTIVA   11A ★
FA: RICHARD ROSSITER AND GAIL EFFRON, 1996.

This route ascends the south-facing wall around to the right from *Automatic Choke*. Begin just right of a roof. Follow thin cracks up a knobby wall and gain a shelf. Start up to the right, then follow six bolts up the steep head wall. Lower off (85 feet) or scramble off to the northwest.

5.   JOINT VENTURE   11a ★
FA: (OF UPPER SECTION) RICHARD ROSSITER AND LEAH MACALUSO, 1998.

Climb a shallow left-facing, right-leaning dihedral to a two-bolt anchor, clip the right bolt, then traverse right and climb into a subsequent dihedral. Work up and left to the arête, then climb straight up and turn a small roof. Five bolts to a two-bolt anchor. Bring a few mid-range pieces for the dihedral.

6.   FEEDING THE BEAST   12A ★
FA: DAN HARE AND ROB STANLEY, 1997. SR.

Climb to the first bolt anchor on *Joint Venture*, then follow the corner up and left past some bolts to an anchor near the top of the wall. A "direct start" has been toproped just right of the *Joint Venture* dihedral. Bolts not placed at time of writing.

ANIMAL WORLD

West Buttress
10.   Free Willie 11b
12.   Wine And Roses 10 ★

East Buttress
15.   Hands Of Destiny 13a ★
19.   Global Gorilla 11b ★ or 12b ★

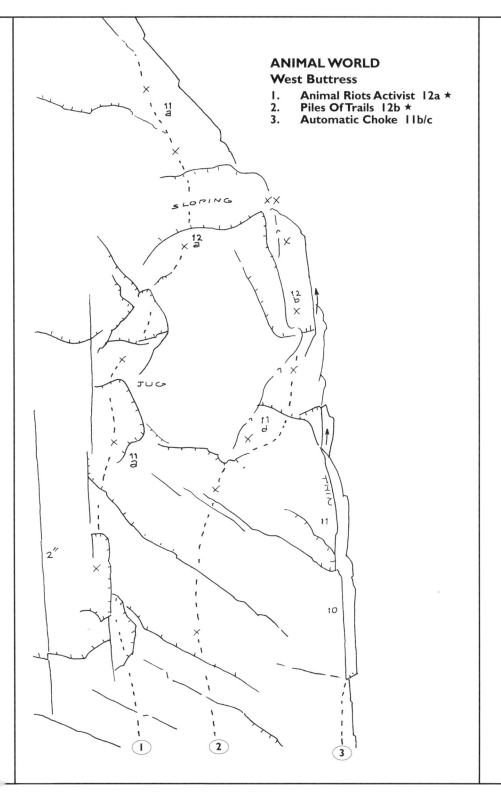

ANIMAL WORLD
West Buttress
1. **Animal Riots Activist** 12a ★
2. **Piles Of Trails** 12b ★
3. **Automatic Choke** 11b/c

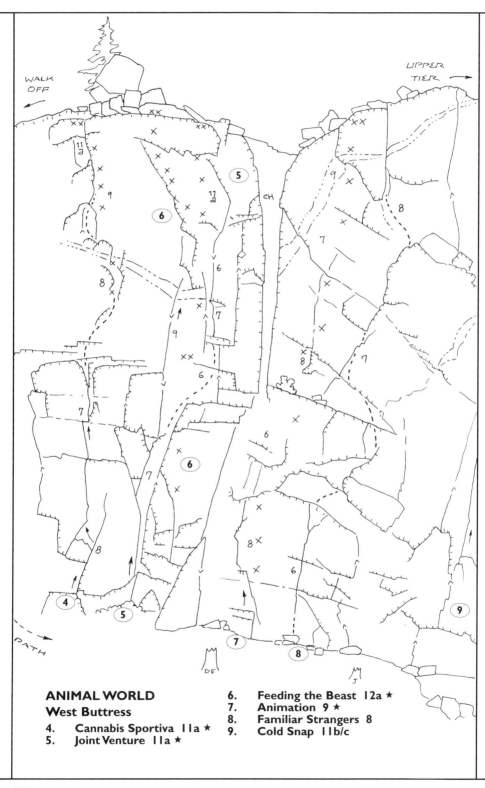

ANIMAL WORLD
West Buttress
4.   Cannabis Sportiva 11a ★
5.   Joint Venture 11a ★
6.   Feeding the Beast 12a ★
7.   Animation 9 ★
8.   Familiar Strangers 8
9.   Cold Snap 11b/c

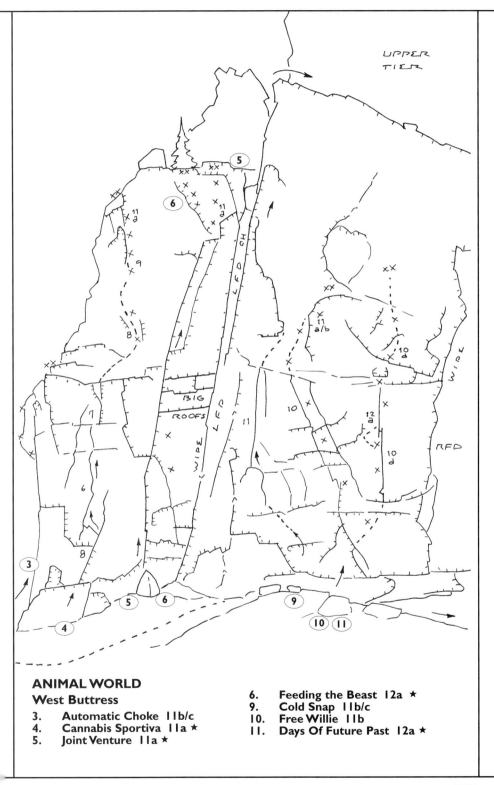

ANIMAL WORLD
West Buttress

3. **Automatic Choke** 11b/c
4. **Cannabis Sportiva** 11a ★
5. **Joint Venture** 11a ★

6. **Feeding the Beast** 12a ★
9. **Cold Snap** 11b/c
10. **Free Willie** 11b
11. **Days Of Future Past** 12a ★

7. ANIMATION 9 ★
FA: RICHARD ROSSITER AND GAIL EFFRON, 1996.

This route ascends the left side of a west-facing wall that forms the right plane of a huge dihedral. Follow excellent holds (with thoughtful pro) along the right edge of an orange streak and gain a perfect ledge. Pull up on a boot-shaped thing (#3 RP) and climb straight up along a white dike. Finish with a short, left-facing corner and belay on the big ledge that divides the east buttress into two tiers. 100 feet. Walk off to the west or east. During Spring of 1997 ten bolts and a two-bolt anchor were placed on this route by an unknown party.

8. FAMILIAR STRANGERS 8
FA: JIM MICHAELS AND DAN HARE, 1979. SR.

Begin at a thin crack just right of the preceding route. Climb the crack and gain a ledge after about 40 feet. Work up and right and climb a wide crack along the left edge of a flake. Climb up and left over steep rock and follow a hand crack through a roof. Belay and descend as for the preceding route.

The following three routes ascend a steep, south-facing wall just around to the right from the preceding routes.

9. COLD SNAP 11B/C
FA: DAN HARE AND DAVID BREWSTER, 1980.

Begin near the center of the wall, to the right of a low roof. Follow a crack for about 20 feet, then traverse left to a crack near the left edge of the face and climb to its end. Move up and right and jam a wide crack in a right-facing dihedral. Finish on the big grassy ledge that runs along the bottom of the upper tier.

10. FREE WILLIE 11B
FA: BOB D'ANTONIO AND GREG HAND.

This route follows a left-leaning crack system up the middle of the steep face, right of the preceding route. Five bolts to a two-bolt anchor.

11. DAYS OF FUTURE PAST 12A ★
FA: BOB D'ANTONIO AND GREG HAND.

Begin as for *Free Willie*, then break right and follow bolts along a seam with a fixed nut. Pass a bulge and continue to a two-bolt anchor. Seven bolts.

To reach the upper tier, scramble up behind (north of) the lower west buttress and gain a big ledge that divides the buttress into upper and lower tiers.

12. WINE AND ROSES 10 ★
FA: DAN HARE AND MASON FRISCHETTE, 1979.

This route is located on the southeast side of the upper tier, about 150 feet east from the high point of the ledge that runs along its base. Climb a thin crack up an inset to a roof, go left over the roof, and up a difficult finger crack to a belay stance. Continue up easier rock to the top of the buttress or down-climb to the west.

13. CENTER
FA: MARC HIRT AND TIM HUDGEL?

Identify a fixed anchor out to the right from the inset on the preceding route. Nothing is known of this route.

EAST BUTTRESS

To reach the east buttress, follow a path along the base of the west buttress and continue eastward for about 100 yards.

14. KRAKATOA 9
FA: Dudley Chelton and Richard Smith, 1973.

This route is assumed to follow the crack and chimney system just left from *Hands of Destiny*. From a "low point," climb a crack and turn a roof, then go up and right to belay on a "slab." Climb up toward a roof, then traverse left to the original crack and follow it to the top. Scramble off to the left and down a gully.

15. HANDS OF DESTINY 13A ★
FA: Bob Horan, belayed by Steve Mestdagh, 1987. Retro-bolted by Horan, 1996.

Begin beneath the crack and chimney system of *Krakatoa*. Follow bolts up the fabulous vertical face at the left side of the east buttress. Twelve bolts. Lower off (100 feet) from a two-bolt anchor or climb a final pitch up the headwall (10a, 40 feet, four bolts). One may also traverse right from the seventh or eighth bolt and lower off (70 feet) from the anchor at the top of *Animal Instinct*.

16. ANIMAL INSTINCT 12B/C ★
FA: Fred Knapp and Dan Hare, 1996.

Climb past the first two bolts on *Sun Dog*, then move left and follow seven bolts up the left side of a sharp, overhanging arête. Lower off (70 feet) from a two-bolt anchor.

17. SUN DOG 12A ★
FA: Ken Trout, Rick Leitner, Kirk Miller.

Begin on a ledge about 20 feet right from *Hands Of Destiny*. Work up through a bulge, then go up and left and climb along the right side of a sharp, overhanging arête. Turn a roof and gain the anchor at the top of *Animal Instinct*.

18. EVOLUTION REVOLUTION 12B/C ★
FA: Mark Rolofson.

This line takes a crack through the big roof between the two prominent arêtes at the southeast corner of the buttress. Nine bolts plus gear.

19. GLOBAL GORILLA 11B ★ OR 12B ★
FA: Rick Leitner and Marc Rolofson.

This spectacular route ascends the arête to the right of *Animal Instinct*. It is the longest single sport pitch in Boulder Canyon; however, it is more easily done in two or three pitches with semi-sling belays. Like *Genesis* in Eldorado Canyon, most parties only climb the "first pitch." Begin at a left-facing dihedral with two bolts. P1. 11b and 11 bolts to a two-bolt anchor at 70 feet. P2. 12b and five bolts to a two-bolt anchor at 120 feet. P3. 12b and six bolts to a two-bolt anchor at 170 feet. 24 QDs are needed to do the route as a single pitch.

The following routes may be reached by following a path around the east side of a broken buttress, then up and left to a ledge below the upper east face, or more directly a few yards right from *Global Gorilla*.

20. ANIMAL MAGNETISM 11C ★
FA: Rick Leitner. Redpoint: Dan Hare, 1996.

Begin at a left-facing dihedral near the lower end of the ledge. Climb about 20 feet up the dihedral, then stretch up and right to clip the first bolt. Continue up the steep wall and finish with the last two bolts on *Global Gorilla*. Lower off (120 feet) from the second anchor on *Global Gorilla* or climb the final pitch (12b).

ANIMAL WORLD

East Buttress

15. Hands Of Destiny 13a ★
16. Animal Instinct 12b/c ★
19. Global Gorilla 11b ★ or 12b ★
24. Pitbull Prowser 11b or 12a ★

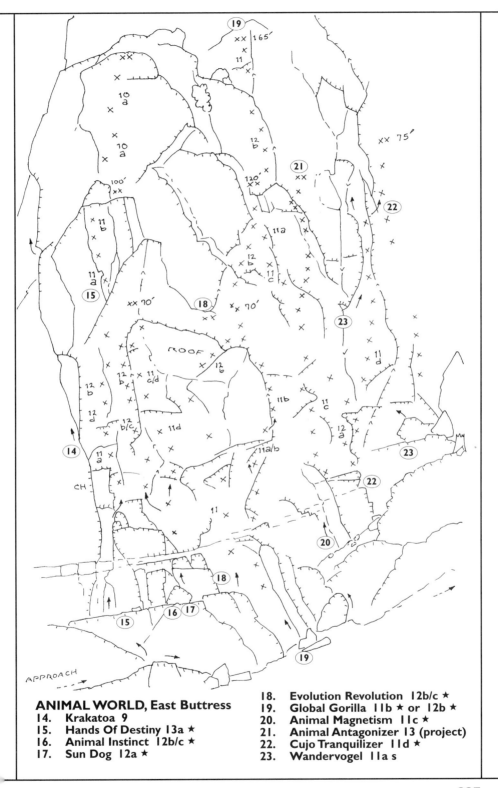

ANIMAL WORLD, East Buttress

14. **Krakatoa** 9
15. **Hands Of Destiny** 13a ★
16. **Animal Instinct** 12b/c ★
17. **Sun Dog** 12a ★
18. **Evolution Revolution** 12b/c ★
19. **Global Gorilla** 11b ★ or 12b ★
20. **Animal Magnetism** 11c ★
21. **Animal Antagonizer** 13 (project)
22. **Cujo Tranquilizer** 11d ★
23. **Wandervogel** 11a s

21. ANIMAL ANTAGONIZER 13 (PROJECT)
TR: INITIATED BY PAUL GAGNER; COMPLETED AS A LEAD BY MARK ROLOFSON.

From the eighth bolt on *Animal Magnetism*, follow bolts up and right over a roof and gain a bolt anchor at 100 feet. 15 bolts.

22. CUJO TRANQUILIZER 11D ★
FA: MARK ROLOFSON.

Begin just right of *Animal Magnetism*. Follow bolts up the steep wall to ledges at the bottom of the *Wandervogel* dihedral. The line originally went up and left to join *Animal Magnetism*. A newer version climbs the right wall of the *Wandervogel* dihedral, then breaks right to join the upper part of *Pit Bull Prowser*.

23. WANDERVOGEL 11A S
FA: HARRISON DEKKER AND CHRIS WOYNA, 1981.

Begin from a large block about 70 feet up and right from *Animal Magnetism*. Traverse left (needs fixed pin) into a large, left-facing dihedral and belay above a perched block (11a, 80 feet). Climb through a roof above and left of the belay, then up the dihedral to finish with a crack in the right wall (11a, 80 feet).

24. PITBULL PROWSER 11B OR 12A A1★
FA: KEN TROUT. REDPOINT: RICK THOMPSON.

This route climbs the steep face just right of the prominent dihedral of *Wandervogel*. P1. 11b and 11 bolts to a two-bolt anchor, 75 feet. P2. 12a A1 and three bolts to a two bolt anchor, 25 feet.

25. NEW BEGINNINGS 11C ★
FA: PAUL GAGNER.

Begin atop a large block just up and right from the preceding line. Follow bolts along a right-facing dihedral and finish with a steep slab on the right. Eight bolts to a two-bolt anchor, 75 feet.

Far East Buttress

This obscure rock is located about 100 yards south of the East Buttress of Animal World. It has a single known route of unknown origin and difficulty. Start up the path as for the preceding routes, then break right and contour east to the bottom of the buttress.

SOUTH FACE 11?
Climb an overhanging hand crack in the middle of the south face, then follow bolts up the steep slab above.

CATS AND DOGS 12
FA: MARK ROLOFSON, 1981.

About 8.8 miles up the canyon and on the north side of the road , hike up the slope a ways and find a small rock with a 20-foot A-shaped roof. Bring small to medium stoppers and TCUs.

ANIMAL WORLD
East Buttress

(ON FACING PAGE)
19. **Global Gorilla 11b ★ or 12b ★**
20. **Animal Magnetism 11c ★**
21. **Animal Antagonizer 13 (project**
22. **Cujo Tranquilizer 11d ★**
23. **Wandervogel 11a s**
24. **Pitbull Prowser 11b or 12a ★**
25. **New Beginnings 11c ★**

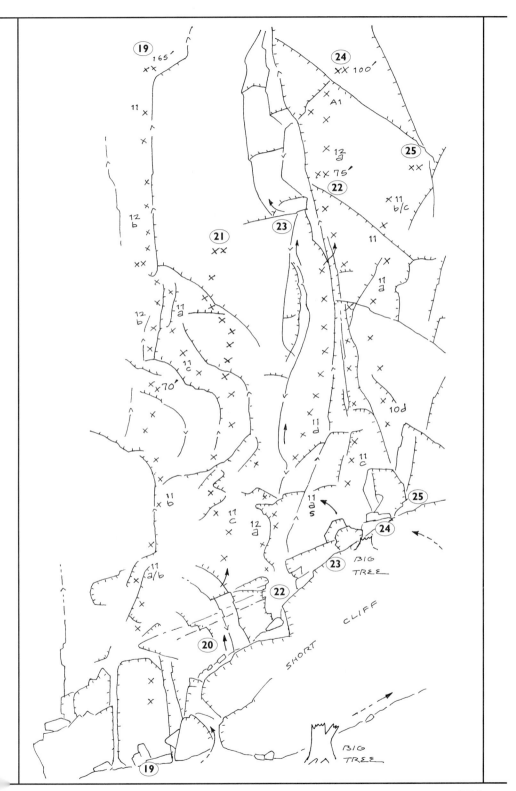

229

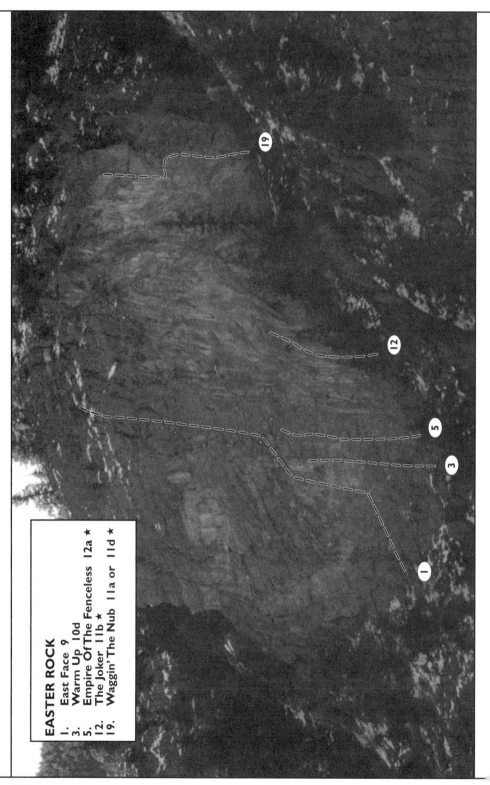

EASTER ROCK
1. East Face 9
3. Warm Up 10d
5. Empire Of The Fenceless 12a ★
12. The Joker 11b ★
19. Waggin' The Nub 11a or 11d ★

PUNK ROCK

About 450 feet west of The Boulderado and on the same side of the road is a sprawling heap of granite that has been named Punk Rock. About 1981, Jim Stuberg and others climbed and named many of the climable features such as *Cope Some Cone* (9), a chimney. Detailed information is not available.

EASTER ROCK

Easter Rock is located at the nine mile mark and on the right (west) side of the road. This large buttress overhangs on its east and north sides and has become a popular "sport climbing" crag. There is a narrow pull-out along the road below the east face, but it is probably better to park at a large pull-out at 8.8 miles. Directly below the east face, a trail zigzags up the slope several hundred feet to the northeast corner of the buttress. Most of the routes are located on the big north face. Typical gear needed: Arms and quickdraws.

1.   EAST FACE 9
FA: LAYTON KOR AND DAVE DORNAN, 1963.

Begin at the lower left side of the east face. Traverse right across a ledge to a slab beneath a large roof. This point may also be reached from the last switchback in the trail. Climb to the roof, then traverse right to near its end, and step around a corner at the bottom of a broken dihedral. Climb the dihedral and subsequent slab to the top of the rock.

2.   ROOF ON A HOT TIN CAT 10 A2
FA: KYLE COPELAND AND MARC HIRT, C. 1986.

Climb an overhanging crack in the middle of the east face to a 20-foot roof. Aid through the roof and belay under the next roof.

Note: The following routes top out at threadable bolt anchors from which one may lower off.

3.   WARM UP 10D
FA: MARK ROLOFSON AND DIANNE BARROW.

Look for a line of five bolts a short way left of the northeast arête.

4.   BARBARIANS 12B ★
FA: RICHARD WRIGHT AND TODD ANDERSON.

Begin in a conspicuous dihedral just left of the northeast arête. Nine bolts.

5.   EMPIRE OF THE FENCELESS 12A ★
FA: KEN TROUT.

This fine route is reminiscent of *Suburban Hangover* on The Needle in Estes Park, but harder. Traverse in from the right and climb the northeast arête. Seven bolts.

6.   TELL-TALE HEART 12B ★
FA: MARK ROLOFSON.

This route, the first sport climb on the wall, follows a left-facing dihedral system about 15 feet right of the northeast arête. Eight bolts.

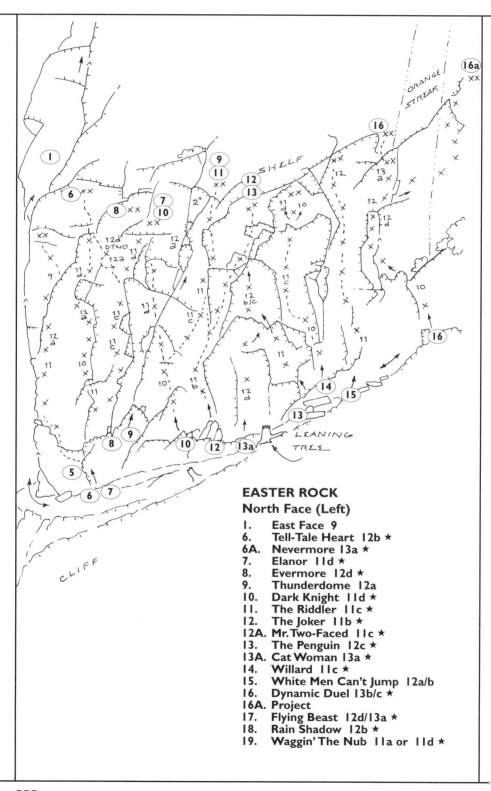

EASTER ROCK
North Face (Left)

1. East Face 9
6. Tell-Tale Heart 12b ★
6A. Nevermore 13a ★
7. Elanor 11d ★
8. Evermore 12d ★
9. Thunderdome 12a
10. Dark Knight 11d ★
11. The Riddler 11c ★
12. The Joker 11b ★
12A. Mr. Two-Faced 11c ★
13. The Penguin 12c ★
13A. Cat Woman 13a ★
14. Willard 11c ★
15. White Men Can't Jump 12a/b
16. Dynamic Duel 13b/c ★
16A. Project
17. Flying Beast 12d/13a ★
18. Rain Shadow 12b ★
19. Waggin' The Nub 11a or 11d ★

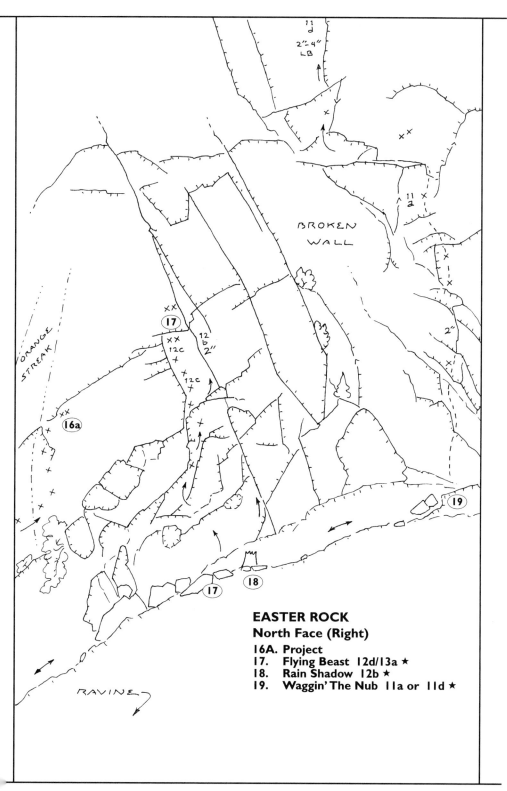

EASTER ROCK

North Face (Right)

16A. Project
17. Flying Beast 12d/13a ★
18. Rain Shadow 12b ★
19. Waggin' The Nub 11a or 11d ★

6A. NEVERMORE 13A ★
FA: MARK ROLOFSON.

Climb to the seventh bolt on *Tell-Tale Heart*, then work up and right (past a bolt) to the crux and last bolt on *Evermore*. Nine bolts.

7. ELANOR 11D ★
FA: MARK ROLOFSON.

This route takes the next left-facing dihedral right of *Tell-Tale Heart*, then goes up and right past two more bolts to an anchor shared with *Dark Knight*.

8. EVERMORE 12D ★
FA: MARK ROLOFSON.

Climb past the sixth bolt on *Elanor*, then work up and left past two more bolts and up and right to an anchor. Eight bolts.

9. THUNDERDOME 12A
FA: CHRIS PEISKER AND DAN HARE.

Follow a corner and crack system up and right to an anchor shared with *The Riddler*. SR plus extra #1.5 and 2 Friends.

10. DARK KNIGHT 11D ★
FA: ALAN NELSON.

This route forms an "X" with *Thunderdome*. Begin left of a spike and follow bolts up and left to an anchor shared with *Elanor*. Six bolts.

11. THE RIDDLER 11C ★
FA: ALAN NELSON AND RICHARD WRIGHT.

Begin as for the preceding route, but break right after the second bolt, then work right and up to an anchor shared with *Thunderdome*. Seven bolts.

12. THE JOKER 11B ★
FA: ALAN NELSON AND RICHARD WRIGHT.

Begin at a spike of rock. Climb straight up, then angle right past the top of a bent tree to an anchor shared with *The Penguin*. Six bolts.

12A. MR. TWO-FACED 11C ★
FA: ALAN NELSON.

Climb straight up past the third bolt on *The Joker* and join *The Riddler*. Seven bolts.

13. THE PENGUIN 12C ★
FA: MARK ROLOFSON.

This route is located behind a tree that leans against the wall. Climb up into a short, right-facing dihedral and continue mostly straight up to an anchor shared with *The Joker*. Five bolts.

13A. CAT WOMAN 13A ★
FA: MARK ROLOFSON.

Begin midway between *The Joker* and *The Penguin* and stick clip the first bolt. Climb straight up past two bolts, then step right and join *The Penguin*.

14. WILLARD 11C ★
FA: MARK ROLOFSON AND DIANNE BARROW.

Begin right of the leaning tree. Follow bolts along a rat-facing dihedral, then crank up and right at a horn. At the last bolt, pull right and up to an anchor (10), or go left and up to a bucket (11d).

15. White Men Can't Jump 12a/b
FA: Alan Nelson.

Begin just left of a small arête and climb up through a right-facing dihedral. The crux is just above a small roof near the top of the pitch. Six bolts.

16. Dynamic Duel 13b/c ★
FA: Mark Rolofson. Redpoint: Peter Beal.

Locate a line of seven bolts a short way up the dihedral of *White Men*. There is a "lowering anchor" below the lip of the big roof, but the climb finishes at a higher anchor after turning the roof.

16A. Project

Climb to the sixth bolt on *Dynamic Duel*, then follow bolts right and up to an anchor just below the lip of the big roof. Twelve bolts.

17. Flying Beast 12d/13a ★
FA: Mark Rolofson.

Begin about 50 feet right of the preceding route and to the right of a hanging flake with bat shit or some sort of nasty-looking ooze above it. Follow bolts along an overhanging, right-facing dihedral. Six bolts.

18. Rain Shadow 12b ★
FA: Dan Hare.

Climb a finger and hand crack through the big roof just right of *Flying Beast*. SR.

19. Waggin' The Nub 11a or 11d ★
FA: Dan Neber and Rick Leitner.

Begin from a narrow ledge at the far right side of the wall. Follow four bolts up a blocky face and belay on a ledge with a bolt anchor (11a, #1 and 2 Friends needed). A second pitch climbs the crack above (11d, #0.5 to #4 Friends needed).

HIGH ENERGY CRAG

This small buttress resides at 9.1 miles, on the left (east) side of the highway, just beyond Easter Rock. It features a series of overhangs above a low-angle slab. All routes require gear; no bolts.

1. Eugenics Wars 12?
FA: Gray Ringsby and partner, 1986.

This route is described as ascending the left side of the crag. Nothing more is known.

2. No Preservatives 10
FA: Skip Guerin, solo, 1981.

Climb the shallow corner left of *Star Span*.

3. Star Span 11 ★
FA: Pat Ament and Roger Briggs, 1976.

At the lower left side of the crag, a block protrudes to form a large roof. Climb the hand crack that pierces the right side of the block.

4. Golden Bull 10
FA: Alec Sharp and Matt Lavender, 1979.

Well around to the right from *Star Span* the wall drops back to form a large, right-facing dihedral. Climb a crack along the overhanging arête at the left edge of the dihedral.

HIGH ENERGY CRAG
2. No Preservatives 10
3. Star Span 11 ★
4. Golden Bull 10
5. Proton 9
6. Neutron Star 10a s
7. Diet Of Worms 10a ★
8. Imp-Passible Crack 11a
8A. Next to Imp-Passible 9

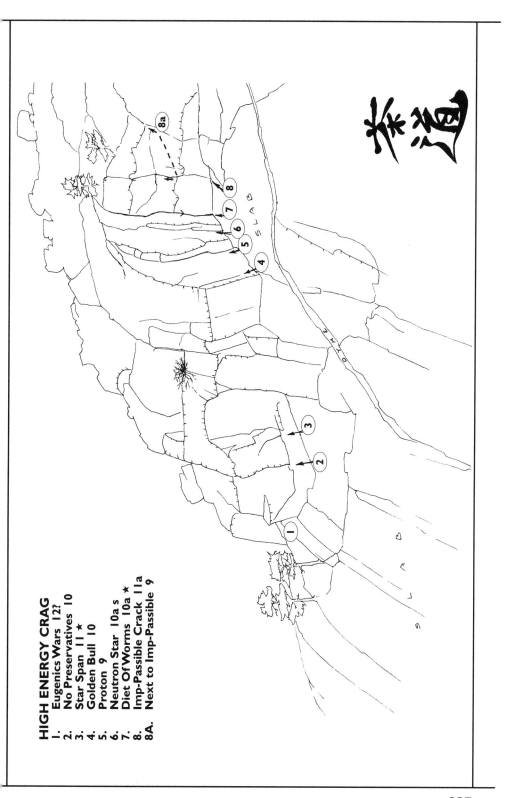

HIGH ENERGY CRAG
1.   Eugenics Wars 12?
2.   No Preservatives 10
3.   Star Span 11 ★
4.   Golden Bull 10
5.   Proton 9
6.   Neutron Star 10a s
7.   Diet Of Worms 10a ★
8.   Imp-Passible Crack 11a
8A. Next to Imp-Passible 9

5. PROTON 9
FA: DAVID BREASHEARS AND ART HIGBEE, 1975.
On the left wall of the dihedral, climb a small, left-leaning corner just up to the right from *Golden Bull*.

6. NEUTRON STAR 10A S
FA: ART HIGBEE, JIM ERICKSON, DAVID BREASHEARS, 1975.
Climb the next small, left-facing corner to the right of *Proton*.

7. DIET OF WORMS 10A ★
FA: JIM ERICKSON, ART HIGBEE, DAVID BREASHEARS, 1975.
Climb a crack up the actual inside corner of the big dihedral.

8. IMP-PASSIBLE CRACK 11A
FA: HENRY BARBER AND PAT AMENT, 1977.
Climb a fist crack and then a hand crack through a roof on the right wall of the big dihedral.

8A. NEXT TO IMP-PASSIBLE 9
FA: ART HIGBEE, SOLO, 1975.
Climb up to the roof of the preceding route, then undercling right.

CONEY ISLAND
Coney Island resides above the highway at the 9.2 mile mark, about one hundred yards south of Easter Rock. It is up on a shelf to the north as the road bends back to the west and is not easily seen in passing. The crag consists of a large upper wall and smaller lower wall that are completely separate from each other. There is room for one or two cars to park on the south side of the road just below the crag, but it is better to park a short way beyond at a larger pull-out (also on the south side).

Lower Buttress
The following routes are located on the smaller, south-facing buttress just above the highway.

1. THE BAIT 11A ★
FA: DAN HARE AND JOHN FORT, 1994.
This route ascends the large dihedral at the west end of the buttress. Bring QDs for four bolts plus a medium stopper or small Friend. Lower off from a two-bolt anchor.

2. TWIST AND SHOUT 13B
This route ascends the left side of the arête along the right margin of the big dihedral. Six bolts to a two-bolt anchor.

3. FLY TRAP 11D ★
FA: DAN HARE.
Begin at a perched block and follow a line of bolts just right of the arête. Five bolts to a two-bolt anchor.

4. FLIES IN THE SOUP 11C
FA: DAN HARE.
Climb past three bolts in the middle of the overhanging wall right of the big dihedral. Lower off.

5. PRONG 12C/D ★
Climb the overhanging wall just left of *Fly Swatter*. Four bolts to the anchor on *Fly Swatter*.

CONEY ISLAND
1. The Bait 11a ★
6. Fly Swatter 10c
11. Joy Ride 12b ★
16. Quintet 10

Upper Buttress

Lower Buttress

239

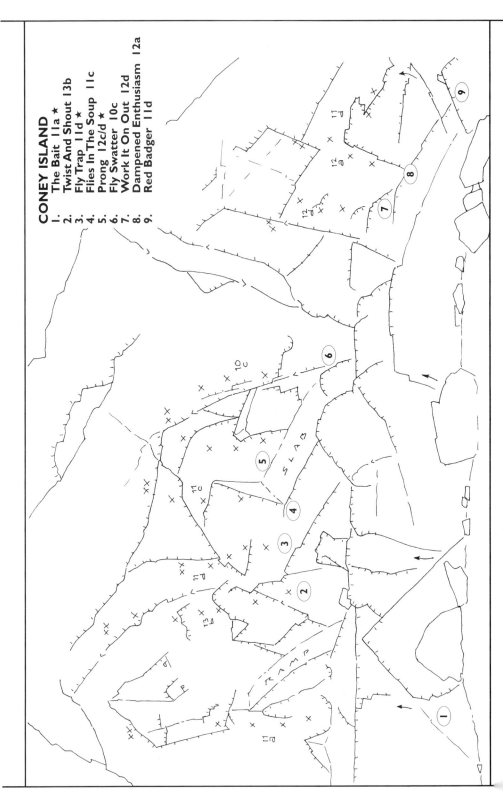

CONEY ISLAND
1. The Bait 11a ★
2. Twist And Shout 13b
3. Fly Trap 11d ★
4. Flies In The Soup 11c
5. Prong 12c/d ★
6. Fly Swatter 10c
7. Work It On Out 12d
8. Dampened Enthusiasm 12a
9. Red Badger 11d

6. FLY SWATTER 10c
FA: DAN HARE.

Follow three bolts up the wall just right of an arête and left of a big, left-facing dihedral. Lower off.

7. WORK IT ON OUT 12d

Follow three bolts up the left side of a smaller overhanging wall just right of a left-facing dihedral. Lower off.

8. DAMPENED ENTHUSIASM 12a
FA: NOEL CHILDS AND DAN HARE, 1991.

Climb up and right past three bolts and gain a two-bolt anchor above the lip of the overhanging wall at the right side of the buttress.

9. RED BADGER 11d
FA: FRED KNAPP, ALAN LESTER, DAN HARE, 1992.

Climb in from the right and join the preceding route at the third bolt.

Upper Buttress

The following routes are located on the larger upper buttress. Most of the routes are slightly over-hanging, intricate and strenuous. Approach by hiking up around either side of the Lower Buttress. The first four routes ascend the west and south sides of a huge block that protrudes from the left (west) side of the upper wall.

10. FEEDING THE BEAST 12b
FA: DAN HARE.

Climb an overhanging fin at the upper west side of the buttress. Four bolts. Lower off.

11. JOY RIDE 12b ★

Follow bolts up the left side of the big block's south face. Seven bolts.

12. DER LETZTE ZUG 12c ★

Follow bolts up the middle of the big block. Six bolts.

13. DIE REEPERBAHN 13b ★

Begin down to the right, beneath a roof. Turn the roof, then follow bolts along the right edge of the block, just left of the arête. Eight bolts.

14. LOADING ZONE 10d s
FA: DAN HARE AND SCOTT WOODRUFF, 1978.

Climb the right-facing dihedral along the right side of the big block and belay on a ledge. Finish with an easier crack and exit left.

15. PSYCLONE 11d
FA: BOB HORAN AND SKIP GUERIN, 1981.

Begin just right of *Loading Zone*. Climb a difficult thin crack, then merge left with *Loading Zone* and belay on the big ledge. Climb the easy crack as for *Loading Zone*, then move right and jam a fist crack through a roof (10d).

16. QUINTET 10
FA: SCOTT WOODRUFF AND DAN HARE, 1978.

Climb in from the right, then follow a right-facing, zigzag dihedral up the middle of the wall. Choose an exit.

CONEY ISLAND

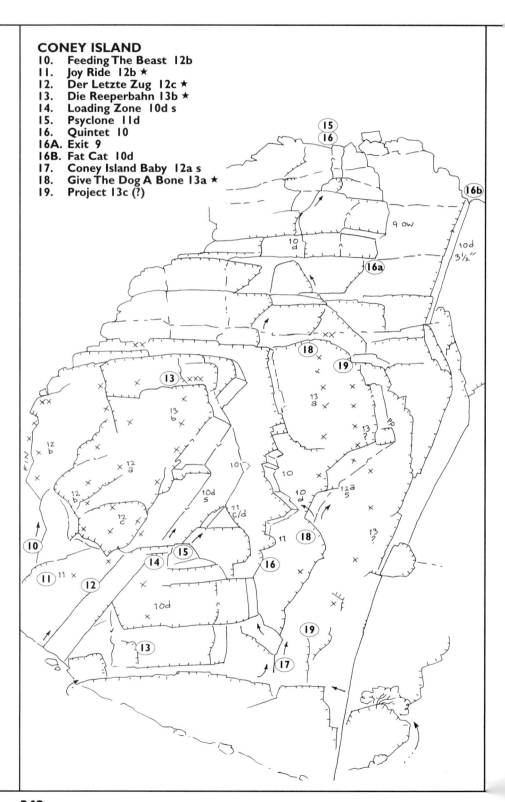

16A. Exit 9
To the right of the fist crack of *Psyclone*, climb an off-width/squeeze type of thing in a right-facing corner.

16B. Fat Cat 10d
FA: Bob Horan and Skip Guerin, 1981.
Climb a fist crack in a right-facing dihedral to the right of the preceding finish.

17. Coney Island Baby 12a s
FA: Erik Eriksson and Mark Rolofson, 1982. SR up through a #2.5 Friend with extra #1 and #2 Friends.
Begin a short way to the right of *Quintet* and follow a crack into a right-arching overhang. Belay or lower off from two pins.

18. Give The Dog A Bone 13a ★
Climb the first 25 feet of *Coney Island Baby* (10), then break left and follow bolts up the head wall. Six bolts to a two-bolt anchor.

19. Project 13c (?)
Begin to the right of *Coney Island Baby*. Climb continuously difficult rock to the roof of the preceding route, turn the roof, and continue to a two-bolt anchor. Nine bolts.

20. Mongouichi 10
FA: Mark Shannon and Doug Robnett, 1980.
Begin at the east side of *Coney Island*. Climb a prominent leaning dihedral to the base of an overhanging, east-facing headwall (5) and belay. Climb the right of two cracks (10). 300 feet.

NIP AND TUCK
At 10.5 miles and on the north side of the highway are two small buttresses separated by a brushy gully. The rocks are obscured by trees along a right-hand bend in the road and are easy to miss. Parking is very limited just below the rocks, but there is plenty of parking just west of Stepping Stones (about 200 yards west of Nip) on either side of the highway.

Nip
The following routes are located on the west of the two buttresses.

1. Ebb Tide 10 ★
FA: Scott Woodruff and Dan Hare, 1979.
Climb the left of two parallel cracks in an overhanging wall at the left side of the crag.

2. Night Train 9+
FA: Dan Hare and Clay Wadman, 1983.
Begin just right of *Ebb Tide*. Follow thin cracks up and right to a roof, turn the roof on the left (wide) and finish in a dihedral.

3. Heart Throb 10 ★
FA: probably Pat Ament, Bob Hritz, Dudley Chelton, mid-1960s. FFA: Dan Hare and Joel Schiavone, 1984.
Climb to the roof as for *Night Train*, then move right to a jug and pull up to clip a bolt. Gain the slab above the roof and finish up to the left.

243

NIP

South Face

1. Ebb Tide 10 ★
3. Heart Throb 10 ★
8. Left-Angling Crack 9 ★
9. Arête 10d ★

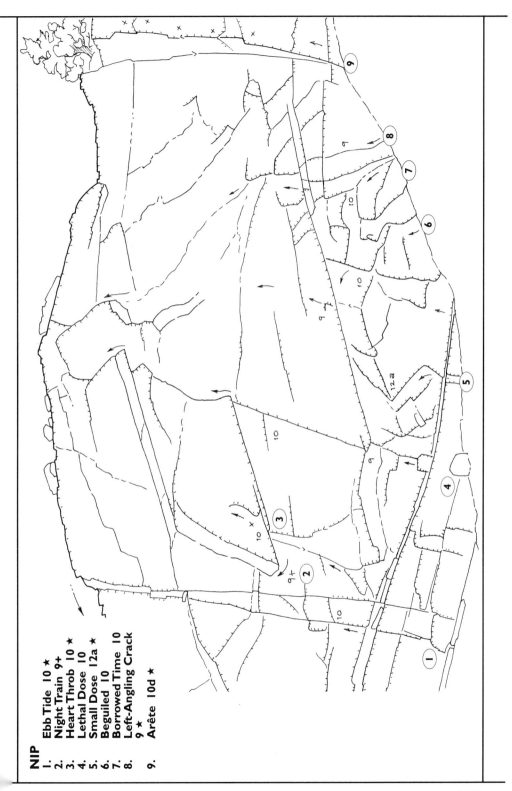

NIP
1. Ebb Tide 10 ★
2. Night Train 9+
3. Heart Throb 10 ★
4. Lethal Dose 10
5. Small Dose 12a ★
6. Beguiled 10
7. Borrowed Time 10
8. Left-Angling Crack 9 ★
9. Arête 10d ★

245

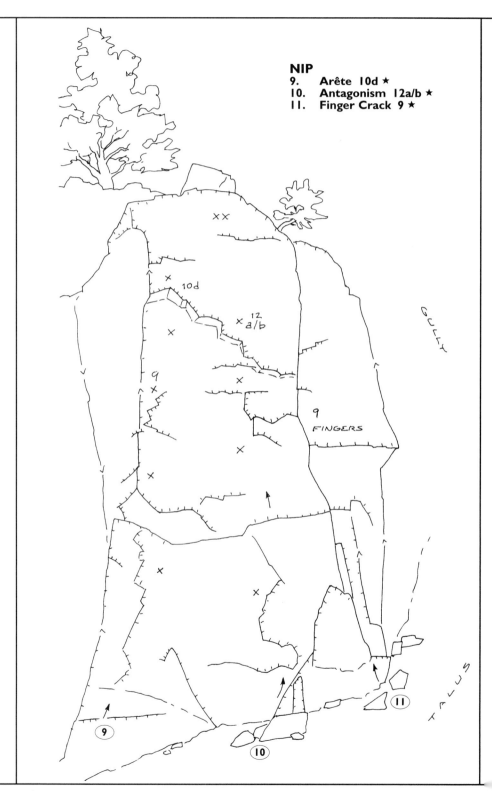

NIP
9. **Arête 10d** ★
10. **Antagonism 12a/b** ★
11. **Finger Crack 9** ★

4.   LETHAL DOSE 10
FA: PROBABLY DAN HARE AND PARTNER.

Begin a short way right of *Heart Throb*. Climb cracks in the right wall of a large left-facing dihedral, clear the big roof, and finish in a crack.

5.   SMALL DOSE 12A ★
FA: DON DEBIEUX, 1991.

Overdose is more like it. Climb a finger-wrecking, overhanging crack a short way right of *Lethal Dose*. Protect via a cheater-placed wire at the lip.

About ten feet right of *Small Dose*, one can boulder up a smooth, rounded arête and down-climb a dihedral to the right.

6.   BEGUILED 10
FA: SCOTT WOODRUFF AND DAN HARE, 1979.

Begin at a short, right-facing dihedral around to the right from *Lethal Dose*. Climb the dihedral and pull around the left end of a long roof, then continue up a slab and finish in the left of two small dihedrals.

7.   BORROWED TIME 10
FA: DAN HARE, SOLO, 1979.

Climb a small leftward arch, then angle left on a slab and finish with a small dihedral.

8.   LEFT-ANGLING CRACK 9 ★

Begin just right of the preceding route. Climb a thin crack in a steep wall, then take a left-angling crack in a slab, and finish in a right-facing dihedral.

The following three routes are located on a large square-cut block that protrudes at the upper east side of Nip. A two-bolt anchor near the top can be reached by scrambling up the gully along the right side of the block or by leading one of the routes.

9.   ARÊTE 10D ★
Climb the steep and beautiful southwest arête of the block. Five bolts to a two-bolt anchor.

10.   ANTAGONISM 12A/B ★
FA: MARC HIRT, TIM HUDGEL, BOB D'ANTONIO, 1986.
Climb the sheer face just right of the preceding route. Four bolts.

11.   FINGER CRACK 9 ★
Climb the obvious finger crack that pierces the right side of the block.

Tuck

The following routes are located on the east of the two buttresses.

1.   SURPRISING SLAB 8
FA: SCOTT WOODRUFF AND RAY SNEAD, 1979.
Climb thin seams on the left and then cracks in the middle of a slab at the far left side of the rock.

2.   HARE BALLS 7
FA: KURT GRAY AND DAN HARE, 1980.
Climb the right of two thin finger cracks just right of the preceding route.

TUCK
1. Surprising Slab 8
3. Dan-D-Line 6
6. Hypotenuse 9+ ★

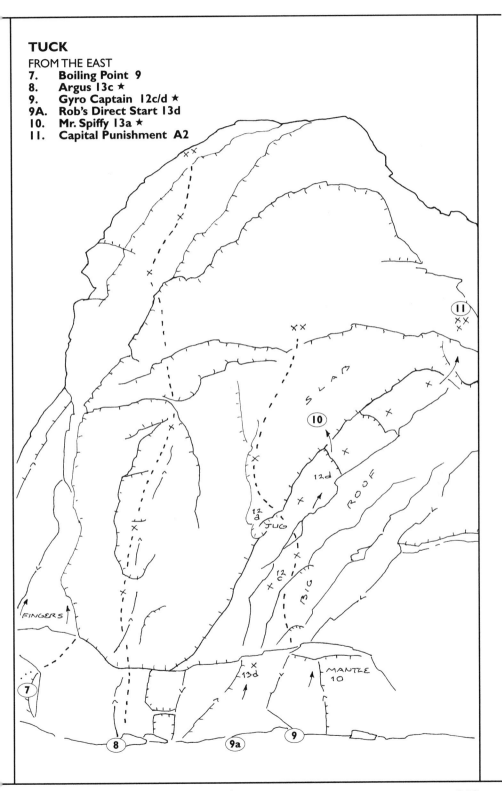

TUCK

FROM THE EAST
7.   **Boiling Point 9**
8.   **Argus 13c ★**
9.   **Gyro Captain 12c/d ★**
9A. **Rob's Direct Start 13d**
10. **Mr. Spiffy 13a ★**
11. **Capital Punishment A2**

3.   DAN-D-LINE 6
FA: CHRIS TAYLOR AND CHARLY OLIVER, 1980.

Begin beneath a west-facing slab to the right of the preceding routes. Climb up through a roof and follow incipient cracks to the top.

4.   SPREAD EAGLES DHARE 9
FA: KURT GRAY AND CHARLY OLIVER, 1979.

Climb the arête that forms the southwest corner of the rock.

5.   CONSTRICTOR 9
FA: SCOTT WOODRUFF, SOLO, 1979.

Begin just right of the arête of the preceding route. Climb a thin overhanging crack that rises out of a small, left-facing corner.

6.   HYPOTENUSE 9+ ★
FA: DAN HARE AND SCOTT WOODRUFF, 1979.

Begin a few feet right of *Constrictor*. Climb a prominent open-book via thin cracks in the right wall.

7.   BOILING POINT 9
FA: PROBABLY DAN HARE AND PARTNER, 1979.

Climb parallel hand cracks along the right side of the south face.

The following routes are located on the lower right side of the buttress.

8.   ARGUS 13C ★

Begin at the low-point of an overhang at the southeast corner of the buttress. Follow bolts up a blunt arête and through a bulge. Six bolts to a two-bolt anchor.

9.   GYRO CAPTAIN 12C/D ★
FA: WILL GADD AND MARK ROLOFSON, 1987.

Begin at thin cracks underneath the big diagonal roof. Work up and left and turn the roof at a jug. Continue past another bolt to a ledge with a two-bolt anchor.

9A.   ROB'S DIRECT START 13D
FA: ROB CANDELARIA.

Begin left of the initial inside corner and climb straight up past a bolt.

10.   MR. SPIFFY 13A ★

Begin as for *Gyro Captain*, but go right at the second bolt to a third bolt and turn the roof. Lower off.

11.   CAPITAL PUNISHMENT A2
FA: DEAVERS AND VALDEZ, 1986.

Begin as for *Gyro Captain*, but continue up and right along a seam beneath the roof.

STEPPING STONES

Just west of Nip And Tuck is a large buttress with a "cobblestone" or "checkerboard" southwest face. A solitary old route ascends this face, however, the long diagonal overhang along its bottom, has become popular for bouldering and is called The Barrio. A pillar up to the right of the cobble-stone wall has several routes of interest. Park along a wide shoulder on the right side of the highway, several hundred feet west of the buttress. Walk back along the highway and follow a flagstone (stepping stone) path to the bottom of the wall.

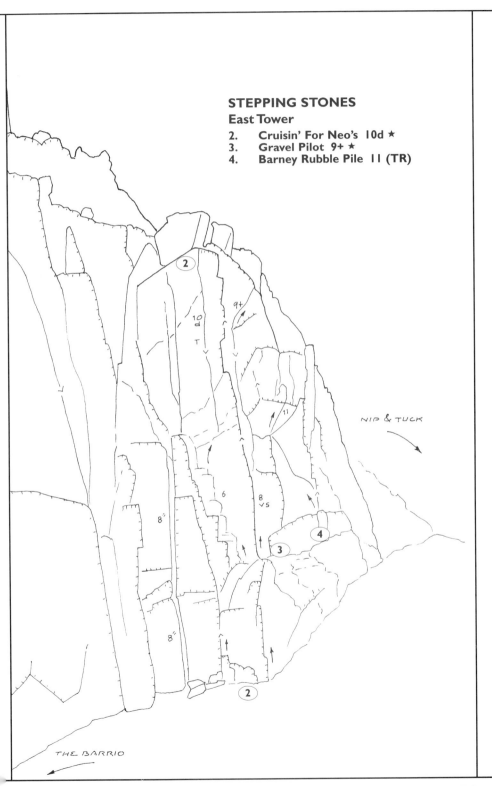

STEPPING STONES

East Tower

2. **Cruisin' For Neo's 10d ★**
3. **Gravel Pilot 9+ ★**
4. **Barney Rubble Pile 11 (TR)**

NIP & TUCK

THE BARRIO

1.   STEPPING STONES 7 ?
FA: Larry Dalke, mid-1960s.

Find a route up the "cobblestone" wall. Exact location is not known. It may pass through the initial roof near the low-point of the southwest face (harder than 7), or farther around to the west, on the left side of an arête.

East Tower

The following routes are on a 70-foot pillar at the upper east side of the buttress.

2.   CRUISIN' FOR NEO'S 10D ★
FA: Don DeBlieux and Paul Lembeck, 1990.

Start below the west side of the pillar, ten feet right of an obvious eight-inch crack. Climb an easy right-facing corner followed by a steep and difficult open-book dihedral with a thin crack (RPs). One may also begin with a thin crack about five feet right of the off-width.

3.   GRAVEL PILOT 9+ ★
FA: DeBlieux and Lembeck, 1990.

Begin as for the preceding route, but stay right and climb a tasteful arête (8 vs) followed by a groove and a bulge.

4.   BARNEY RUBBLE PILE 11 (TR)
FA: Lembeck, 1990.

Begin around on the south side of the pillar. Follow thin cracks through a large overhang. This is probably a free version of *How Would We Know*.

5.   HOW WOULD WE KNOW 6 A2
FA: Pat Ament, Dudley Chelton, Bob Hritz, 1968.

Climb a steep, south-facing wall and a big roof.

Castle Rock Area

The most westerly group of crags in Boulder Canyon begins with Castle Rock (11.8 miles) and ends with Surprising Crag (12.4 miles). All features lie on the south side of the highway with the exception of Cenotaph Crag (12.0 miles) which is on the north side. Broken Rock, Mountain Rose Crag and Frisky Cliff can be reached by crossing a bridge at the southeast corner of Castle Rock. See individual approaches for each crag.

CASTLE ROCK

Castle Rock is one of Boulder's most famous crags with a long history of ascents by many distinguished climbers. The beehive-shaped crag is located on the south side of the highway at 11.8 miles and is encircled on the west and south by an older, unpaved section of the same road. Castle Rock features routes at all levels of difficulty and of great variety. The few routes based mostly on bolts are pretty scary (mostly). To descend from the summit, scramble to the north side and follow your nose down ramps, ledges, and short cracks. See Route 1.

1. NORTH FACE CLASS 4
This is the standard descent route. From the north side of the summit, follow well-worn ramps, ledges and short cracks to a small saddle, then continue down a gully to the west. In wet conditions, one may rappel from trees.

2. WEST FACE 5
Begin below a pinnacle that sits halfway up the west side of Castle Rock. Climb a slot or a crack to the left and belay on a ledge with a tree. Climb the chimney behind the pinnacle and follow cracks to the summit.

3. BIG DEAL PINNACLE 9
FA: PAT AMENT AND CARL DIEHL, 1975.
Also known as *Square Diehl*, this route ascends the pinnacle in the middle of the west face. Climb the first pitch of the *West Face* route and belay at the tree. Move right, then climb a steep slab and a hand crack through the right side of a roof. Finish on the summit of the pinnacle.

4. POLYESTER LEISURE SUIT 11A ★
FA: PETE ZOLLER AND ED MCKIGNEY.
Begin a short way right of the preceding route. Climb an easy dihedral, turn a roof, and climb the face above past three bolts. Rappel 75 from a tree. Gear up to one inch needed.

5. TIMES PAST 9
FA: ALEC SHARP, CHRIS DALE, MURIEL SHARP, 1980.
Climb a shallow groove that leads to the right side of the pinnacle.

6. ANOTHER ROADSIDE ATTRACTION 10
FA: ED WEBSTER AND PETE ATHANS, 1986.
Climb the face and thin crack about 20 feet left of *Skunk Crack*.

7. SKUNK CRACK 9+
FA: HARVEY CARTER AND CAREY HUSTON, 1960.
Down and right of the pinnacle the wall forms a buttress, then cuts back into the deep corner of *Bailey's Overhang*. Climb the left of two cracks on the west side of the buttress.

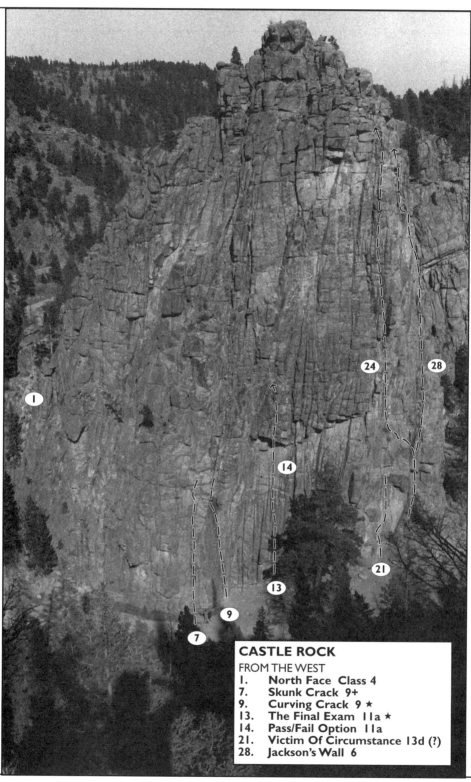

CASTLE ROCK

FROM THE WEST
1.   North Face Class 4
7.   Skunk Crack 9+
9.   Curving Crack 9 ★
13.   The Final Exam 11a ★
14.   Pass/Fail Option 11a
21.   Victim Of Circumstance 13d (?)
28.   Jackson's Wall 6

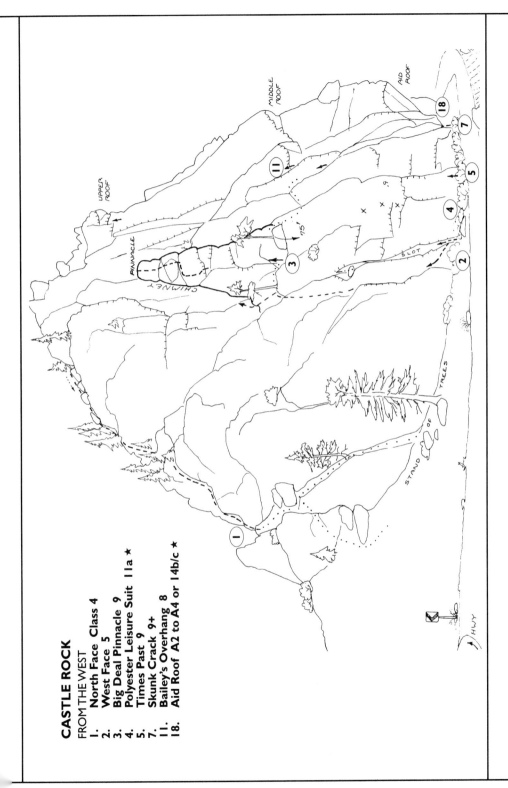

CASTLE ROCK

FROM THE WEST

1. **North Face Class 4**
2. **West Face 5**
3. **Big Deal Pinnacle 9**
4. **Polyester Leisure Suit 11a ★**
5. **Times Past 9**
11. **Skunk Crack 9+**
11. **Bailey's Overhang 8**
18. **Aid Roof A2 to A4 or 14b/c ★**

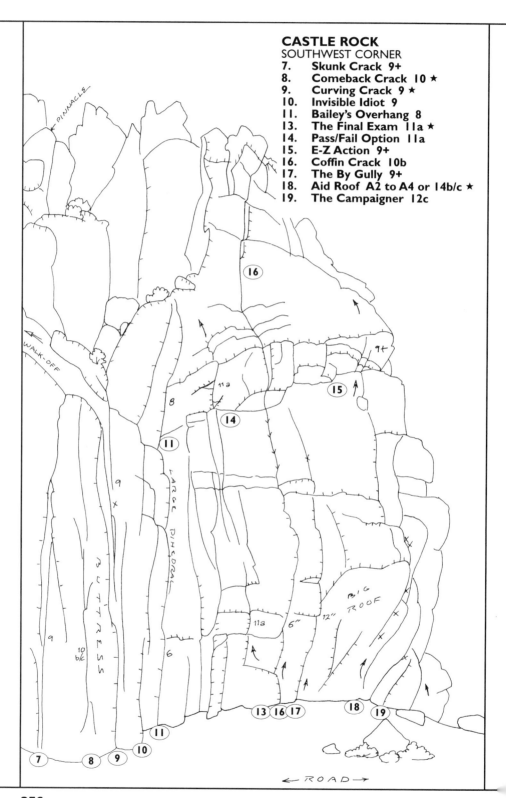

CASTLE ROCK
SOUTHWEST CORNER

7. **Skunk Crack 9+**
8. **Comeback Crack 10 ★**
9. **Curving Crack 9 ★**
10. **Invisible Idiot 9**
11. **Bailey's Overhang 8**
13. **The Final Exam 11a ★**
14. **Pass/Fail Option 11a**
15. **E-Z Action 9+**
16. **Coffin Crack 10b**
17. **The By Gully 9+**
18. **Aid Roof A2 to A4 or 14b/c ★**
19. **The Campaigner 12c**

PINNACLE

WALK-OFF

LARGE DIHEDRAL

BUTTRESS

BIG ROOF

← ROAD →

CASTLE ROCK

FROM THE SOUTHWEST
19. The Campaigner 12c
21. Victim Of
    Circumstance 13d (?)
24. Cussin' Crack 7 ★
28. Jackson's Wall 6
31. Tongo 11a s ★

8.   COMEBACK CRACK 10 ★
FA: PAT AMENT AND JIM ERICKSON, 1972.

Hands and fingers, just right of *Skunk Crack*.

9.   CURVING CRACK 9 ★
FA: TINK WILSON AND PARTY, 1961. FFA: PAT AMENT AND DAVE REARICK, 1964.

Climb a crack that curves up and left, just right of the buttress of the preceding route.

10.   INVISIBLE IDIOT 9
FA: JIM ERICKSON, SOLO, 1978.

Climb an overhanging dihedral between *Curving Crack* and *Bailey's Overhang*.

11.   BAILEY'S OVERHANG 8
FA: WALTER BAILEY AND PARTY, 1950s.

Climb the big dihedral and roof to the right of *Curving Crack*.

12.   DEAD MOUSE TRAVERSE 10
FA: ALEC SHARP AND DAN HARE, 1979.

Start up *Bailey's Overhang*, then angle up and right passing along the lip of the Practice Roof. Eventually gain the long dihedral of *Cussin' Crack*.

13.   THE FINAL EXAM 11A ★
FA: ROYAL ROBBINS AND PAT AMENT, 1964.

Climb a thin crack through a bulge to the right of *Bailey's Overhang*.

14.   PASS/FAIL OPTION 11A
FA: MARK SHANNON, 1980.

From the top of *The Final Exam*, follow a crack up through a roof.

15.   E-Z ACTION 9+
FA: MORRIS HERSHOFF.

Climb through the roof 45 feet right of *Pass/Fail Option*.

16.   COFFIN CRACK 10B
FA: DAVE REARICK AND PAT AMENT, 1964.

Climb the off-width-squeeze to the right of *The Final Exam*, and continue in the same system all the way to the top of Castle Rock.

17.   THE BY GULLY 9+
FA: ROYAL ROBBINS AND PAT AMENT, 1964.

Climb the 12-inch slot to the right of *Coffin Crack* and continue in the same system to the top of the rock.

18.   AID ROOF A2 TO A4 OR 14B/C ★
FA: DALE JOHNSON, PHIL ROBERTSON, BOB SUTTON, 1953. FFA: ROB CANDELARIA, 1996 OR JERRY MOFFATT, 1997.

Aid a crack/seam out the big roof on the southwest side of Castle Rock. The finger crack toward the right side of the roof is the easiest aid line and has been climbed free with the addition of three bolts.

19.   THE CAMPAIGNER 12C
FA: KEN DUNCAN, 1970s.

Begin beneath the right edge of **The Aid Roof** and follow a very difficult crack with some pins up and left around a bulge.

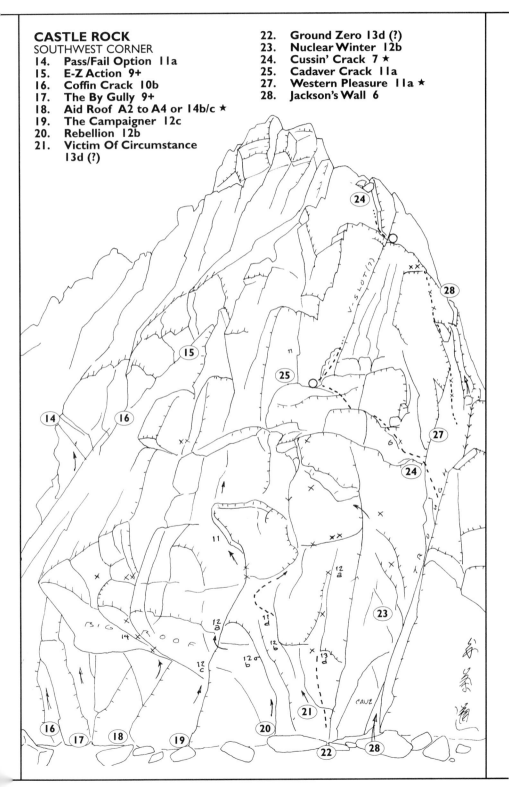

CASTLE ROCK
SOUTHWEST CORNER

14. **Pass/Fail Option 11a**
15. **E-Z Action 9+**
16. **Coffin Crack 10b**
17. **The By Gully 9+**
18. **Aid Roof A2 to A4 or 14b/c ★**
19. **The Campaigner 12c**
20. **Rebellion 12b**
21. **Victim Of Circumstance
     13d (?)**

22. **Ground Zero 13d (?)**
23. **Nuclear Winter 12b**
24. **Cussin' Crack 7 ★**
25. **Cadaver Crack 11a**
27. **Western Pleasure 11a ★**
28. **Jackson's Wall 6**

20. REBELLION 12B
FA: KYLE COPELAND AND JOE BURKE, 1984. FFA: MARK ROLOFSON AND ARTHER STOKES BAKER, 1986.

Begin a few feet right of *The Campaigner*. Climb a thin crack up to a piton, then cut left (crux) to *The Campaigner*.

21. VICTIM OF CIRCUMSTANCE 13D (?)
FA: ALEC SHARP AND MAT LAVENDER, 1982.

Begin just right of the preceding route. Climb a left-leaning crack past a bulge, then angle left toward *The Campaigner*. Undercling back right and lieback around a roof. Originally rated 12b, above rating is from a recent ascent by Jerry Moffatt.

22. GROUND ZERO 13D (?)

Begin just right of the preceding route. Follow a seam to a horizontal break, then climb an overhanging right-facing dihedral. Three bolts to a two-bolt anchor.

23. NUCLEAR WINTER 12B
FA: KYLE COPELAND AND MARK HIRT, 1984. FFA: ALEC SHARP AND DAN HARE, C. 1991.

Begin back in the cave at the beginning of *Jackson's Wall*, then follow bolts up and left to the finish of the preceding route.

24. CUSSIN' CRACK 7 ★
FA: HAROLD WALTON AND PARTY, EARLY 1950S.

This route is a real classic and still popular. P1. Climb up through the cave as for *Jackson's Wall*, but after about 60 feet, balance left along a tricky traverse and belay at the bottom of a long, V-shaped dihedral. P2. Climb the slippery and deceptive dihedral and belay at right after a long pitch. P3. Continue up the steep corner past a roof to big ledges near the summit.

25. CADAVER CRACK 11A
FA: RICHARD NIXON, GEORGE LEHMKUHL, BOB WHITE, 1970. FFA: CHRIS REVELEY AND DAVE O'MELIA, 1973.

Follow *Cussin' Crack* to the belay ledge beneath the long, V-shaped dihedral. Climb the hand crack in the steep wall on the left.

26. STICKY FINGERS 10D S
FA: ALEC AND MURIEL SHARP, 1980.

Follow *Cussin' Crack* into the leftward traverse of the first pitch, then climb up to and around the right side of a roof and belay on a ledge. Climb steep cracks in the wall above.

27. WESTERN PLEASURE 11A ★
FA: DAN HARE AND ALAN BRADLEY, 1984.

Begin about 100 feet up into the trough of *Jackson's Wall* beneath a shallow dihedral with a couple of pins. Climb up to a small triangular roof, pass it on the left, and continue up the wall past two bolts (crux). From a belay on a good ledge, climb unprotected (8) to gain a finger crack and continue with exciting moves to the summit. An earlier start to this climb took a (8) roof a little farther up to the right.

28. JACKSON'S WALL 6
FA: DALLAS JACKSON AND CHUCK MERLEY, 1953.

This is a very old and popular route, but most of the climbing is not very aesthetic. Begin in a deep cleft/cave at the southwest side of Castle Rock, just left of a giant block. One may squirm up the chimney in the back, climb the outside of the block, or better, climb the slab that makes the right side of the cleft (8). Continue up a trough to a belay ledge in a left-facing corner. Move up toward a roof, cut left past a wobbly block (crux), then go up and right to easier terrain.

CASTLE ROCK
24. Cussin' Crack 7 ★
41. South Face 10a ★
45. Athlete's Feat 11a ★
47. Country Club Crack 11c ★
50. Tourist's Extravagance 12d/13a

29. ACROBAT'S OVERHANG 12
FA: JOHN GILL, 1960s.

Begin just left of the squeeze chimney of *Circadian Rhythms* and hand traverse out onto the south-west side of the big block at the start to *Jackson's Wall*. Move up and left around a bulge.

30. CIRCADIAN RHYTHMS 9+
FA: PAT AMENT AND GREG FINOFF, 1984.

At the right side of the big block and just left of *Tongo*, climb a squeeze chimney that leads up to a thin crack.

31. TONGO 11A S ★
FA: PAT AMENT AND WILL BASSETT, 1963. FFA: PAT AMENT AND ROGER BRIGGS, 1967.

Begin just right of *Circadian Rhythms*. P1. Follow a ramp up and right and belay in a short, left-facing dihedral (10a s). P2. Climb the dihedral, then follow a difficult crack up and left to a ledge.

31A. DIRECT START 8 S

From the start of *Tongo*, climb up and left over unprotected but moderate terrain to the start of *Cussin' Crack*. This was pioneered by Alec Sharp as a direct start to *Sticky Fingers*.

32. AFTER FOREVER 11C S
FA: KURT SMITH AND RICK LOVELACE, 1987.

Begin just left of a large tree to the right of *Tongo*. Climb straight up to the middle of the ramp on *Tongo*. Continue up the wall past a bolt and gain the traverse on *Cussin' Crack*. Move up to the right of *Sticky Fingers*, turn a roof, and follow a thin crack past a bolt. Move right, then up over a bulging headwall to the ledge on *Western Pleasure*. A two-bolt rappel anchor is in place.

33. ENDANGERED 10
FA: KYLE COPELAND AND TIM HUDGEL, 1984.

Begin with *Tongo*, but after the initial hand traverse, climb straight up past a "stray" bolt, reach a narrow ledge, move right, stretch up to a mantle, and finish at the top of *Tongo*. This may overlap *After Forever*.

34. ATLAS SHRUGGED 11D S
FA: DAN HARE AND MARC VENERY, 1987.

Begin at a seam between an old fire scar and the aforementioned tree. Climb unprotected (10a) up to a couple of very tricky nut placements (a #2 RP followed by a #1 Rock extended on another wired piece), move up and right a bit past a couple of bolts, then traverse straight left at two pins in a horizontal crack and crank up to the belay on *Tongo*. A second pitch takes a left-angling crack system between the finish to *Jackson's Wall* and the second pitch of *Western Pleasure*.

35. BLACK CRACK 9+

Climb a crack just right of an old fire scar, after which one may lower off or continue up and right over a bulge to connect with the second pitch of the *South Face* route.

36. GILL CRACK 12A ★
FA: JOHN GILL (AS A BOULDER PROBLEM), MID 1960s.

Climb the thin, finger-wrecking crack just right of *Black Crack*, then step left and down-climb the easy part of *Black Crack* (6).

37. THE STING 11 S
FA: ROB CANDELARIA, 1976.

From the top of *Black Crack*, angle up and left to the belay on *Tongo*.

CASTLE ROCK

SOUTH FACE LEFT

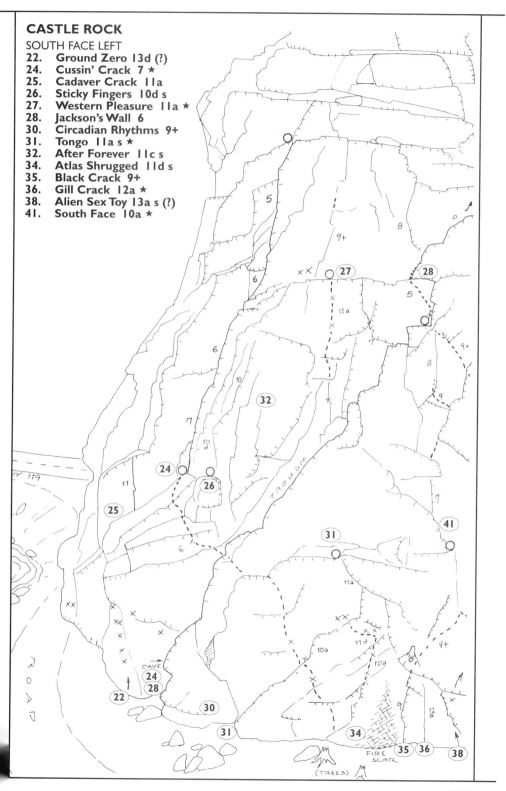

38. ALIEN SEX TOY 13A S (?)
FA: CHARLIE FOWLER AND KYLE COPELAND, 1986.

Begin at a left-leaning flake just right of the *Gill Crack*. Climb over a bulge (crux), then move right past some bolts to the *South Face* route.

39. CLOSE TO THE EDGE 12A/B ★
FA: ROGER BRIGGS AND DAN HARE, 1995.

Begin about 15 left of *Boot Lead*. Climb the vertical wall past three bolts. The third clip is very difficult.

40. BOOT LEAD 12A VS
FA: LARRY AND ROGER DALKE, 1965. FFA: SKIP GUERIN AND CHIP RUCKGABER, 1983.

Begin about 30 feet left from the start to the *South Face* route. Climb up and right into a right-facing flake/seam (crux) and continue with no pro to a ledge on the *South Face*. Continue with *Corinthian Vine* or go get yourself a good stout. You earned it.

41. SOUTH FACE 10A ★
FA: GEORGE HURLEY AND CHARLES ROSKOSZ, 1961. FFA: LAYTON KOR.

A classic, also known as *Jackson's Wall Direct*. Begin at a short, right-facing dihedral toward the right side of the south face. P1. Climb part way up the dihedral, then make strenuous moves up and left to a ledge (10a). Continue left to a vertical crack, and climb to a belay on a small ledge. P2. Steep cracks and corners lead to a belay shared with *Jackson's Wall* (9 or 9+). P3. Finish with the last pitch of *Jackson's Wall* (6).

42. KNIGHT WITH THE SHINING STICK A4

Begin with the right-facing dihedral of South Face and follow it as it arches right. Continue right to *Never A Dull Moment* and belay as for *Athlete's Feat*. Ascend a system of shallow corners and seams between *Athlete's Feat* and *Englishman's Home* and belay on the big ledge at the top of *Country Club Crack*. Full aid rack including hooks and RURPs.

43. CORINTHIAN VINE 12D ★
FA: TOM RUWITCH AND ROGER BRIGGS, 1968. FFA: ALEC SHARP LED THE ROUTE FREE BUT FOR THE ROOF ON THE SECOND PITCH, 1981. COMPLETE FREE ASCENT UNKNOWN.

This is a stupendous route up the smooth wall between *South Face* and *Never A Dull Moment*. P1. Begin with *South Face* or *The Boot Lead* and climb to a ledge. P2. Climb a right-facing dihedral with a roof or take the face on the right with two bolts and belay on a ledge with a two-bolt anchor. P3. Climb the steep wall above the belay and turn the crux roof. Go up and left along a ramp to easier terrain.

44. NEVER A DULL MOMENT 12A S ★
FA: ALEC SHARP AND ANDY PARKIN, 1979.

Begin just to the right of *South Face*. P1. Traverse up and right past two bolts to the first belay on *Athlete's Feat*. P2. Move left into a steep and difficult crack and belay on *Athlete's Feat*. P3. Step left again and climb a shallow left-facing corner with two bolts. P4. Climb the arête past a bolt, then work up and left to the ramp at the top of *Corinthian Vine*.

45. ATHLETE'S FEAT 11A ★
FA: STAN SHEPHERD AND DON DAVIS, 1961. FFA: ROYAL ROBBINS AND PAT AMENT, 1964.

In 1964 this was probably the hardest free climb in North America, maybe in the whole Universe. Begin at a pointed boulder just up and left from the bridge at the southeast corner of the rock. Climb up past a pin, stretch up to clip a bolt and make a difficult mantle (crux). The route is obvious from here as it simply follows the bulging right-facing dihedral system to a ledge near the top of the rock. From this ledge (the fourth belay), jam a (9+) crack directly above or move left and climb a right-facing corner (8).

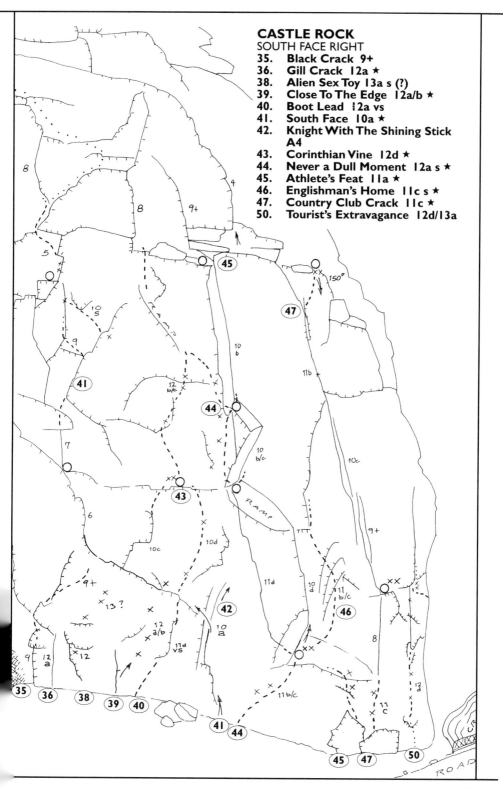

CASTLE ROCK
SOUTH FACE RIGHT
35. **Black Crack 9+**
36. **Gill Crack 12a ★**
38. **Alien Sex Toy 13a s (?)**
39. **Close To The Edge 12a/b ★**
40. **Boot Lead 12a vs**
41. **South Face 10a ★**
42. **Knight With The Shining Stick A4**
43. **Corinthian Vine 12d ★**
44. **Never a Dull Moment 12a s ★**
45. **Athlete's Feat 11a ★**
46. **Englishman's Home 11c s ★**
47. **Country Club Crack 11c ★**
50. **Tourist's Extravagance 12d/13a**

46. ENGLISHMAN'S HOME 11c s ★
FA: ALEC SHARP AND BILL FEIGES, 1979.
Begin with *Athlete's Feat* or *Never a Dull Moment*, but from the first belay, climb up and right into a series of short, right-facing dihedrals. Work up and left through these corners (crux) to a small ledge and belay. Lieback and stem a shallow, right-facing dihedral to the crux section of *Country Club Crack*.

47. COUNTRY CLUB CRACK 11c ★
FA: TED ROUILLARD, CLEVE MCCARTY, 1956. FFA: PAT AMENT, MIKE STULTS, TOM RUWITCH, 1967. SR WITH EXTRA MID-RANGE GEAR AND A #4 FRIEND.
This is one of the best crack climbs in the Boulder Area. The crux is a smooth face at the bottom of the first pitch requiring very delicate footwork. Begin at a large block immediately right of the large spike at the base of *Athlete's Feat*. P1. Climb up into a flared crack and belay at right. P2. Follow a series of cracks up and left to a roof. Pull around to the left and jam a smooth hand crack (11a) to a ledge with boulders. Climb an easy chimney to the summit or rappel 150 feet to the ground.

48. SPIN OFF 11c s
FA: BILL MYERS AND MARK SONNEFELD, 1987.
After the face moves on the first pitch of *Country Club Crack*, move left to a small, right-facing corner and roof that lead back right to the first belay.

49. DOMESTIC ABUSE 12a s
FA: ERIC DOUB, LIDIJA PAINKIHER, JOHN AARON, 1987.
From the roof just before the crux of *Country Club Crack*, traverse right and go around the buttress into a 10-foot crack, then back to the edge to belay. Continue up to the ledge at the top of *Country Club*. The first ascent party climbed *Englishman's Home* to reach the roof.

50. TOURIST'S EXTRAVAGANCE 12d/13a
FA: BOB BOUCHER AND BOB SANDAFER, 1962. FFA: CHRISTIAN GRIFFITH, 1985.
Begin down to the right of *Country Club Crack*. Climb the steep face past two bolts and a fixed pin, then step left to the first belay on *Country Club Crack*. One could also finish with *Radio Andromeda*.

51. RADIO ANDROMEDA 11b
FA: PAT AMENT AND ROGER BRIGGS, 1972. SR TO A #4 FRIEND.
Begin at the edge of the stream, just right of the preceding route. Climb the first pitch of *First Movement* to a roof, then traverse left (11a) and belay from a fixed anchor. Climb a very difficult hand and fist crack to a ledge. Easier terrain leads to the summit.

52. FIRST MOVEMENT 10 s
FA: STAN SHEPHERD AND GREG BLOMBERG, 1962. FFA: JIM ERICKSON AND PAT AMENT, 1972.
Also known as *Sonata Allegro*. Climb tricky flared cracks and belay at the bottom of a slot. Climb the slot.

53. ROUTE 66 8+
FA: PAT AMENT AND JOHN AUTRY, 1963.
Begin from the stream, a couple of yards right of *First Movement*. Climb a flared chimney and belay in a slot. Traverse right beneath a roof and follow a left-facing dihedral to the summit.

BROKEN ROCK
Across the stream and southeast of Castle Rock, is a large irregular buttress that has occasionally drawn the interest of rock climbers. The name says something about the nature of the crag; never-the-less, if overhanging cracks are your version of fun, Broken Rock is worth a visit.

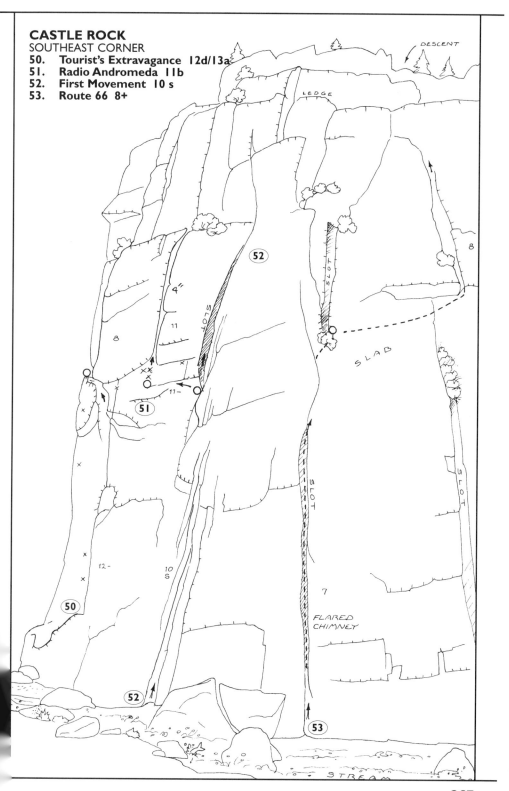

CASTLE ROCK
SOUTHEAST CORNER
50. **Tourist's Extravagance 12d/13a**
51. **Radio Andromeda 11b**
52. **First Movement 10 s**
53. **Route 66 8+**

DESCENT

LEDGE

52

SLOT

8

SLAB

51

17 –

12 –

10
S

SLOT

SLOT

7

50

FLARED
CHIMNEY

52

53

STREAM

1. UNDERCLING 9
FA: DUDLEY CHELTON AND TOM GRIES, 1971.

From the bridge beneath *Country Club Crack* walk east a short way and ascend the following features: a low-angle trough/corner with a small tree that leads up to a roof, an undercling around the roof, a crack on the right that leads up to a small tree, a sloping ledge 15 feet to the right, a belay at the base of a large overhang, an undercling to the right that leads to a ledge, and easy slabs above and left. To descend, hike east and then north.

2. WHIMSEY 11A
FA: DAN HARE AND SCOTT WOODRUFF, 1978.

From the bridge walk east a short way and scramble up easy slabs to a ledge with trees. Climb a big, square overhang with a flake into a shallow groove.

3. COSMIC WHIMP-OUT 11A
FA: MARK WILFORD AND BILL ALEXANDER, 1977.

Cross the stream at the bridge and walk up to the low point of the rock. Climb a clean hand and fist crack through a roof.

4. TREE TRIMMER 11B/C
FA: SCOTT COSGROVE AND GEORGE SQUIBB, 1987.

Thirty feet or so to the right of *Cosmic Whimp-Out*, a fir tree stands near the wall. Behind the tree, practically obscured by its limbs, is a roof problem with two bolts.

5. HUNG JURY 9+
FA: DAN HARE AND JOHN WARREN, 1983.

Climb a hand crack over a roof behind a tree and about 40 feet left of *Momentum Operator Crack*.

6. OUT TO PASTURE 10A
FA: DAN HARE AND ALLEN WOOD, 1980.

Ten or fifteen feet to the left of the *Momentum Operator* jam over a bulge and master a roof via parallel cracks.

7. MOMENTUM OPERATOR CRACK 11A ★
FA: ROGER BRIGGS, BRIAN KEW, STEVE KENTZ, 1971.

Begin about 80 feet up and right from the stream. Climb two parallel cracks and a bomb-bay chimney. "It ain't very pretty, but it's pretty hard." That's what she said.

8. CRACK UP 9 ★
FA: DUDLEY CHELTON AND BOB CULP, 1973.

Climb a hand and fist crack in an overhanging dihedral about 20 feet up and right from the preceding route. Bring extra gear in the two-to-three-inch range.

9. EULOGY 9+
FA: DAN MICHAEL AND DAN HARE, 1982.

Climb an overhanging, left-facing corner to the right of *Crack Up*.

10. SUE'S SONG 10C
FA: DAN HARE AND DAN MICHAEL, 1982.

Ascend to a jutting flake and move left to a wide crack.

11. TURKISH REVENGE 10
FA: CARL HARRISON AND AL TORRISI, 1982.

Lieback a large flake to the right of *Momentum Operator*.

BROKEN ROCK
4. Tree Trimmer 11b/c
7. Momentum Operator
8. Crack 11a ★
9. Crack Up 9 ★
9. Eulogy 9+
10. Sue's Song 10c

Moe Hershoff on *Animal Instinct*. Photo by Richard Rossiter.

The Overlook

This is the upper-most tier of Broken Rock. The following two routes are located around on the north side above a grassy ramp.

12. OBSCURITY RISK 12A
FA: DON DEBIEUX, 1993.

Climb an overhanging wall just right of an arête, finish in an easy dihedral on the left. Two fixed RPs and a knifeblade. Bring additional gear.

13. FLAKE RIGHT 7
FA: DEBLIEUX, SOLO, 1993.

Begin 25 feet right of *Obscurity Risk*. Climb a flake and a crack.

MOUNTAIN ROSE

The following routes are located on two small buttresses above the aqueduct, south of Castle Rock. To reach these features, walk across the bridge and up a faint trail just west of Broken Rock. I have listed the recent first ascent data for this area, but some of the easier routes (such as *Better You Than Me*) were climbed around 1983 by Joyce Rossiter and me, if not others.

Left Buttress

1. MOUNTAIN ROSE 10A s
FA: JOHN AUGHINBAUGH AND MIKE DARRAH, 1990.

Begin at the east side of the buttress. Climb along diagonal roofs and short corners to a bulge. Climb a crack through the bulge or escape to the left.

2. TOP ROPE 10

Climb straight up the face a short way right of *Mountain Rose*.

3. TOP ROPE 11

Begin to the right of the preceding route. Angle up and left past a white dike.

4. THE ANCIENT OF DAYS 9 vs
FA: RICHARD ROSSITER, SOLO.

Begin just left of a large, open-book dihedral and boulder over a bulge (10a) or start around to the right. In either case, work up a moderate slab, turn a small roof and climb straight up the steep wall (9) to a short dihedral. Turn a bulge with good holds and gain a ledge with an old pine tree. Scramble off to the east. This route would require about five bolts to provide a safe lead.

5. TIME LORDS 7 s
FA: ROSSITER, SOLO.

Begin as for *The Ancient Of Days*, but work up and left to a break in the roof, then climb a shallow dihedral and finish at the old pine tree as for *The Ancient of Days*.

6. HUMMING BIRD 5
FA: MIKE DARRAH AND CHUCK MCGROSKY, 1989.

Start up a large open-book dihedral, then work up and right and turn a small roof.

7. WAR DRUMS 9
FA: DARRAH AND MCGROSKY, 1989.

Begin left of a tree and climb straight up past two bolts in the right wall of a large, open-book dihedral. Rappel 80 feet from a tree.

8. SICK PUPPY 12b/c
FA: MIKE DARRAH AND JOHN AUGHINBAUGH, 1990.
Begin well to the right of the big open book. Begin with a finger-tip mantle, then follow four bolts up a rounded arête.

Right Buttress

1. HEAT WAVE 10c
FA: MIKE DARRAH, 1989.
Begin about 40 feet right of a manhole or round opening in the aqueduct. Climb the arête along the left wall of a conspicuous, right-facing dihedral. Three bolts plus gear including RPs.

2. SHORT BUT SWEET 8
FA: MIKE DARRAH AND DAVE DOW, 1989.
Climb an easy right-facing dihedral, then go left around a roof.

3. BETTER YOU THAN ME 8 vs
FA: DARRAH AND DOW, 1989.
Begin just left of some trees at the right side of the buttress. Start up a short crack, then pull right and climb a small buttress to the top.

THE ICE FALL AREA

About one-quarter mile west of Castle Rock and on the same side of the road is a cliffy area that has become popular for ice climbing during winter. The origin of the water (ice) is a series of leaks in an aqueduct about 200 feet above the stream. This is a great practice area with many possible routes of varying difficulty. It is also quite popular. Though there is a wide shoulder just below the area and another good pull-out just below Cenotaph Crag, parking currently is limited to a large pull-out about 200 yards up the highway and on the right (12.2 miles). To descend from the aqueduct at the top of the ice formations, hike west until an obvious trail leads back down to the stream.

1. THE WINDOW WI3
Climb the second gully left of the prominent central buttress.

2. CENTER WI3
Climb a short vertical section and gully along the left side of the prominent central buttress.

3. THE RAMP WI2
Climb a low-angle ramp just right of the prominent central buttress.

Ice Blob

The following lines ascend the broad ice apron to the right of The Ramp.

4. GRADE ONE GULLY WI2
Climb a gully along the left side of the Ice Blob.

5. BLAME JAMES WI3
Climb the next gully to the right.

6. OVERNIGHT SENSATION WI3+
Climb the steep wall in the center of the formation.

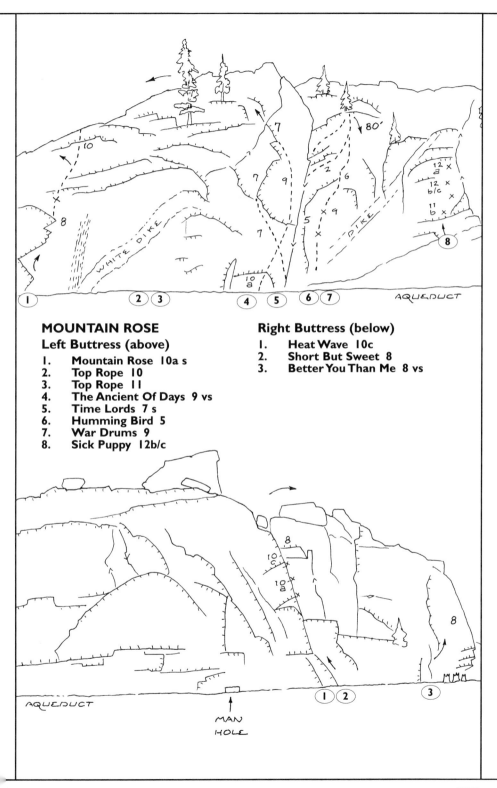

MOUNTAIN ROSE

Left Buttress (above)

1. Mountain Rose 10a s
2. Top Rope 10
3. Top Rope 11
4. The Ancient Of Days 9 vs
5. Time Lords 7 s
6. Humming Bird 5
7. War Drums 9
8. Sick Puppy 12b/c

Right Buttress (below)

1. Heat Wave 10c
2. Short But Sweet 8
3. Better You Than Me 8 vs

7.   COOL ROOF M8 TO M4 (RIGHT)
Climb icicles through a big roof, just right of center.

8.   WALK IN THE PARK WI3
Climb steps just right of *Cool Roof* to a tree belay.

9.   GULLY WI3
Climb a gully between two small rock ribs.

10.   OVER BEFORE IT STARTED WI3+
Begin from ledges up to the right and climb a short steep section.

11.   PHOTON TORPEDO WI4-
Climb a series of pillars on a separate formation to the right of the Ice Blob.

CANDLESTICK AREA
This is a small area a short way farther upstream from the preceding routes. The two newer routes on the left top out at a three-bolt anchor. The lower ice wall to the right of The Candlestick features many top-rope possibilities.

1.   SEX, DRUGS AND CHEAP THRILLS WI5-
Climb the left of two 40-foot pillars. Lower off from a bolt anchor.

2.   THRILLER PILLAR WI5-
Climb the right of two pillars, just left of the big tree, to a bolt anchor.

3.   THE CANDLESTICK WI4 TO WI5
Climb the prominent pillar that hangs from a small roof, just right of the large tree.

FRISKY CLIFF
Just above the aqueduct and to the right of the Ice Fall Area is a buttress with an impressive north-facing overhang. To reach this cliff in the summer, hike up the descent trail for the winter ice climbs or hike up the talus slope south of Castle Rock to the aqueduct, then walk west.

1.   SINOPIA 13A ★
FA: PETER BEAL, 1997.
Begin near the upper left side of the crag. Climb a very steep wall and pass a bulge. Six bolts to a two-bolt anchor.

2.   THE ORB 13A ★
FA: PETER BEAL, 1996.
Begin 40 feet down and right from the preceding route. Follow eight bolts along two disjunct arête/dihedrals and gain a two-bolt anchor.

3.   LAST TANGO 10C
FA: DAN HARE AND MASON FRISCHETTE, 1986.
Begin beneath a break in the middle of the wall. Climb a left-leaning crack and finish with an overhanging, left-facing dihedral.

4.   FRISKY 10A
FA: DAN HARE AND ALLEN WOOD, 1980.

Begin just left of a really big overhang and below a break in the middle of the wall. Climb up through the break, then work up the right wall around an overhang and finish in a thin crack.

5.   THE BORG 13C ★
FA: JESSIE GUTHRIE. REDPOINT: BEN MOON, C. 1993.

This route ascends the big roof above where the aqueduct enters a tunnel. Begin just right of the tunnel, then climb back up and left into the line. Five or six bolts.

6.   RUMORS OF GLORY 13B ★
FA: JESSIE GUTHRIE.

Begin as for *The Borg*, but go up and right from the right side of the tunnel and continue out the right side of the big roof. Three bolts.

CENOTAPH CRAG

About one-half mile west of Castle Rock and on the north side of the road, locate a small west-facing buttress hidden in the trees. The most prominent feature on the west face is a right-leaning, right-facing dihedral. Cenotaph is only about 150 feet above the road, but is very difficult to see while driving up the canyon. So plan on missing it, turning around, and finding it on the way back down. There is a perfectly good pull-out right below the crag, however, it has been designated "no-parking" for no apparent reason.

1.   GOIN' DOWN IN IT 9 VS
FA: FRED KNAPP AND DAN HARE, 1991.

Climb the black streak at the left side of the west face. Bring RPs and Tri-cams, or just toprope it.

2.   ETHEREAL 9
FA: DAN HARE AND DAVE HURST, 1986.

Climb the first crack right of the black streak.

3.   APPARITION 11A ★
FA: DAN HARE AND NOEL CHILDS, 1987.

Begin about 8 feet left of the arête along a big, right-facing dihedral. Climb double cracks over a small roof and continue up the face past a pin and two bolts. Lower off from a two-bolt anchor.

4.   PHANTASM 11C
FA: DAN HARE AND FRED KNAPP, 1991.

Begin with *Apparition*, then break right and follow bolts along the arête. Four bolts to a two-bolt anchor.

5.   RIGHT TO LIFE 10B
FA: JIM ERICKSON, SOLO, 1976.

Follow a crack up the big dihedral in the middle of the rock.

Note: The bolts on the following two routes appear to have been removed.

6.   PHAEDRA 11C S
FA: MARC GAY AND DAN HARE, 1986.

Not far right of the big dihedral, climb up past three bolts and gain a thin crack. Lower off from a two-bolt anchor.

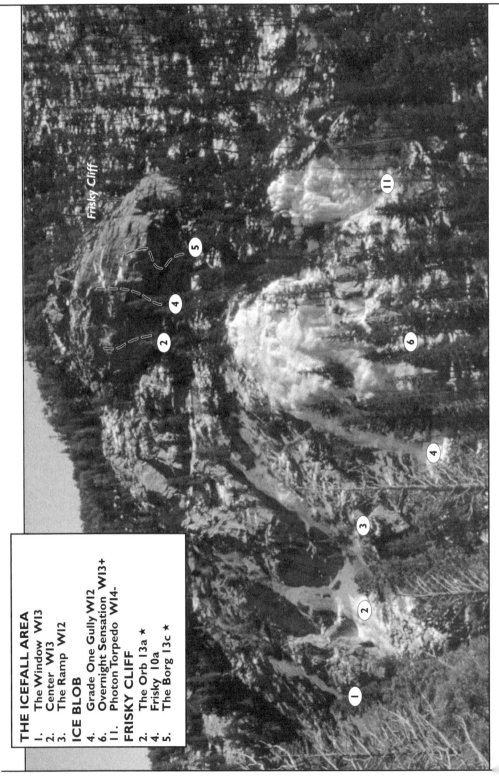

THE ICEFALL AREA
1. The Window WI3
2. Center WI3
3. The Ramp WI2

ICE BLOB
4. Grade One Gully WI2
6. Overnight Sensation WI3+
11. Photon Torpedo WI4-

FRISKY CLIFF
2. The Orb 13a ★
4. Frisky 10a
5. The Borg 13c ★

Frisky Cliff

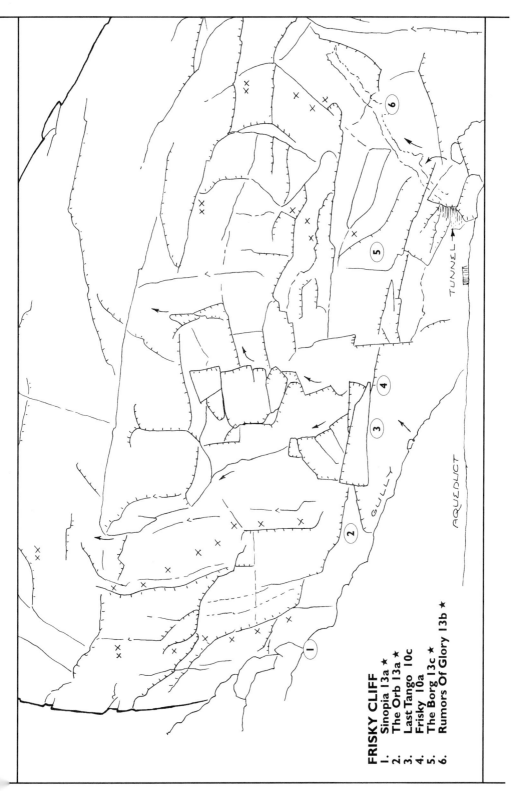

FRISKY CLIFF
1. Sinopia 13a ★
2. The Orb 13a ★
3. Last Tango 10c
4. Frisky 10a
5. The Borg 13c ★
6. Rumors Of Glory 13b ★

TUNNEL

GULLY

AQUEDUCT

7. EUPHORIA 11c s

Begin just right of *Phaedra*. Climb past three bolts, then move up and left into the thin crack of *Phaedra*. Lower off.

8. UP ABOVE IT 10D

Climb a thin crack just right of the preceding route.

9. FIVE-EIGHT CRACK 8

FA: PROBABLY SOLOED BY ERICKSON, 1976.

This is the next feature to the right.

CENOTAPH TOWER

A short way south of Cenotaph Crag, just above the highway, is a small rock tower with a single known route on its west side.

HAREBELL 10A

FA: TED ANDERSON. GEAR PLUS TWO BOLTS.

This route ascends the left side of the west face to a two-bolt anchor with chains.

SURPRISING CRAG

Surprising Crag is located about a mile west of Castle Rock, on the south above a sharp right bend in the highway. Routes have been completed on two features: a buttress at lower left called Overhang Wall, and the prominent west-facing buttress up to the right. Overhang Wall features pure sport climbs, and the upper buttress features mostly crack and seam routes. Park at a pull-out below the crag. Cross the stream on some old planks and hike up the hillside. During high water, it may be possible to cross on a log bridge downstream from the buttress.

Overhang Wall

This wall is located above a steep ramp that is always wet due to a leak in an aqueduct above the crag. The wall faces west and features big overhangs with bolt protection. It would be a good winter crag, except that the ramp is completely covered with ice until late spring.

1. UNKNOWN

Climb to the first bolt on *Whipping Post*, then follow bolts up and left under the big roof. Five bolts to a two-bolt anchor.

2. WHIPPING POST 12B

Begin from a block below the left side of the big roof. Five bolts to a two-bolt anchor.

2A. WHIPPING-FACTOR 12B ★

Climb to a "ledge" above the third bolt on *Whipping Post*, then move right and finish with *Warf Factor*. Six bolts.

3. WARF FACTOR 12A ★

Begin from the right side of the block mentioned in *Whipping Post*. Climb through the middle of the big roof. A knee-lock is possible at the fifth bolt. Six bolts to a two-bolt anchor.

3A. WARF-POST 11A ★

Climb to a "ledge" up and left from the fourth bolt on *Warf Factor* and finish with *Whipping Post*. Six bolts.

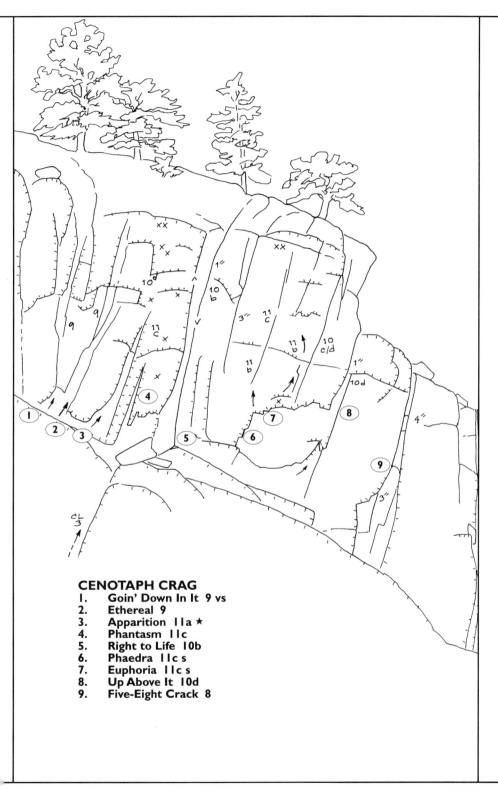

CENOTAPH CRAG
1. Goin' Down In It 9 vs
2. Ethereal 9
3. Apparition 11a ★
4. Phantasm 11c
5. Right to Life 10b
6. Phaedra 11c s
7. Euphoria 11c s
8. Up Above It 10d
9. Five-Eight Crack 8

SURPRISING CRAG

Overhang Wall
3.   Warf Factor 12a ★
4.   Warm-Up 11c

Upper Buttress
7.   Heart Like A Wheel 10a
11. Amber 11b ★

Upper Buttress

Overhang Wall

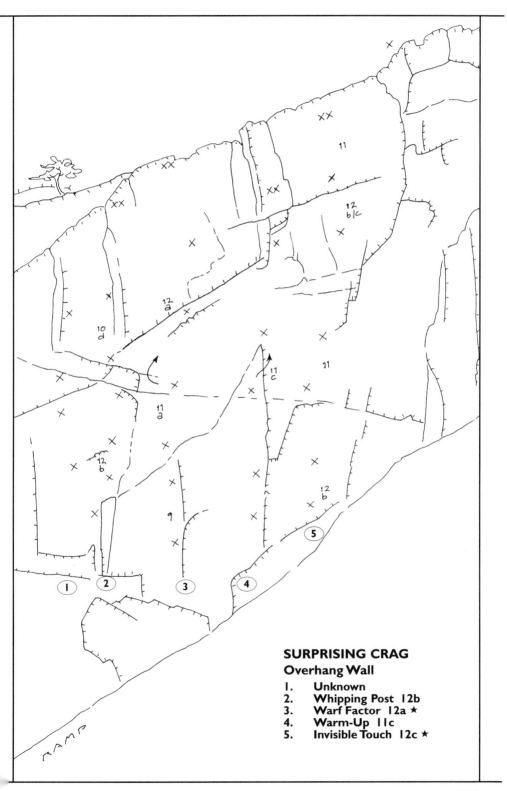

SURPRISING CRAG
Overhang Wall

1. Unknown
2. Whipping Post 12b
3. Warf Factor 12a ★
4. Warm-Up 11c
5. Invisible Touch 12c ★

4.   WARM-UP 11C

Climb a prominent left-facing dihedral and the steep wall above. Lower off from a two-bolt anchor.

5.   INVISIBLE TOUCH 12C ★

Follow bolts up the steep wall just right of *Warm-Up*. Five bolts to a two-bolt anchor.

Upper Buttress

This cube-like formation is located up and right from Overhang Wall and features a steep, west-facing wall with a big, left-facing dihedral on the right.

6.   ENTRAPMENT 10D S

FA: DAN HARE AND JOEL SCHIAVONE, 1982.

Near the left side of the wall, climb an overhang to a small tree at its lip. Step left and follow thin cracks to the top.

7.   HEART LIKE A WHEEL 10A

FA: DAN HARE AND PAT HEALY, 1982.

Climb the overhang of *Entrapment*, then climb straight up along a flake, follow thin cracks up and left and around the left end of a roof.

8.   MARVIN GARDENS 11A

FA: JUDY AND BEAR WHEATON AND JOHN PAYNE, 1989.

Climb cracks right of the preceding route. Exact location unknown.

9.   BURIED ALIVE 10D S

FA: GREG DAVIS AND DAN HARE, 1982.

Begin at a left-facing corner beneath a prominent black streak in the center of the wall. Climb up to the lip of a long low roof, then traverse left at a flake and follow cracks up and left to the top.

10.   POWER LINE 11 ★

FA: BILL FEIGES AND KENT LUGBILL, 1980. RIGHTHAND FINISH: TOM BALLARD.

Begin just right of a prominent black streak in the middle of the wall. Ascend thin cracks to a small overhang, traverse left and finish in a slot. Or move right and follow a difficult thin crack to the top.

11.   AMBER 11B ★

FA: DAN HARE AND MIKE HANKINS, 1987.

Begin a few feet left of the big, left-facing dihedral at the right side of the wall. Follow a series of seams and shallow dihedrals to the top of the wall. Three bolts plus gear to a two-bolt anchor.

12.   NORTH CRACK 8+

FA: PAT AMENT AND JIM ERICKSON, 1970.

Jam the wide crack in the big, left-facing dihedral at the right side of the main wall.

13.   SOUTH CRACK 8

FA: JIM ERICKSON AND PAT AMENT, 1970.

Climb a crack on the south side of the big block at the right side of the buttress.

14.   FORBIDDEN FRUIT 10

FA: DAN HARE AND MASON FRISCHETTE, 1979.

Begin above and right of *South Crack*. Climb an overhanging hand and fist crack through a block, scramble a short way, and finish with a hand crack.

SURPRISING CRAG
Upper Buttress

6. Entrapment 10d s
7. Heart Like A Wheel 10a
8. Marvin Gardens 11a
9. Buried Alive 10d s
10. Power Line 11 ★
11. Amber 11b ★
12. North Crack 8+
13. South Crack 8

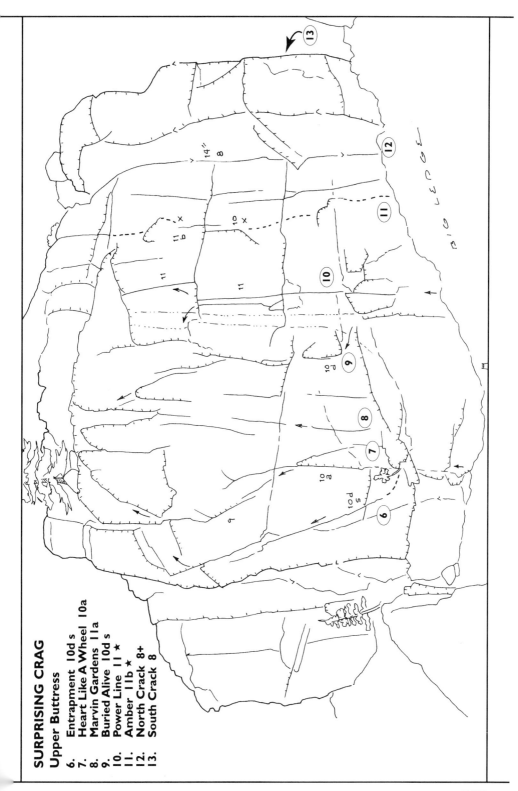

Scott Reynolds on *Empire of the Fenceless*. Photo by Richard Rossiter.

Old Stage Wall

Lefthand Canyon winds its way into the foothills about five miles north of Boulder. In the lower part of the canyon, an impressive cliff called Old Stage Wall was developed by climbers during the mid 1980s. The cliff is on private land and currently closed to climbing. For information on climbing prospects, contact the Access Fund in Boulder.

To reach this area from Boulder, drive 4.5 miles north on Highway 36 from its junction with Broadway. Turn west up Lefthand Canyon and proceed for 1.5 miles. The cliff comes into view to the east across a stream. Park along the road, ford the stream, and climb a steep footpath to the base of the wall.

1.   DRAGON LADY 12A ★
FA: BOB HORAN, 1986. REDPOINT: MARK ROLOFSON, 1987.

This is a direct start to *Alex In Wonderland*. Climb left out of a cave/roof and join the original line at a diagonal seam. Four bolts to the seam; eight bolts in all. Lower off 80 feet.

2.   ALEX IN WONDERLAND 11C/D ★
FA: BOB HORAN AND CINDY PIEROPAN, 1986.

Climb up and right along a right-facing dihedral, turn a roof, and follow six bolts up the overhanging face. Lower off 80 feet.

3.   UNKNOWN CRACK 11B S
FA: SCOTT REYNOLDS, 1985.

Begin below the roof in the middle of the wall. Climb a slightly rotten crack with a wide section to the top of the wall.

4.   SOLSTICE 12D ★
FA: BOB HORAN, 1987.

Begin from a ramp beneath the right side of the wall. Turn a six-foot roof and follow bolts straight up the face. Eight bolts to a two-bolt anchor. Lower off 80 feet.

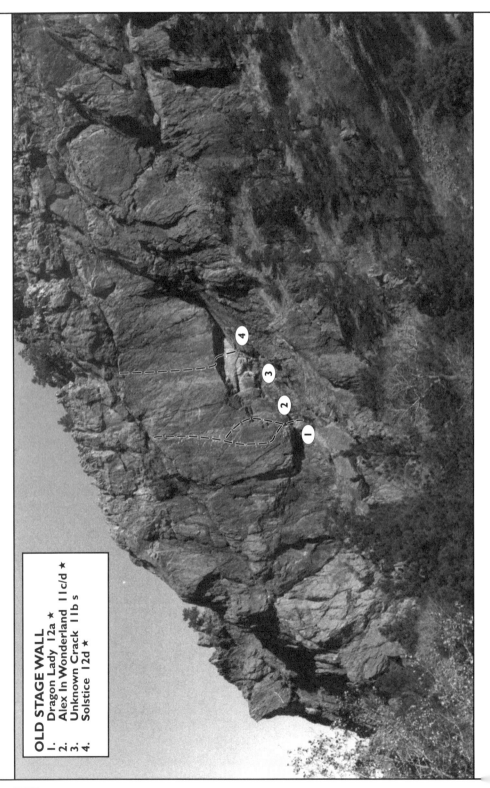

OLD STAGE WALL
1. Dragon Lady 12a ★
2. Alex In Wonderland 11c/d ★
3. Unknown Crack 11b s
4. Solstice 12d ★

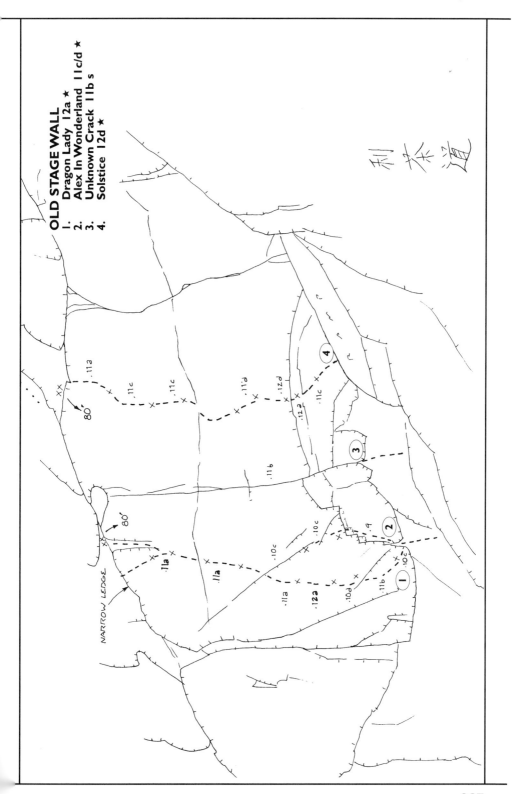

OLD STAGE WALL
1. Dragon Lady 12a ★
2. Alex In Wonderland 11c/d ★
3. Unknown Crack 11b s
4. Solstice 12d ★

飛 杯 道

NARROW LEDGE

.11a
80'
.11a
.11a
.11a
.10c
.10c
.12a
.10d
.11b
①
②
.10q
q
③
.11b
.11c
.12d
.12?
.11c
④
.11a
.11c
.11c
.11a
80'

Rated Route Index

5.12B

5.13C

5.13D

5.14C

Route Name Index

A

X, Y, Z

Your **HANDS**

ARE the most **IMPORTANT**

piece of

CLIMBING GEAR

you own.

PAMPER them.

Use Climb On!™ Hand Bar to take care of your most valuable climbing gear—your hands. Formulated from natural ingredients to heal your wounds, prevent scarring and to keep your hands tough but supple, Climb On!™ will keep you on the rock or get you back on in a hurry. Great for gobis, hangnails, split fingertips, flappers and rope burns. It also works wonders on chapped lips, skin cracks and sunburn. Find Climb On!™ and all our other climbing gear at your favorite climbing shop, or call us direct.

EXTRAORDINARY CLIMBING GEAR®

TRANGO®

A DIVISION OF GREAT TRANGO HOLDINGS, INC.
800.860.3653 ‣ WWW.TRANGO.COM
BOULDER ‣ COLORADO ‣ USA

SCRAMBLES OVER EASY.

FILA OUTDOOR™